A Coach's Influence
Beyond the Game

Grant Teaff

The Social Issues Initiative
Presented by the American Football Coaches Association
and the American Football Coaches Foundation

To all the football coaches who influenced me to play, coach, and love the game.

To all the coaches who gave generously of their expertise and knowledge to the creation of this book.

To Bill and Inez Teaff, who lovingly gave me a set of values and a work ethic that created a foundation for my life.

Other books by Grant Teaff:

I Believe (Grant Teaff with Sam Blair)
Winning (Grant Teaff with Louis and Kay Moore)
Seasons of Glory (Grant Teaff and the Baylor Bears)
Coaching in the Classroom (Grant Teaff)
Grant Teaff with the Master Coaches (Grant Teaff)

Audio and video tapes:

The Master Motivator
The Christian Family with Grant and Donell Teaff
Winners without Drugs
The David Principles

About the Coach, Association, and Foundation

About the Author

Grant Teaff, as a player, coach, and executive director of the American Football Coaches Association, has spent his life immersed in what he calls, "the great game." Like many coaches who have invested their lives in the game, he has seen and lived through many changes in the game and our society.

Combining his knowledge and experiences into *A Coach's Influence: Beyond the Game*, he explores the changes in our society and how they have negatively affected many of America's youth. Teaff also relies on the generosity and expertise of hundreds of coaches in creating this book as a reservoir of experience, techniques, and knowledge to serve coaches and teachers as they strive to influence beyond the game.

A native of Snyder, Texas, Teaff served as the head football coach of McMurry University, Angelo State University, and Baylor University. He won 170 football games while becoming a national leader and spokesman for the game of football.

Coach Teaff has been inducted into eight Halls of Fame, including the College Football Hall of Fame and Texas Sports Hall of Fame. In addition to *A Coach's Influence: Beyond the Game,* he has written five books, *I Believe, Winning, Seasons of Glory, Coaching in the Classroom,* and *Grant Teaff with the Master Coaches.*

As a nationally known author and motivational speaker, Teaff enthusiastically shares his belief that a coach's influence should and does go far beyond the game.

About the American Football Coaches Association

The American Football Coaches Association (AFCA) is the only national organization solely dedicated to improving football-coaches through ongoing education, interaction, and networking. Its primary goal is to provide resources for personal and professionaldevelopment among the football coaching profession. The AFCA membership includes over 11,000 members and represents coaches and several stakeholders within the game of football. Any high school, junior college, international, semi-professional, or professional football coach is eligible to become a member of the AFCA. Founded in December of 1921 by 43 coaches in a meeting at the Hotel Astor in New York City, the AFCA has continued to push the envelope in regard to the growth of the profession. The AFCA strives to maintain the highest possible standards in football and the profession of coaching football, as well as to provide a forum for the discussion and study of all matters pertaining to football and coaching. The flagship event of the AFCA is its national coaches' convention, which takes place annually during the second week in January. More than 6,000 coaches attend the four-day event. Each year, more than 100 speakers lecture on topics such as concussion management, X's & O's, practice and program organization, media relations, and career development. Attendees can earn professional development hours that can help with school district recertification, salary points, and other career-related opportunities

About the American Football Coaches Foundation

The American Football Coaches Foundation was established in 1998. One of the twenty major goals set by Grant Teaff for the American Football Coaches Association in 1994 was to create an educational foundation that would provide funds to assist the American Football Coaches Association in all of its educational venues. The Foundation's financial contribution to the annual AFCA convention benefits the rank and file of AFCA membership. Fees for convention and membership are kept at a minimum, while providing funds for publications and the educational website. The premise for intense education of coaches is simple; a trained, educated and developed coach will invariably have a more positive influence on those they teach and coach.

The Board of Directors of The Foundation consists of men from the business and corporate world, the NCAA, lawyers, representatives of the NFL and the NCAA, a former governor and a former president of the Fellowship of Christian Athletes. The Board is a strong, hard-working group who care about the game and those who coach and play. The Foundation hosts two golf tournaments and the prestigious CEO Coach of the Year award and dinner. Anyone can contribute to The Foundation and many have in appreciation of a specific coach, and many coaches have contributed to show appreciation for the education they have received. In the spirit of giving back, Coach and Mrs. Teaff (Donell) have given this book and its proceeds to the American Football Coaches Association Foundation.

Contents

Part IV
Solutions

·

Foreword

I believe Grant Teaff and I have as much in common as any two coaches in America. Over the many years that we have known each other, every time we get together we talk about what it takes to be a "successful coach." Our backgrounds are strikingly similar, Grant from Texas, me from Alabama. We both place our relationship with God as a first priority. We both played at small colleges, and coached in small colleges before taking over major college programs, Baylor University and Florida State University. Something else we agreed on was that we should use our position of leadership to coach and teach "beyond the game."

In *A Coach's Influence: Beyond the Game*, Grant writes about coaches being role models for their players. Being a role model is a must in our society. Within the last team I coached in 2009, 65% of my players were from fatherless homes. I emphasized to our coaches, "We must live our lives and coach in such a way that we will be role models for our players. In some cases we will be the dad the player 'never had.' Role modeling is an essential part of teaching values and developing positive character traits."

This book points out the importance of a coach's influence with his players. Personally, after my own father, my coach was the most influential person in my life. For several years now, surveys in America indicate teachers and coaches are held in high esteem by young people, because of their positive influence. Throughout my fifty-seven years as a college football coach, I always reminded my players that if they didn't have a dad, they needed to remember they were loved by me and their coaches, and they had a Father in heaven who loves them.

Mark Schlabach authored a book about me in 2010 entitled *Called to Coach*. That's another point that Grant and I agree on: coaching is a "calling." If as coaches we embrace the calling, we must accept the responsibility of being the best coach, leader, and role model possible. *A Coach's Influence: Beyond the Game* is enlightening and challenging for coaches and provides usable solutions that are already proven to be successful. This book is about the basics of the most important job we have as coaches, emphasizing values and building character. In football, the basics are blocking and tackling. If you fail to master those two basics, you can forget the strategy. If we fail to teach the basics of succeeding in life, then we are failing in our calling.

Grant covers in chapters 4, 5, and 6 how a coach's successful personal development can be handed down to players. Chapters 7–13 are comprised of the most comprehensive and applicable solutions to negative social issues found in one resource. Besides being great references, those chapters showed me the concern coaches have for their players and their innovative ways of changing negative social behavior through the game and by emphasizing that their players are physical, mental, and spiritual. By helping our athletes develop in all three areas, we will produce men who will be great leaders, husbands, and fathers.

This book is a must resource for coaches in all sports, as well as teachers. I would wholeheartedly recommend it to CEOs, business leaders, or in fact, anyone building a business, a football team, or a family. Finally, this book is clear in its challenge that all coaches and teachers must influence "beyond the game."

Bobby Bowden
Former Florida State Head Coach

Acknowledgments

This book was born out of a need expressed by members of the American Football Coaches Association. Over one hundred coaches contributed to this book through the generosity of their wisdom and experience.

Special heartfelt thanks are due to the following:

- the AFCA and AFCF staff who assisted and encouraged
- Jenny Hunt, Diane Smith, and Baylor University Press for excellent work
- Dan Knotts and Donnelley Publishing for a great job
- Josh Bookbinder for his research and compilation of statistics
- The Foundation Board for caring about coaches' education and development.

Thanks is not enough for Donell, my best friend, wife, and coaching partner. For fifteen months, she has sacrificed our time together while encouraging me, as she has for every book written, and in all these books she has served as my personal editor.

Introduction

A Coach's Influence: Beyond the Game

In January 1993, at the American Football Coaches Association's national convention in Atlanta, Georgia, I was asked to give a keynote speech. This followed the conclusion of my coaching career with my Baylor football team playing the University of Arizona. It was a good ending, as we were fortunate to beat my friend Dick Tomey and his Desert Storm defense in the Sun Bowl.

Thinking this would be my last opportunity to speak to the profession that I loved about the game that had been my life since a sophomore in high school, I expressed appreciation for the football coaches in my life who had influenced me profoundly with their knowledge of the game and the importance they placed on my development "beyond the game."

Emphasizing how important it is for the game to be used to teach life's lessons and how deeply the game is loved, I paraphrased a quote from Douglas MacArthur. It was his last speech to the cadets at the U.S. Military Academy: "Today marks my final roll call with you. But I want you to know that when I cross the river, my last conscious thought will be of the game, and the game, and the game. I bid you farewell."

Little did I know that six months later I would be thrust back into the game in a different role than playing or coaching. I accepted the position of executive director of the American Football Coaches Association in July 1993 and took over my responsibilities in January 1994.

As executive director of the AFCA, many hats were to adorn my head in the months and years to come. But none was more important to me than making sure that the AFCA continued to be the guardian of the game. Who better to protect, guard, promote, and develop our great game than the football coaches? Another hat symbolic of the role I wanted to play was planning and executing the finest educational venues for the members of the AFCA. Technical and philosophical training are extremely important; however, to me, the most important venues for education would be the personal and professional development of each member coach. My motivation stemmed from first-hand knowledge of the power of a coach's influence, in my own life, both as a recipient of that influence and, for thirty-seven years, a conveyer.

The idea of coaches being prepared and committed to making a difference in the lives of their players by using the game as the great classroom and encouraging each player to become the best man he can possibly be has always been a part of the thinking of great coaches.

Around one hundred years ago, the great Michigan coach Fielding H. Yost outlined clearly what the end result of a coach's influence should be:

> "To me no coach in America asks a man to make any sacrifice. He requests the opposite. Live clean, come clean, think clean. Stop doing all the things that destroy you, mentally, physically, and morally, and begin doing those things that make you keener, finer, more confident."

Amos Alonzo Stagg, one of the founders of our Association and one of the most innovative coaches of all time, said, "Winning isn't worthwhile unless you have something finer and more noble behind it." As the author of the original Code of Ethics of the AFCA, Coach Stagg said to the membership, "To me the coaching profession is one of the noblest and most far reaching in building manhood." Building manhood, of course, means influencing "beyond the game."

During 2010, I spoke with several coaches from the high school level through the professional ranks and all shared a deep concern with me: "Today's athletes are affected by a changed American society." The problem was described in different ways: social issues, negative behavior, indifference, and negative attitudes.

The request from coaches was consistent, "We need more education that will help us deal with today's 'social issues.'" That clarion call set in motion an effort that would span two years and six months of research, identifying social issues and finding solutions to these issues, as well as writing this book.

Researching the cause for the surge of negative social issues and surveying 12,000 coaches showed evidence and statistics that clearly indicated that changes in the American society are producing an inordinate number of children with a myriad of social issues.

The membership of the AFCA identified and prioritized six social issues that needed to be addressed. They were the negative effect of some homes, disrespect, lack of accountability, negative peer pressure, attitude of entitlement, and the issue of character. Research also indicated that institutions of higher education prepared teachers and coaches curriculum-wise; however, many fall short in preparing their graduates to deal with the challenges of negative social behavior.

This book is a result of an effort to provide solutions to social issues and to challenge coaches to accept the responsibility of mentoring and often serving as father figures. The professional development chapters featured in the book are designed for the personal improvement of the individual coach that allows, when mastered, the coach to teach and role model mind control that includes attitude, effort, motivation, and leadership to those in his charge.

This book would not have been possible without the generosity and willingness of the Association's members who shared their wisdom and expertise, bringing *A Coach's Influence: Beyond the Game* to fruition.

Part I

The Facts

— I —

The Consequences of a Changed Society

My love for the United States of America is very strong. In fact, I am what can be unabashedly referred to as a red, white, and blue patriot. While I love this country for many reasons, I particularly love the freedom we have as citizens to dream dreams and work toward making those dreams our goals. We also have the freedom to make our goals a reality.

At the beginning of my sophomore year of high school in Snyder, Texas, two new football coaches arrived in town, and my life has never been the same. At that moment in time, I already had a strong value system that was ingrained in me by my family. Subsequently, my high school teachers opened the door for me to grow intellectually. My two new coaches, however, taught me how to achieve success on the football field, and then transfer what the game taught me into successes in my life.

After playing organized sports for a year, I publicly proclaimed that I knew what I wanted to do with my life, which was to be a football coach. My underlying rationale was straightforward: I wanted to be like my coaches, teaching others as I had been taught.

The Dream

As I began to share my dream with my teammates, I upped the ante by further expanding on the vision of my future. My enhanced goal was to be a head football coach in the Southwest Conference, which was, at the time, the premier athletic conference in America. My fifteen-year-old brain had deduced that since coaching in the Southwest Conference had to be the highest level of coaching, that's where I wanted to be.

Near the end of my senior year, the high school annuals arrived. I was surprised, yet somewhat pleased, as I opened the annual and found the page dedicated to prophecies about the senior class. Beside my name, in bold print, was the prediction, "Grant Teaff will be the head football coach at the University of Texas." Whenever that story is brought up, I always say, tongue-in-cheek, "Heck, I only missed it by 100 miles." Waco, Texas, the home of Baylor University, is approximately 100 miles from Austin and the University of Texas. The other major goal that I had set for myself in my formative years was also quite direct: "I just want to make a difference." Although that goal was set at a relatively early age, it is still my number one goal in everything that I do. "Make a difference."

After playing eight years of high school and college football, coaching for 37 years, and serving as executive director of the world's largest football coaches association for almost two decades, I feel I am eminently qualified to say that coaching is absolutely a profession that allows players and coaches to make a difference.

On numerous occasions during my tenure as executive director of the American Football Coaches Association (AFCA), I have been introduced as a person who coaches the coaches. Frankly, I honestly think it's the other way around. Either way, one factor has not changed about the coaching profession: coaches coach other coaches, as well as their players.

A Special Profession

Coaching is a special profession. To be truly successful, a coach must exhibit leadership with his staff, with his players, and in his community. In addition to handling the technical aspects of football, a coach has a number of other core responsibilities, including teaching values, developing a sound work ethic with colleagues and athletes, and emphasizing to the players the benefits of receiving an education. The coach has the opportunity to teach meaningful life lessons through the game of football.

Some individuals claim that engaging in sports does not build character in those who participate. I adamantly disagree with these naysayers, because I know from my own experience of playing the game that my involvement in football had a meaningful impact on my character; furthermore, over the course of my coaching career, I saw many young men develop their character as a result of their participation in the game of football.

Unfortunately, in today's society, building character, changing lives, and even producing top academic students does not guarantee job security for a coach. In reality, coaches must win in order to keep their jobs, in order to pursue making a difference in the lives of the individuals they coach.

Missed Opportunities

On all competitive levels of coaching football below the professional ranks, coaches are helping mold their players into the men they will eventually become. Over the years, football coaches have always risen to the challenge of dealing with the needs of their players. Beginning in the early 1960s, American society began to change. A transformation occurred that created issues that coaches had not dealt with previously. As a result, over the last few decades, as society changed, more coaches and teachers in the educational system in America have been forced to address the by-products of this changed society.

When I first achieved my goal of coaching in the late 1950s, social issues were almost nonexistent. At that time, only a few of my players needed to strengthen their work ethic and adjust their level of personal discipline. Furthermore, very few athletes thought they were entitled. Mostly, my athletes had an attitude of "I know I have to earn it."

As a rule, most human attitudes tend to need some degree of adjustment. A lot of individuals, then and now, have attitudes that are negative, simply because human nature facilitates such an approach to life. I personally learned very quickly in life about the advantages of having a positive attitude. Accordingly, I made a concerted effort to address that factor early in my coaching career.

Recently, I became aware of the fact that during my first year as a head football coach in 1960, I fell short in the attitude area. In later years an email arrived from a man who had been a member of my first football team at McMurry College in 1960. He wrote to apologize for what he called his "crappy" attitude he had as a McMurry Indian. He said, "For years, I wanted to come to see you personally and apologize for my bad attitude." Frankly, I did not remember him. Obviously he dropped out of the program at McMurry and has lived with regret all these years. Writing him back, apologizing, I took responsibility for not helping him adjust his attitude. In my email, I reminded him of my own youth at that time, and then remarked, "Youth is no excuse for doing a poor job." Even though attitude was a high priority for me, I had somehow failed to change his negative attitude.

One of the many responsibilities of a coach is to discover what holds his players back from reaching their full potential on and off the field. It was obvious to me that I had totally missed this particular freshman's negative attitude so many, many years ago. Instead of regretting his negative attitude for a lifetime, his narrative might have been much different if I had done a better job as his coach.

Thinking back, I remember how proud I was of my first team, which, in my opinion, had an outstanding attitude. In his case, however, I had failed. It reminds me of the old adage, "You can lead a horse to water, but you can't make him drink." As such, the following point seems relevant: the members of the coaching and teaching profession need to remember that the water, which is a metaphor for the knowledge we serve our players, is only effective if our players drink it in. Another truism that I've heard most of my life further sums up the key point: "As a coach, it's not what you know, but what you teach."

Better Coaches

Most players and young coaches are taught by their mentors that when a problem exists, they must find the source of the problem and fix it. Since assuming the role of executive director of the American Football Coaches Association (AFCA), I have placed a strong emphasis on professional and personal development for the AFCA membership through educational venues, publications, unlimited resource material on the website, and a convention lasting three and a half days, featuring 392 mostly educational events. My passion is for every football coach to be "better tomorrow than today." As a coach, one of my major goals was to encourage every player to improve in some area each day. If that goal is accomplished on a daily basis, then at the end of a week, a month, a year, or even a lifetime, an individual will be the very best that he or she can be at the conclusion of each one of those time periods.

Help Needed

Over the last twenty years, the AFCA has provided speakers and information for coaches that help them to do a better job coaching with the techniques and philosophy of the game, along with mentoring and leadership. In that regard, the AFCA has always been very open to suggestions from its members concerning the AFCA convention program. In recent years, we have heard more and more from coaches asking for help dealing with students who lack values, have bad attitudes, or engage in negative behavior and inappropriate activities. These "four horsemen of the apocalypse" are the results of what the AFCA now calls "social issues" facing teachers and coaches on a daily basis.

Discovery

As the conversation about social issues expanded across the AFCA, it was determined that most coaches were in need of assistance. Concurrently, coaches who had already identified social issues discovered certain solutions to specific ones. The resulting plan, developed by the AFCA, was very simple: identify the key social issues facing coaches and prioritize them, while searching for the underlying causes of the issues. As a result, in early 2010, a survey/questionnaire was sent to every member of the AFCA. The questionnaire was straightforward, asking, "What social issues are prominent with the players on your level?" The responses began to pour in. Frankly, I was surprised to see a final list of social issues totaling 32. The AFCA staff picked six major issues and placed the remaining under those six. During membership registration at the 2011 AFCA convention in Dallas, Texas, each coach registering was asked to prioritize the list of the six key social issues, based on their personal experiences.

The Issues

The final list of social issues, as defined and prioritized by the AFCA membership, was as follows:

- *Peer pressure*—drugs, alcohol, gangs, criminal activity, premarital sex
- *Disrespect*—authority, coaches, teammates, parents, women
- *The home*—fatherless, no positive male role model, poor parenting, parental pressure
- *Entitlement*—selfishness, lack of dedication, "the-world-owes-me" attitude
- *Accountability*—personal behavior, attitude, responsibility, self-discipline
- *Character*—dishonesty, untruthfulness, questionable integrity, a quitter, lack of values.

The total number of votes for each prioritized social issue was quite similar. Accordingly, it was concluded that all six categories of social issues should be addressed equally. The variance between the six categories could probably be found to result from either the unequal sizes of the high schools or the differing socioeconomic statuses of the schools. On the college level, because players are chosen, it would seem logical that the extent of the social issues would be less. That conclusion, however, does not seem to be the case, based on a recent story in *Sports Illustrated* that pointed out criminal behavior occurring among the top programs in the Football Bowl Subdivision.[1] The story confirmed the observation that both high school and college coaches must deal with the social issues created by a changed society.

The Cause

Successful coaches identify problems, find solutions to these predicaments, and then develop a plan to implement the appropriate solution. It is apparent that an escalation of social issues on the high school and college levels has been caused by a changed society. In that regard, the relevant question is, "What has changed in American culture and society since 1960?" The answer is, in fact, that "just about everything has changed." For example, television has gone from a few black-and-white network channels to over three hundred channels on cable. Furthermore, over the years, more adult programming has crept into the afternoon and evening time periods. At the same time, television has been called upon to help raise a number of latchkey children. In the process, it has provided uncensored programming for the unsupervised.

Social media is contributing to the changes in American society. It has provided a broad platform for instant communications. Media such as Facebook, Twitter, texting, and the Internet place unsupervised children in an unrestricted environment in which they can read or watch anything.

Another factor is the development and availability of electronics, such as cell phones, iPad-type devices, and audio players. The music and words of some of the tunes currently blasting the airways have also played a role in changing our society. Tabloid newspapers and magazines, often with provocative pictures and headlines, can be seen and read by anyone in the checkout line at the grocery store. And oh yes, movies have ratings. Look around at a PG-13 or R movie showing and observe who is in attendance.

Two other major contributors to the rise of current social issues are a diminished work ethic and vanishing values. In that regard, a number of coaches have expressed concern for the growing feeling of entitlement that is exhibited by some of their players, based on the athletes' belief that they are deserving—entitled—to certain privileges without having to work for them.

In reality, the litany of possible causes for the changes in American society pales when compared to what many experts claim is the major problem in our country, the fatherless home.

A National Crisis

Speaking about the fatherless home in America, Wade Horn, at that time director of the National Fatherhood Initiative, said, "This is a national crisis. In fact, I believe it's not just one of many national crises, but it's 'the' national crisis because father absence drives almost every other social problem we experience." Former Governor Roy Romer of Colorado remarked, "I think it is a national crisis. We spend 40 percent less time as parents with children than we did a generation ago. That's very serious, and it's mainly because of absentee fathers." Governor Romer also noted, "Every child needs a role model that is both male and female." Ronald Mincy of the Ford Foundation (Philadelphia) observed that "it's a national crisis . . . that has to be dealt with with a great deal of care, and delicacy, and I'm glad that we're finally paying attention to it."[2]

The following statements from the Head Start program of the U.S. Department of Health and Human Services clearly back up the many individuals who believe in the importance of fathers:

> Scholars now know that boys and girls who grow up with an involved father, as well as an involved mother, have stronger cognitive and motor skills, enjoy elevated levels of physical and mental health, become better problem-solvers, and are more confident, curious, and empathetic. They also show greater moral sensitivity and self-control. As they grow, well-fathered children are substantially less likely to be sexually involved at an early age, have babies out of wedlock, or be involved in criminal or violent behavior. They are much more likely to stay in school, do well there, and go to college.[3]

In addition, statistics clearly back up the many individuals who believe that the fatherless home is a national crisis:

- 65% of youth suicides are from fatherless homes.
- 90% of all homeless and runaway youths are from fatherless homes.
- 85% of children who exhibit behavioral disorders are from fatherless homes.
- 71% of high school dropouts are from fatherless homes.
- 70% of youths in State institutions are from fatherless homes.
- 75% of adolescent patients in substance abuse centers are from fatherless homes.
- 85% of rapists motivated by displaced anger are from fatherless homes.[4]

The following statistics were gathered by the U.S. Census Bureau in 2009:

- 13.7 million single parents in America.
- 22 million children raised by single parents (more than one-quarter of all children).
- 82.2% of custodial parents were mothers.
- 36.8% of custodial mothers had never been married.
- 76.0% of single mothers had full-time jobs.
- 30.4% of custodial mothers and their children lived below the poverty line.[5]

David Popenoe, professor of sociology at Rutgers University and author of *Life without Father*, was interviewed in 1996 by David Gergen, editor-at-large at *U.S. News and World Report*. Dr. Popenoe argued that the real change in America has come since 1960. He makes the point that in 1960, "17 percent of the children in America went to bed at night without their natural father at home." In 1996 that number was up to 36 percent. Dr. Popenoe also stated, "The best evidence is that children coming from non-intact families have a risk factor of two to three times various problems befalling them as they become teenagers and young adults, compared to children from intact families. And that means juvenile delinquency . . . dropping out of school . . . having a bad marriage . . . teenage pregnancy."[6]

The other side of the story, Dr. Popenoe observed, is that, "in general, I think you can say that a society that has a lot of single men running around without family responsibility [—you've] got to worry about that society." During the discussion, Gergen mentioned that Dr. Popenoe's book emphasized the "high divorce rate and the high illegitimacy rate as being the product of a changing culture, [a] radical individualism that's taken hold." Popenoe responded, "I think you probably have to change both . . . there has to be a cultural shift, and then we have to back away from the kind of 'expressive individualisms,' one term, or 'me generation.' . . . looking at the data . . . we've gone too far in that direction."[7]

Charlayne Hunter-Gault, newspaper reporter and broadcast journalist, was a national correspondent for the Public Broadcasting Service (PBS) in the 1990s and reported on numerous national issues related to the fatherless home. She observed the following:

[Life without father is] being called one of America's most urgent and fastest-growing social problems. The 1990 Census counted 19 million children in families without fathers. Today, that number has increased to some 23 million. The National Commission on Children reports that fatherless children are five times more likely to be poor and ten times more likely to be extremely poor. Their risks are greater for dropping out of school, alcohol and drug use, adolescent pregnancy and child bearing, juvenile delinquency, mental illness, and suicide.[8]

As if the aforementioned statements, statistics, and proclamations deploring the fatherless home as a "national crisis" were not enough to point out the seriousness of the issue, the National Center for Fathering further clarified the gravity of the problem with a report entitled "The Consequences of Fatherlessness," citing a number of important studies and noting that "Some fathering advocates would say that almost every social ill faced by America's children is related to fatherlessness."[9]

Documented Social Ills

The following social ills have been documented at Fathers.com, the website for the National Center for Fathering:

Poverty—Children in father-absent home are five times more likely to be poor. In 2002, 7.8 percent of children in married-couple families were living in poverty, compared to 38.4 percent of children in female-householder families. In 1996 young children living with unmarried mothers were five times as likely to be poor and ten times as likely to be extremely poor. Almost 75 percent of American children living in single-parent families will experience poverty before they turn 11 years old. Only 20 percent of children in two-parent families will do the same.

Drug and alcohol abuse—The U.S. Department of Health and Human Services states, "Fatherless children are at a dramatically greater risk of drug and alcohol abuse." Children growing up in single-parent households are at a significantly increased risk for drug abuse as teenagers. Children who live apart from their fathers are 4.3 times more likely to smoke cigarettes as teenagers than children growing up with their fathers in the home.

Physical and emotional health—A study on nearly 6,000 children found that children from single-parent homes had more physical and mental health problems than children who lived with two married parents. Additionally, boys in single-parent homes were found to have more illnesses than girls in single-parent homes. Children in single-parent families are two to three times as likely as children in two-parent families to have emotional and behavioral problems.

Educational achievement—In studies involving over 25,000 children using nationally representative data sets, children who lived with only one parent had lower grade point averages, lower college aspirations, poor attendance records, and higher drop-out rates than students who lived with both parents. Fatherless children are twice as likely to drop out of school. School children from divorced families are absent more, and more anxious, hostile, and withdrawn, and are less popular with their peers than those from intact families.

Crime—Children in single-parent families are more likely to be in trouble with the law than their peers who grow up with two parents. In a study using a national probability sample of 1,636 young men and women, it was found that older boys and girls from female-headed households are more likely to commit criminal acts than their peers who lived with two parents. A study in the state of Washington using statewide data found an increased likelihood that [a child] born out of wedlock would become a juvenile offender. Compared to their peers born to married parents, children born out of wedlock were 1.7 times more likely to become an offender and 2.1 times more likely to become a chronic offender if male . . . and 10 times more likely to become a chronic juvenile offender if male and born to an unmarried teen mother.

Sexual activity and teen pregnancy—Adolescent females between the ages of 15 and 19 reared in homes without fathers are significantly more likely to engage in premarital sex than adolescent females reared in homes with both a mother and a father.[10]

Children out of Wedlock

Fathers leaving home—and avoiding responsibility for their out-of-wedlock children—is becoming its own national crisis.

Regarding that issue, Hope Yen, an Associated Press reporter, recently wrote that nearly half of American dads under 45 years of age said they have at least one child who was born out of wedlock. Furthermore, the share of fathers living apart from children has more than doubled in recent years.[11]

A recent Pew Research Center report highlighted the changing role of parents, as U.S. marriage rates in traditional family households fell to new historic lows. The report, entitled "A Tale of Two Fathers," found sharp differences based on race and education. Black and Hispanic fathers were much more likely to have children out of wedlock, at 72 percent and 59 percent, respectively, compared to 37 percent of white males. Among fathers with at least a bachelor's degree, only 13 percent had children outside of marriage, compared to 51 percent of those with high school diplomas and 65 percent of those who did not finish high school. Three-fourths of fathers who were aged 20-24 had children born out of wedlock.[12] The findings come as the latest census data show that marriages have fallen to a record low, pushing the share of U.S. households with married couples below 50 percent for the first time ever.[13]

Another contributing factor to the fatherless home is that it has been discovered that many biological fathers who might want to be part of a child's life are denied that opportunity. As the Children's Bureau of the U.S. Department of Health and Human Services recently noted, "Historically, unmarried fathers have had fewer rights with regard to their children than either unwed mothers or married parents."[14]

Call to Action

In reality, football coaches across America have been dealing with children from fatherless homes for many years. Not surprisingly, statistics confirm the fact that coaches often serve as surrogate fathers for many of their players. This is consistent with an observation I made in a speech to the AFCA in 1994, the year I took over as the organization's executive director. I remarked, "In the future, coaches will have to accept the fact that they will be the father-figure to many of the young men they coach."

Tom Osborne, former head football coach at the University of Nebraska and a former United States Congressman from the state of Nebraska, asserted the following to over four thousand coaches at a recent AFCA convention:

> I want to say just a word or two about influence. I think that you are all aware of this, but our culture has changed. I started coaching in 1962. In 1962 the out-of-wedlock birth rate was 5 percent; today it is 37 percent. When I went out recruiting in 1962 and 1963, we would occasionally run across somebody from a single-parent family, but if we did, it was usually because one parent or the other was deceased. Today, over half of our kids are growing up without both biological parents.

Tom then continued,

> The drug culture, the alcohol issue, the gangs, and the violence have shifted tremendously. The biggest factor that we are dealing with is homes without fathers. About 25 million kids in our country have no father. When you don't have a dad, just about every kind of dysfunction doubles and triples. So, in many cases, you're the dad. You're taking the place of something that the kid has missed in his life. It is a tremendous responsibility. Typically what happens is you've got a single mom who's working hard and can barely keep her head above water and can't really discipline and pay attention to some of those kids, try as she might. She does a great job in many cases. . . . A lot of kids don't know much about discipline. As coaches, you've got to teach them about discipline. A lot of them don't value education. They don't realize they're not going to go very far if they don't have some kind of marketable skills.

Coach Osborne then paused for a moment, looked directly into the eyes of the coaches in the audience and said, "You are the only guy who can make them understand this."[15]

That statement was a direct challenge to every coach and teacher by one of the greatest football coaches of all time. Coaching goes beyond winning football games and is more than character-building losses, more than graduating 100 percent, more than blocking and tackling. The coach has a responsibility to influence beyond the game.

— 2 —

Coaching: Beyond the Game

On my trusty iPad, I recently asked *Merriam-Webster's Dictionary* for the definition of the word *coach*. Certainly, the first definition to come up on my screen was not what I was looking for: "a large, usually closed horse-drawn carriage." The second definition that appeared was more to my expectations: "one who instructs or trains; especially one who instructs players in the fundamentals of a competitive sport and directs team strategy." In my opinion, that definition is what a lot of folks think coaching is, instructing players in the fundamentals of the game, coming up with offenses and defenses, strategies, and so forth. Coaching involves more . . . much more. In reality, the roles and responsibilities attendant to being a coach encompass several dimensions.

The Coach

One individual who understands the expansive nature of being a coach is David Brandon, former CEO of Domino's Pizza and currently the athletic director at the University of Michigan. David has great respect and love for those who coached him. As a quarterback at the University of Michigan, he was coached by the legendary Bo Schembechler.

In January 2007, David was named the American Football Coaches Foundation CEO Coach of the Year. The individuals honoring Mr. Brandon that night at the Waldorf Astoria in New York City collectively donated over one million dollars to the American Football Coaches Foundation, which was established by the American Football Coaches Association (AFCA) in 1998 to fund its educational mission. In his acceptance speech, David paid tribute to the profession of coaching when he stated,

> When it's all said and done at the end of all of our lives, we look back and try to figure out how many peoples' lives we've changed for the better. Certain people are in positions to do more of that than others. I can't think of a profession that has the ability to transform lives and change those lives for the better any more than that of the coaching profession. Any good coach I've ever known can measure the lives they've changed in the hundreds and thousands. I have great reverence for coaches. I think it's one of the noblest of professions. It's a hard job, it's a punishing job that requires a lot of sacrifice, but it's well worth it, based on the influence coaches have and the positive effect they have on the lives of those they coach.

Since 2006, beginning with Jeffrey Immelt, the CEO of General Electric, the American Football Coaches Foundation has recognized an outstanding corporate CEO by honoring him at a dinner in New York City at the Waldorf Astoria. The money raised at the dinner has had a huge impact on the ability of the AFCA to educate its 12,000 members. The dinner is always awe inspiring for a number of reasons, as the Who's Who of the corporate world and the athletic world attend to show their appreciation for the CEO being honored. For me, the highlight of the dinner is when I hear how each of these great leaders, at the pinnacle of his world, was impacted and influenced by one or more coaches.

In 2008, David Sokol, the former Chairman of the Board of MidAmerican Energy Holdings Company, was named the CEO Coach of the Year. In 2009 and 2010 Mark Hurd, CEO of Oracle, and Fred Smith, the innovative CEO of FedEx, received The Foundation's award. In 2011 T. Boone Pickens, Chairman of BP Capital, was the Foundation's honoree. Boone, who played basketball at Oklahoma State under the renowned Henry Iba, came close to entering the coaching profession himself. Frankly, he would have been a great coach had he chosen to go that direction, because he is an extraordinary leader. Like the other CEOs who received the award before him, Boone has great appreciation for the role that coaches play in the lives of those whom they coach. The 2012 CEO Coach of the Year was the commissioner of the NFL, Roger Goodell. He was unanimously selected by both the AFCA and the Foundation Board because of the leadership he exhibited in protecting the players in the NFL and the game itself through his innovative and strong leadership.

Each of the Foundation's CEO Coaches of the Year have had something very positive to say about the influence their coaches had on their lives. These exceptional leaders in the corporate world took for granted that their coaches knew how to teach the fundamentals of the game and inspire their teams to win. The chorus of praise coming from the honorees, however, made it abundantly clear how their coaches influenced beyond the game.

The Road to Coaching

A long, arduous journey starts when an individual decides to make coaching his life's work. While getting into coaching is hard, it's not as difficult as staying in coaching. The demands on a football coach to achieve success on the football field are very high and getting higher.

A young person desiring to go into coaching must be given the opportunity to learn the nuances of successfully coaching the game. Unfortunately, this opportunity cannot be addressed through a formal education. At the present time, no college or university offers an undergraduate, master's, or doctoral degree in coaching football. As a result, the game must be learned over a period of time through preparation and participation. Young coaches are forced to learn from their peers who have experience, because the game is complex. Fortunately, coaches, in general, have a deep sense of responsibility to give back to the game by sharing their knowledge and expertise with other coaches. His-torically, most coaches have been more than willing to share their approach to methods of problem-solving with other coaches. Across the board, from the founding fathers of college football, like Knute Rockne of Notre Dame and Amos Alonzo Stagg of the

University of Chicago, to representatives of today's exceptional coaches, like Mack Brown of the University of Texas, Nick Saban of the University of Alabama, and Les Miles of LSU, coaches have consistently and consciously given back to the game.

Given the pay-it-forward attitude of the coaching community, as well as the educational venues afforded by the AFCA, each coach needs to assume the responsibility of taking advantage of available educational opportunities. All coaches ask their players to improve every day to be better tomorrow than they are today. In that regard, coaches have a responsibility to practice what they preach.

Taking over as the executive director of the AFCA in 1994, I presented twenty major goals to the Board of Trustees. They approved all of them during that first meeting. The first thing on my agenda was to communicate to the members of the Association two main points. First, as a football coach, you are a member of one of the greatest professions in America. Accentuating that point, I said, "Take pride in your profession, your dress, your language, and always act as a professional." Second, AFCA will provide you with educational opportunities that cover all aspects of the game of football, as well as ensure that you have opportunities for personal and professional growth. Frankly, no reason exists that would preclude a coach from becoming the best he can be, not only as a football coach, but more importantly, as a leader, and ultimately as a husband and a father. As such, coaches should never be satisfied with how much they have learned. In fact, opportunities for learning abound. Football is a classroom, from which coaches will continue to learn and use as a platform to teach.

Never Stop Learning

At one time, Gordon Wood, who coached successfully at several Texas high schools, was the winningest interscholastic football coach in Texas history. Coach Wood exemplified the spirit of the tagline "learning has no off-season." Even in his later years, while retired in Brownwood, Texas, after a career in which he won nine state championships at different schools, he still attended college games on the weekends.

In fact, on a number of occasions, Coach Wood, while still coaching, would show up at Baylor Stadium, watch a game, and then drive the three hours back to Brownwood that night. I remember one game in which we had run the option particularly well and defeated a very good football team. As was my custom, I arrived at my office about 5:30 on Sunday morning to review the video of the previous game before going to the television station to record my TV show. It was very dark, and when I walked into the waiting room next to my office, I immediately saw someone on the couch. I walked over, looked down, and saw Coach Wood. I placed my hand on his shoulder to awaken him; he immediately sat straight up on the couch. I said, "Coach Wood, what in the world are you doing here?" He said, "I loved the play you ran last night with the fullback, so I stayed over to watch the film with you this morning, so I could get all the details." Nine championships and still learning! What an example for coaches everywhere.

Master the Fundamentals

If asked to describe myself as a football coach, I would quickly reply, "a fundamentalist." The word *fundamental* is defined in the dictionary as "serving as a *basic*, supporting existence, or determining essential structure or function."

Sometimes, the best thing that a coach can do after a devastating loss is to have his team go back to the basics or fundamentals. In football, that course of action refers to blocking and tackling, wrapping up the football, looking the ball in, taking a proper stance, making perfect snaps, and so on. On offense, most teams have three or four plays that are the basis for their offense. On the defensive side of the ball, going back to the basics involves having the defenders line up in their basic defensive scheme and physically defeat the man in front of them.

Beginning the Dream

One of the fundamentals from the AFCA's perspective is to encourage aspiring young football coaches to jump in with both feet. Each coach is exhorted to make learning an integral part of his life and to enhance the process of professional growth by taking advantage of the educational venues of the AFCA.

Every year during the Association's convention, the NCAA and the AFCA host thirty aspiring young coaches, each of whom has been selected to attend the Future Coaches Academy. The Academy features three days of outstanding curriculum for these aspiring coaches' personal development. Personally, I look forward to speaking first on the program.

The first thing I always say to attendees is likely a little shocking to them: "If you're getting into the coaching profession, and your major goal is to become a millionaire head football coach, you are making a huge mistake." Their eyes open wide when I tell them that the majority of football coaches in the profession make a little over minimum wage when the number of hours coaches work are figured into the paycheck. Of course I tell them, "You should still strive to be the best in everything you do, and particularly, coaching. If your best takes you to the lofty financial spot, that's great, but the odds are greatly against you. Rather, the driving inspiration should be more than the money. The calling should be to use the game to teach life's lessons."

Fundamentals for a Beginning Coach

Concluding my time at the podium, I always end with the following statement: "Seize every opportunity for self-improvement and be conscious of the little things for your continued personal development." Each aspiring coach is given a "Do" list.

The Beginner's "Do" List

- Listen, learn, and make yourself indispensible through your effort and work ethic.
- Control your emotions. When angered, remain quiet and in control.
- Remember that there's always a time and place for everything. Develop the attributes of self-control.
- Force yourself to be organized. Plan each day. Set goals in all areas of your life.
- Leave nothing to chance. Do not assume. Ask if you don't know.
- Have total loyalty to the staff, your supervisors, the institution, and those individuals you coach.

- Express your own opinion when appropriate, but when a decision is made, totally support that decision.
- Stay out of staff, office, and institutional politics.
- Start each day with a positive attitude, and keep it.
- Look for the good when bad things happen.
- Emulate the admirable traits in the coaches with whom you work.
- Be yourself, and do not try to be someone else (God only made one Bear Bryant).
- Keep copious notes from staff meetings.
- Set aside a part of each day for self-improvement (example: work on your vocabulary).
- Give total effort in everything you do.
- Be willing to help others, but not at the expense of your own assignments.
- Periodically ask your supervisor, "Where can I improve, and how can I do my job better?" The impression you make with those you work with will have an effect on your future.
- Learn the names of the support staff in the office. Try to speak to them daily, and call them by their names.
- Treat everyone with respect, especially individuals with menial jobs.
- Make personal phone calls, emails, Facebook entries, and texts on your own time.
- Remember Facebook is far from private, and what you say and the pictures you put up could come back to haunt you.
- Have a daily quiet time.
- Bloom where you're planted.
- Don't spend your time looking over the fence for the next job.
- Do the job you have with passion, and your next job will find you.

If an aspiring coach learns to take responsibility for his own personal development and advancement in our profession, his likelihood of achieving success skyrockets. Every person is given the breath of life with different talents and abilities. For instance, I love music and would give almost anything to be able to sing, but I cannot. Unless a miracle occurs, I will never be able to do more than make a joyful noise. My set of circumstances, however, does not deter me from enjoying the music of others. In fact, like most people, I have talents that others may not have. Accordingly, one of my responsibilities in life is to develop my own talents to their fullest. Whenever feasible, coaches should emulate positive traits that they admire in others. Positive and admirable traits are much like gold; once refined, they will prove their value again and again.

Successful Traits

To be a successful coach one must develop positive personal traits. If coaches adopt these traits and develop them to the fullest, they will maximize the likelihood of prospering as a husband, father, leader, and coach. The following four attributes serve as the fundamental platform for coaches:

1. *Commitment*—Faithfully adhering to a set of basic precepts (persistence with a purpose)
2. *Compassion*—The emotional capacities of empathy and sympathy, particularly for the suffering of others
3. *Leadership*—The ability to influence the behavior and actions of others to achieve an intended purpose
4. *Perseverance*—A demonstrable work ethic characterized by a high level of industriousness and a desire to see the job through to its completion

Ethics and Integrity

Ethics and integrity should be a vital part of every individual's core value system. Historically, ethics and integrity have been the foundation of the AFCA. Early on, one of the bedrock underpinnings of the AFCA has been to ensure that all members understand their responsibility regarding ethics and integrity in every aspect of the game. In fact, the precept "coaches teaching beyond the game" has its roots in ethics, integrity, and character.

On December 27, 1921, a group of football coaches gathered at the Hotel Astor in New York City to discuss the feasibility of a formal organization of football coaches. Subsequently, in 1922, under the leadership of Major Charles D. Daly of the U.S. Military Academy, that same group of football coaches formed an association of head football coaches that is known today as the American Football Coaches Association.

For that initial group of forty-three head coaches, ethics and integrity were a high priority. The renowned Amos Alonzo Stagg of the University of Chicago was given the responsibility of drafting for this fledgling group what would eventually evolve and become the AFCA's Code of Ethics. Proper sportsmanship and ethical integrity in coaching were among the first fundamental cornerstones laid by the founders of the AFCA. In the process, the concepts and principles of coaches exhibiting mutual honor and respect among their peers and those athletes they coached were entrenched in the profession.

Since 1923, the AFCA has had an Ethics Committee. The first committee Chairman was Amos Alonzo Stagg. The Ethics Committee is the most important committee in our Association, and I was honored to serve for twelve years as the Chairman of that committee. The committee Chairman and committee members take this awesome responsibility very seriously. Bill Curry, who served on the Ethics Committee during my tenure, tells the following story:

> Coach Teaff, the Chairman of the Ethics Committee, always gave the committee, prior to their first meeting of the year, what he called "The Charge." In emphasizing the responsibility each of us had in dealing with the cases that involved peers who were alleged to have broken the AFCA Code of Ethics, Coach Teaff said that besides confidentiality, making honest and fair judgments for those charged is essential. As a part of the charge at my first meeting, Coach Teaff said that all committee members had to obey all NCAA rules and the Code of Ethics. During a break, there was no one around, so I asked Coach Teaff if he really meant "all the rules." Coach Teaff looked me squarely in the eye and said, "Yes, Bill, ALL the rules."

In fact, that's Bill story, and he's sticking to it. For me, nothing has changed. I still feel that way and believe that as coaches, we have a responsibility to live what we teach.

In the beginning, Coach Stagg and his committee presented the Board with ten ethical standards to which coaches should adhere. The original Code of Ethics was written in 1952, and was subsequently revised in 1973 and yet again in 1996. Since those steadfast beginnings in 1922, generation after generation of football coaches have proclaimed through the Code of Ethics and the AFCA Ethics Committee that ethics, honesty, and integrity are major responsibilities that should be accepted by anyone who enters the profession of coaching football.

During 2011 and 2012, college football took hit after hit. Great institutions and well-known coaches suffered the consequences of poor decision-making. As disheartening as the negative headlines are, I am uplifted by the knowledge that for every negative in college, there are hundreds of positives. A large majority of football coaches believe strongly in doing things the right way, with character and integrity. Adhering to the AFCA Code of Ethics and the NCAA rules is fundamental to teaching the importance of honesty and integrity to those we coach.

The Master Coaches on Ethics and Integrity

Tom Osborne, currently the athletic director at the University of Nebraska and formerly the head football coach for the Cornhuskers, as well as a Nebraska Congressman, said,

> I think that players really appreciate integrity, and they sense if you are leveling with them. Of course, the worst thing a coach could ever do is offer some illegal inducement. I know that you all understand this, but this is a profession, and it really lives and dies with the ethics and the public perception of those in the profession. I've spent a little time in politics. Politicians are held in very low regard today, and that has a lot to do with ethics. I hope that's never the case in our profession.[16]

Vince Dooley, former head football coach at the University of Georgia, served as the Chairman of the AFCA Ethics Committee for a decade. He recently made this statement, speaking of his Georgia teams:

> We had values in our mission statement from Georgia, and we started with the value of integrity. If you don't have integrity,

you don't have any worthwhile values at all. Integrity has to be number one, then you go from there to team leadership, team and personal development. All are so important, and that part of our responsibility never lessens, but we have to start with integrity.

One of my longtime friends, an individual who became one of the most beloved and outstanding football coaches of his time, was Tom Landry. Tom coached the Dallas Cowboys to national prominence. He said this about values and ethics,

> I don't think there's any question about the fact that values and ethics are so very important. When you start talking about values and ethics, you are actually talking about character. When you have a team with character, then you have a team that is going to be a winner in life and on the football field.

When the legendary, professional Don Shula appeared before the AFCA convention as a Master Coach, he shared his deep belief in the importance of leadership and integrity in our coaches. To the assembled group, he stated,

> Leadership-wise, I think the three most important things you as a coach are responsible for as a leader are integrity, credibility, and communication. Once your credibility is questioned as a leader, your ability to lead will be diminished.

John Cooper, a successful head football coach who held positions at a number of institutions, including Ohio State, once said, "As a head football coach, it is your responsibility to make sure that you, your coaches, and the people who work for you and with you don't cheat."

Hayden Fry, who had a very successful career that included head football coaching stints at SMU, North Texas, and Iowa, once remarked,

> As a coach, you make a commitment that you're going to do things the right way, and then you explain to your staff and to the players the rules of the game, and the Code of Ethics from the AFCA. Let the players know that, as coaches, we are going to follow the rules and we are asking and demanding our players follow the rules as well.

Another Chairman of the Ethics Committee for the AFCA was Fisher DeBerry, formerly the head football coach of the Air Force Academy, who stated, "At the Air Force Academy, we try to live the core value of the Academy, which is, 'Integrity, first, above all that we do.'"

Coach DeBerry then eloquently summed up the coaches' responsibility to live what we teach by referring to a poem penned by the extraordinary poet Edgar A. Guest, "I'd Rather See a Sermon."

I'd rather see a sermon
than hear one any day;
I'd rather one should walk with me
than merely tell the way.

The eye's a better pupil
and more willing than the ear,
Fine counsel is confusing,
but example's always clear;

And the best of all the preachers
are the men who live their creeds,
For to see good put in action
is what everybody needs.

I soon can learn to do it
if you'll let me see it done;
I can watch your hands in action,
but your tongue too fast may run.

And the lecture you deliver
may be very wise and true,
But I'd rather get my lessons
by observing what you do;

For I might misunderstand you
and the high advice you give,
But there's no misunderstanding
how you act and how you live. . . .

Coach DeBerry went on to say,

I think when they call you coach, that title means we are to be ethical. We are to have core values. I think we have to operate a daily program that teaches character, integrity, and leadership. That will result in our guys becoming good husbands, good fathers, good officers, and certainly contributing to the betterment of society. Football is the best game, as we know, to teach life's lessons. Frankly, that's why the majority of us coach. The highlight of my Christmas was a call I got from a player's dad, who happens to be a very successful high school football coach. He said, 'I just want you to know I sent you a boy, and you sent me back not just a man, but a man with values.' To me that was about the highest compliment I think I could ever have been paid.

To teach values, character, and integrity effectively, the coach must live what he teaches. It is our responsibility that the players see character and integrity in what we do and what we say.

Father Figure—Positive Male Role Model

Over the years, I have heard a number of celebrities say, "I don't want to be a role model." Truth be known, I have never heard a football coach say that. While some coaches might prefer not to have the responsibility of being a father figure to some of their players, the majority of the coaching community does, if the situation warrants it. The reality is, the changes in American society have wreaked havoc on the American home. The absence of a positive male role model in homes is fully understood by most coaches. Coaches also understand that in many cases the buck will stop with them.

In reality, in a free society there are three institutions that are critical to the positive development of children. The three institutions are the home, the church, and the educational system. Stunning statistics in recent years have pointed to the demise of the home in America. The demise of the home has surely contributed to the alarming article published in 2005 in the *Journal for the Scientific Study of Religion* by C. Kirk Hadaway and Penny Long Marler.[17] These two scholars report that the percentage of the American population attending religious services each week is around 21 percent, instead of the approximately 40 percent reported by pollsters. With the decline of the American home, and the decrease in families attending church, education becomes the frontline for developing children intellectually and preparing them to face the realities of life. In far too many cases, skills to be successful in life must be taught as well.

Sports in the educational system have a developmental role to play as well. The athletic field becomes an extension of the classroom. If that classroom is conducted properly, what should have been taught in the home and at church will be conveyed by teachers and coaches.

Football in particular as a classroom or a laboratory provides a setting in which players can overcome social issues. Coaches have an important role in preparing their athletes for wise leadership and personal achievement.

Those of us in education have all known exceptional mothers who have done an outstanding job raising their children without the assistance of a positive male role model. However, many of those successful moms were assisted greatly by a male family member, pastor or youth minister, family friend, teacher, or coach.

Experience tells us that the majority of young men from single-parent homes are in need of a positive male role model or father figure. This reality has created a need for coaches to become reinforcing role models and, in many cases, father figures.

Experience has taught me that the coach as the father figure is indeed a fact. I was blessed with a great father who was a role model and mentor to me, and a man I deeply respected. He always encouraged me to play sports and to follow my dream. He once said to me, "You will spend more time with your teachers and coaches during your education than you will with your family." He was absolutely right in that observation. His comment is equally true for those we coach. They will spend more time with their coaches, trainers, strength coaches, academic support staff, and teammates than they will with their families.

My father was a living example of having a values-based orientation and a strong work ethic. My coaches in high school and college verified my family's emphasis on always adhering to values and exhibiting a work ethic. The discipline I had been taught at home was reinforced and upheld by my teachers and coaches. Frankly, I love them all for their efforts in that regard, because they verified the importance of what I had been taught at home. I had friends who did not have the kind of background I had. Fortunately for them, their coaches and teachers, through their examples and words, had a huge impact on their lives. As a leader and starter on my team, I was constantly reminded by my coaches that I had to earn my right to lead and my starting position on the team. I was not entitled to start or to be a leader, but I had the opportunity to work hard for it. I constantly am reminded of the following words of my coaches and my father: "There are no free lunches."

One particularly memorable example of a coach as a father figure in my life occurred during my junior year at Snyder High School. It was a bright, crisp Friday morning, and just as I drove into the parking lot at the high school, thinking about the big game to be played that night and my potential role in it, I had an epiphany: "I should not be distracted from my concentration on the upcoming game by going to class." In the parking lot, three of my teammates subsequently approached me. As we talked about the game to be played that night, I shared my newfound philosophy: "In order to be mentally prepared to play our best game, we really should not be distracted by having to sit in those classrooms, walk down the hallways, and talk to classmates, because we need to focus on the game." My teammates agreed, so we left the campus and went to a spot about a mile and a half away on Deep Creek. That particular spot had ample grass to lie on, to let the sun's rays warm our bodies. After having our pre-game meal late that afternoon, we reported to Tiger Stadium. As I look back, the stadium was very unimpressive, as was our makeshift dressing room. After World War II, the school system bought a few Quonset huts from the military, one of which was moved to the end of the football stadium to serve as our football dressing room.

Feeling very good about ourselves and the game, and being energized by our focus and rest during the day, the four of us walked joyfully into the dressing room. Our happiness soon turned to fear and concern, because standing in the middle of the room, waiting for us to enter, was Coach Mule Kayser. Coach Kayser was our offensive and defensive line coach. His face was red, glaring at the four of us. He said loudly, "Gentlemen, might I ask you where you have been the entire day?" Stammering and stuttering, I said, "Well, Coach, I thought it would be better for us mentally to go down to Deep Creek and rest, and not be distracted by sitting in classes all day."

His face seemed to turn redder. He reached down into a sack of kindling wood that he had purposely brought into the room, and he uttered the words, "For every action, there is a consequence. Bend over," he said. Dutifully we did. We then thoroughly understood the consequence of our action. Pieces of kindling wood were flying all over the room, as our teammates were ducking and dodging the errant missiles. Coach Kayser helped turn a mediocre team into a very good team by making examples of four starters. The excuses I conjured up to do the wrong thing didn't hold water with Coach Kayser, nor would they have with my father. Without thinking, I had disrespected what my family would have wanted me to do and what my coach knew I should have done. Hurting more than the licks administered was what Coach Kayser subsequently said as he looked me in the eye: "Grant, I am very disappointed in you."

I realized at that moment that Coach Kayser was a father figure to me. It hurt me as deeply to disappoint him as it would have to have disappointed my own father. Truth be known, he taught me the importance of self-discipline in a swift and decisive way on that fateful Friday.

Unsolicited Wisdom

Over the past twenty years, I have conducted interviews with 36 of the greatest coaches of all time during the AFCA convention with over 4,000 coaches in attendance. The session is the most popular event on the convention program. For conference attendees to have the opportunity to sit at the feet of the masters of the game and listen to those icons in our profession is a blessing that provides a wealth of knowledge. During those interviews, I never asked any of the Master Coaches their opinion on the responsibility of a coach to be a father figure. However, during those hour-and-a-half conversations, almost every coach interviewed had something to say about that responsibility.

Don Shula, whose exploits as the head coach of the Baltimore Colts and the Miami Dolphins are renowned, once said,

> Young men in particular look to coaches as father figures or examples. A lot of the young people in certain neighborhoods don't have fathers, so the coach becomes that father figure.

Make sure that you utilize every opportunity you have to help these young men move on successfully in life. Always think about the example you set for your players and for fans who are watching you and your teams. You are responsible, and everything you do should be done in a first-class way.

Over the years, a number of noteworthy coaches have shared their thoughts on the coach–athlete interaction. R. C. Slocum, former head football coach at Texas A&M, added his thought on the matter when he stated, "The player has to believe that you have his best interests at heart. We get guys, unfortunately, who have not had the benefit of a strong father figure. They've never had anyone who said, 'You can't act like that, son. That's bad for you. You're disgracing your family, this program, and yourself.'"

Terry Donahue, formerly the head football coach at UCLA, reflected, "Players today need positive reinforcement; because so many come from split or fatherless homes. In America today, players really need a pat on the back more than athletes ever have needed it in the history of football. Society, as a whole, is different."

Don James, the legendary former head football coach at the University of Washington, commented, "Coaches have to realize that kids listen to you. It's incredible. I got a three-page letter from a former player recently about the impact I had on his life. It was humbling."

John Gagliardi, head football coach at one of the winningest programs in all of football, Saint John's University, said, "Well, I certainly think that the coach has to be a role model. I don't drink or smoke or carouse, and I raise my kids that way. I don't really have a lot of rules for them, but they saw that I didn't smoke or drink. I think that meant something to them, because I never told them not to do those things, yet they didn't do them."

The aforementioned Gordon Wood made the following observation, "In the final analysis, if you're just out there to coach players to win games, we're not in a very good profession. We should all coach kids to help them, that's what I've told our coaches. If we're not in here to help kids, then what are we doing?"

During the 2011 convention that was held in Dallas, Texas, Bobby Bowden, who was serving on a panel addressing the social issues that coaches face, made the following emphatic plea to the members of our Association,

Some say the closest bond a boy can have is with his daddy. That's the closest bond there is. It's also been said a young man's first concept of God is probably his relationship with his dad, because his dad is the one who takes care of him. His dad is the one who sees he has something to wear. His dad is the one who sees he gets to school. His dad protects him.

Bobby continued,

Now, some of you men were lucky enough to have had a dad, but so many of our kids don't have that. I feel for them, you know? It gets around to this: if the number one bond between a boy is his dad, what if he doesn't have a dad? There is no doubt who is next. Coaches. Just think of yourself as a boy. When you came up, who would you listen to more than anybody in the world? Your coach. Now, I love my daddy, but if he told me to do something, and my coach told me to do something different, it'd be a struggle.

The unsolicited testimony offered by these renowned members of football's coaching community should be more than enough insight and motivation for every coach to consider the fact that a serious problem exists in our society. In turn, a major part of the solution to that problem is for coaches to accept and undertake the role of father figure.

Without exception, the coaches and teachers who have been a part of the coaching profession for a few years are aware of the multitude of responsibilities they have, beyond merely teaching fundamentals and strategies of the game of football. On the other hand, individuals who are just entering the field might be somewhat overwhelmed by the responsibilities that often accompany the title "Coach."

The primary focus of this chapter was to point out some of the major responsibilities that coaches have. In reality, however, a number of others also exist, including the following:

- Serving as the guardian of the "family," including the players and the coaches, as well as staff members and their families
- Ensuring the safety and well-being of the student-athlete

- Taking advantage of the opportunity to mold young people during the formative years of their lives
- Teaching respect (note: respect must be given in order to be received)
- Teaching personal responsibility and accountability to the players
- Teaching players in a positive way (note: there are no free lunches)

When individuals begin their journey as football coaches, it's impossible for them fully to understand the magnitude of their influence. That wonderful gratification will be an unsolicited reward that is bestowed on a coach, time and time again, as he continues his journey, with the relatively simple title of "Coach." Eventually, he will understand the power of his influence. In so doing, the coach will never regret using the power of his influence "beyond the game."

— 3 —

The Power of Influence

Coaching is a very special profession. For me personally, it was never a job. It is an honor to be referred to as "coach." My alma mater bestowed a doctorate upon me, and I was extremely honored, but I have never used the title, because I much prefer coach. The impact and the influence my high school coaches had on me created a burning desire to follow in their footsteps and to someday influence others as they were influencing me. I often refer to those in our profession as teachers/coaches, because the best teachers coach their students and the best coaches are great teachers. Because of the nature of the sport of football, the practice field and the games are added classrooms, as they provide for the development of an individual as a total person, one who has felt the sting of defeat and the exhilaration of success. More importantly, there is an opportunity to teach life's lessons by the very nature of the game. There is no entitlement on a football field. Everything has to be earned. A coach's greatest influence is not so much in what he teaches, but in how his players recognize what he teaches in the way he lives his life.

Coaches have a greater opportunity than ever before to be positive influences in today's society. Coaches are able to use practice and games to teach values and develop positive character qualities in their players. Validation of the lessons taught will be provided by the values and character of the teacher.

Home for the Association

In 2001 the Board of Trustees of the American Football Coaches Association (AFCA) agreed with me that we needed to build a national headquarters. We were very excited because it would be a functional office and would make a statement about the relevance of AFCA to the game of football.

Selecting the architects and working with them to design the type of building we needed was step number one. My role was to be meticulous about every part of the building, including the exterior and the grounds. In front of the building, we designed a beautifully landscaped area with shrubs and plants. In the back of the building, the area was to be enclosed with stone walls. And inside those walls, a green space with flowers and trees. Little did I know, on a trip to New York City, that the green space would cease to exist because it would take on a much more important role.

A Place of Honor

In December my wife Donell and I flew to New York City for my induction into the National Football Foundation College Football Hall of Fame at the Waldorf Astoria. Being inducted into the College Football Hall of Fame is looked upon as the epitome of a college coach's accomplishments. Each year, one hundred or more college head coaches attend the dinner, as do current members of the Hall of Fame. They join an audience of 1,600 to recognize and honor those deemed "The Best of the Best." As the time neared for the moment of my induction, my thoughts turned to those in my life responsible for me receiving the Hall of Fame ring.

I thought of my family, my assistant coaches through the years, the hundreds of players, and finally, I thought about the influence of my high school and college coaches and how proud they would have been for me receiving Hall of Fame recognition. As I thought about their influence on me, I realized that none of them had ever been inducted into any kind of Hall of Fame, though they, like thousands of other coaches, had spent their lives positively influencing hundreds and hundreds of young men. I could not hold back the tears, wishing there was a place where coaches could be honored for the sheer power of their influence.

The next morning, while waiting to go to the airport, Donell and I walked down a street near the hotel and happened to walk by a store that sold artwork. Glancing in the window, I saw something that stopped me in my tracks. Instantly, I knew the art that I saw in that window had to go to Waco with me.

Following me into the store, Donell heard me ask the clerk to retrieve a statue from the front window. The two-foot statue was of a young boy with a football under one arm and a helmet under the other. Without asking the price, I muttered to the clerk, "He's going to Waco, Texas."

On the plane ride home, Donell began to question me about the statue and why I was so attracted to it. I replied, "That little boy was me and every other boy who dreamed of playing football. He had a ball and a helmet, but needed instructions. In my imagination he's looking up at a coach saying, 'Teach me how to play the game, teach me how to live life.'"

As the conversation fell silent, I began to jot down words that helped me continue to explain to Donell the emotion that caused the instant connection between me and the little boy. The words became an ode to "a coach's influence."

A COACH'S INFLUENCE
by Grant Teaff

I dreamed a dream, but I had my doubts.
"You can do it," he said. "I'll teach you how."
I tried and tried, he said I should.
I gave it my best, he knew I would.
Lessons taught on the field of strife
Have been invaluable, as I've faced life.
When challenges come my way,
I always think, what would he say?
His inspiring words I hear even now,
"You can do it. I taught you how."
Now, others dream, and have their doubts.
I say, "You can do it, I'll teach you how."

The influence continues.

The trip from New York City was fruitful for many reasons, but by the time I stepped off that plane, I was committed to creating a place at the AFCA headquarters to honor coaches on all levels who had spent their lives positively influencing those they coached.

The green space would become the Plaza of Influence—the designated place where anyone who had been influenced by a football coach could recognize and honor that coach in one of several different ways. The Plaza had space for a thousand bricks, benches in the Plaza to be inscribed, as well as wall plaques, and one hundred capstones. The Plaza of Influence was born.

In preparation for the opening of the new building and the Plaza, I felt that something special needed to be said about it. I put into words what the Plaza meant to me, and those words are in bronze on the Plaza gate.

The Plaza of Influence

The Plaza of Influence is a special place
where football coaches are honored by those
whose lives they have inspired. These coaches
range from the obscure to the nationally
known. The common bond is their profound
influence on lives—touched and changed.

—The American Football Coaches Foundation

On a few occasions since the completion of the Plaza and the building, I have emotionally welled up with tears in my eyes, as I realize what the Plaza of Influence has meant to those who are honored and to those who have made the effort to honor the coaches who influenced their lives.

A few years after the Plaza was opened, our staff received a request from a retired high school coach desiring to honor his high school coach. The information was taken, and in a few weeks the brick was placed at an appropriate spot in the Plaza; the older coach had now been recognized by someone he had influenced. Shortly after the brick was put in place, the staff received a telephone call from the retired coach asking if his coach's brick was in place. The answer was yes. Three days later, the retired coach, his wife, and his former coach arrived to see the brick.

The three were ushered into the Plaza by a staff member and shown the location of the brick. I joined the trio just as the one being honored stood directly behind his brick for the historical picture. He stood motionless, head held high, waiting for his picture to be taken on this momentous occasion. His eyes were filled with tears. To him, he must have felt like he had just been inducted into the College Football Hall of Fame.

I too was filled with emotion, realizing that the idea of the Plaza, and the time, effort, and money spent on it, was worth it for this one moment. A 93-year-old coach and his 66-year-old former player shared a moment where the "thank you for the power of your influence" was expressed without a word being said. Ever so often, I step out into the Plaza, walk around, and read the inscriptions. It always motivates me to see how many lives have been touched and changed by the power of their coaches' influence. Individuals and teams have honored their coaches, and the inscriptions mention many different ways in which coaches have influenced their players.

Take a walk with me now through the Plaza of Influence to share some of the inspiring inscriptions dedicated to the power of a coach's influence.

The Plaza of Influence

Forty-five former players placed the following on a bench dedicated to their coach, Coach Jimmie Keeling (Hardin-Simmons University, Abilene, Texas):

"In honor of the tremendous influence you had on all of us. You have made each and every one of us better men, because we have known you. You made us believe we could achieve. Your influence did not end with our last playing day. Your influence continues."

Mike Farley of the University of Wisconsin-River Falls has been honored by his former players:

"Coach Farley taught us how to compete and to never expect a free lunch. He taught us how to handle adversity. He taught us how to react to a loss with grit and determination. He taught us how to win with humility. He often said, 'We're number nothing,' knowing that he was challenging all of us to prove ourselves. 'The team comes first.' This was the only motto he displayed in his office. We learned that individual accomplishment and recognition had to be sacrificed for the greater good of the team. From the lessons he taught us on the football field, we learned how to live life. 'One play and one day at a time.'"

Coach Al Vanderbush, Hope College, 1946–1954:

"Coach Vanderbush refused to let us settle for less than our best. He taught us to play with intensity and with respect for the rules and our opponents. In his daily life he modeled the man of Christian character, discipline, intellect and integrity, as effectively as it continues in our hearts to this day."

Several years ago, an eighth grade team wanted to honor their coach in the Plaza of Influence. I was so impressed I asked them to present the wall plaque to Coach Steve Wickwar at the AFCA convention in San Antonio, Texas. Coach Wickwar had been severely injured in an automobile accident and left paralyzed; however, the power of his influence never diminished.

"Coach Wickwar taught us how to play the game and continues to show us how to live life through his courage, his faith and his perseverance. Coach's recovery after a paralyzing auto accident inspires us every day."

—8th grade football team, Bush Jr. High,
San Antonio, Texas

Coach Tyrone Willingham honored his high school coach, Coach Gideon (Gid) T. Johnson with these words:

"He nurtured boys into men."

Dal Shealy, who was the head coach at Mars Hill College, Carson-Newman College, and the University of Richmond, was honored by his former assistant coaches and players, who simply said,

"Coach Shealy maintained his high moral values while teaching success on the football field."

Coach John Steigman, a defensive coach at Princeton during two undefeated seasons, was deeply admired by his players for his real-life courage, driving a landing craft onto Normandy Beach on D-Day during World War II. That selfless, courageous act gave credence to his simple points for success: no excuses, keep it simple, be devoted to your cause. The inscription his former players wanted on his wall plaque was this:

> "Coach Steigman was never interested in excuses. His way was simple: get results and be devoted. His influence changed our lives."

Coach Aldo "Buff" Donelli coached at Columbia University from 1957 to 1967. His champs of '61 had this to say on his plaque:

> "The greatest teacher who ever lived. He coached us because he cared about us. He knew the game. He loved the game. He made a difference in our lives."

Coach Don Drinkhahn was honored by the senior team of 2003, South Dade High School:

> "We honor you here so all may see the respect you earn. The field is the best classroom."

Mike Ayers honored his coach, Tom Dowling, with this inscription:

> "Great coach, great teacher, great friend. You were a difference-maker. Not just for a season, but for a lifetime. Thanks."

Tivy High School of Kerrville, Texas, 1955–1961, had as their coach Tom C. Daniel. One of his former players, Bill Womack, placed this plaque in the Plaza for his coach:

> "Remember the fundamentals taught here: anything worth having requires a lot of hard work and intestinal fortitude to obtain."

Ray's Boys from 1972 to 1994 honored their coach, Ray Solari of Menlo College, with Coach Ray's own words to them:

> "Take care of the little things and the big things will take care of themselves."

The Plaza has many nationally known coaches, such as Darrell Royal, who is honored by Red McCombs, a great alumnus of the University of Texas. He honored Coach Royal with a fountain simply inscribed *"Builder of men."* The two beautiful oak trees in the Plaza point out the uniqueness of the Plaza as it honors the obscure and the nationally known. One oak tree was dedicated to Coach Bear Bryant and the other to Tyrone Willingham's high school coach.

The Plaza will always be a place where coaches can be recognized and honored for "The Power of Their Influence."

For me, this chapter on the power of coaches' influence is the most inspirational chapter in this book. I particularly want young coaches coming into our profession to be inspired to use the influence that comes with the title of coach in such a way that those they coach learn the nuance of the game and what it takes to be successful on the football field. Our players will leave the presence of our influence, but they take with them the positive lessons and principles taught. Hopefully we will have been a model and what we taught can help them become better husbands, fathers, citizens, and leaders. If that happens, the influence will continue.

The Power of Influence Award

In 2002 the AFCA and the American Football Coaches Foundation felt it was time to implement a national award for high school head coaches. High school football associations were asked to nominate one coach from their association who most typified the power of a coach's influence. The award was not to be based on win/loss record, but merely on the power of the individual coach's influence on his school, his community, and particularly his team. The thirty to forty nominations we receive each year narrow down to the five most impressive. At the spring Foundation board meeting, the entire board is given the top five nominations. Over a couple of days, they read the information and vote on the coach they feel deserves the award. Because of the quality of the men honored, the American Football Coaches Foundation Power of Influence award has become the number one national high school award.

A certificate is given to each coach and their association in honor of the nomination. Each nominated coach who is not selected is automatically put into the pool for the following year. As a footnote, although winning football games is not a criteria for winning the Power of Influence award, it is quite interesting to note that in each of the states' associations, the coach who members identify as most influential is among the leading winners of football games in the state, if not *the* winner.

Part of the nomination process is to have letters testifying to the influence the nominee had on individual players and the community. For ten years now, over 150 high school coaches have been nominated and AFCA has accumulated hundreds of inspiring letters from former players recommending their coaches because those players were positively affected and molded by their influence.

Tributes to the Coaches of Influence

The following is a random selection of letters accompanying nominations for the Power of Influence award.

Aaron Zimmerman writes of his coach, Craig Beverlin of Kamiakin High School (Kennewick, Washington),

"Growing up in a home where drugs and verbal abuse were commonplace, it was easy for a teenager to slip into a world of low self-esteem and self-doubt. That was the world I was in when I first became a member of Coach Bev's football program. Early on, Coach recognized in me a desire for the better life and that he had an opportunity to keep at least one young man on the right side of the fence. His challenge to me was to hang in there and work hard to get out of my home situation. Most importantly, Coach taught me not to accept excuses for quitting. After four years in the program, I realized I didn't have to continue the generational curse and that I could change my whole world if I had the heart to commit to it. The principles and values that were instilled while I was at Kamiakin High School were carried into a highly successful military term of service. I have earned my bachelor's degree, been promoted to the position of bank manager, and most recently, head coach for the Ellensburg Bulldogs, Grid Kids football team. Because of my time with Coach Beverlin, I have learned that I can go further than I ever thought and that I could leave a world that I despised behind me. It makes me proud that that life is no longer a part of who I am, and that more importantly, my own son will never have to experience it."

Rick Wimmer of Fishers High School (Fishers, Indiana) was recommended highly by Zack Wells with these words,

> "Coach Wimmer was the father figure to many players I
> played with and has continued to be that for thousands more
> over the course of his career. With the absence of a father in
> my own life, Coach Wimmer became a much-needed positive
> male influence. Having been raised by my mother and kicked
> out of my first high school for fighting, I entered Coach's pro-
> gram as a sophomore and quickly understood that dedication,
> hard work, and respect were the foundation of his program.
> My teammates and I still talk about how lucky we were to
> have coaches who cared for us, as players and men. Many of my
> teammates looked to have great childhoods from the outside,
> but it was the guidance and structure of football under the
> direction of Coach Wimmer that kept us all on the right path
> and has allowed us to experience great success as men, heads
> of our own families."

When Nathan Stratton was eight years old, his parents separated.
Nathan's dad raised Nathan and two brothers. Nathan says in
his letter honoring Russell Isaacs of Snider High School (Fort
Wayne, Indiana),

> "My dad was a single parent, and unfortunately, I took advan-
> tage of that. I'm sure my dad did his best, but once my mom
> moved out, he fell into a pretty deep depression. When I was 14,
> peer pressure got the best of me and I started drinking. I had
> every excuse to fail, to not try, and I used them all. If anyone
> ever stood up to me and told me I was underachieving or being
> disrespectful, I would simply blame my situation and the fact
> that my parents' separation was simply too much. It was my
> convenient 'get out of jail free' card. Up until the summer of my
> sophomore year, it had worked great. It was Wednesday, and I
> was tired, just trying to survive. I looked up to see Coach Ike
> running toward me like I had just stolen his playbook. 'Why
> is your helmet off, Stratton? Get that helmet back on!' I told
> him that I couldn't run anymore, I was going to puke. I looked
> right into that famous scowl, and through clenched teeth he
> said, 'You can throw up all you want, but you are putting your
> helmet back on and you're getting back on that line.' So I put
> my helmet back on, lined up, sprinted 40 yards, then threw up
> again, with my helmet on I might add. After practice, Coach

found me on the way to the locker room. He was much calmer and actually had a slight smile on his face. 'I knew you could do it.' It was right then that everything changed. It was that moment that really opened my eyes, not only for who I was, but who I wanted to be. I went from an attitude of living my life trying to find the easy way out, to living to challenge myself to never quit. Two years out of high school, I went through a challenge in my life where I had to make up my mind to quit or finish the race. Coach Ike taught me that you don't quit and you don't give up. I didn't have a choice. I must succeed. I had a challenge I had to handle. It was the same, in many ways, as finishing that 40 yard dash . . . just a whole lot bigger. I decided what type of husband and parent I wanted to be. I knew that life would be a challenge, but that I was ok with that, thanks largely to Coach Isaacs and the role that football played in my life. Had I been the same quitter I was before Coach Isaacs turned me around, I would have lost a great opportunity to be a father to my wonderful daughter. I also decided I wanted to have the same effect on kids' lives that Coach Isaacs had had on me. I have taught hundreds of young men the values that I learned from Coach Isaacs, and I have already seen several of my former players become coaches. I know he knew I could finish those sprints, but I wonder if he knew that, because he made me finish, he has changed the lives of so many families down here in Whiteland, Indiana. The influence continues."

This letter from Marcelyn Ponder praises Coach Isaacs for what he did to help her son. She writes,

"My son, Dave, had a lot to deal with in his life. Because of where we lived and the temptations that surrounded Dave every day, his future could have been one of crime and jail time. I think that I owe my son's life to Coach Isaacs. Because of Coach and his leadership and guidance, my son became a productive young man, especially after his dad died of cancer in his freshman year at Snider. I dread to think what direction he might have taken if it hadn't been for Coach Russell Isaacs."

Another letter for Coach Isaacs from a grateful parent, Jenny Fisher, reads,

"Coach, I want to say thank you. I'm amazed at the number of times my son recounts the messages of living with integrity that you passed on to him during his football days. His high school years were tough, not only due to finding his way in life, but because of his father's and my divorce. Recently during a conversation he said, 'If you wouldn't do it in front of your mom, then don't do it.' So, Coach, you see some young men take it to heart, not for an hour, a day, or a football season, but for life. So, thank you for your dedication and your life's work to the kids in our community. It has made a difference."

Dick Dullaghan coached at Carmel High School (Carmel, Indiana), and Paul Estridge's words about his coach are deeply inspiring.

"Few people in my life knew then and even today (Coach Dullaghan included) that the 16-year-old boy he met in 1973 was a very troubled and lost soul. Nearly bankrupt of self-esteem and confidence, my life would never be the same after he reached out and shook my hand. It's been 28 years since I have captained one of Coach's teams; however, not a week goes by in my life that I fail to reflect on his teachings and how my life has been completely and totally transformed for having known and played for him. Coach Dullaghan continues to impact my life. Therefore, for the lives of my children, my employees, and thousands of customers, I owe a debt of gratitude for the principles he taught me and the power of his influence."

Joseph Wells, who also played at Carmel High School, wrote,

"I will always remember you, not just for your coaching, but for your teaching of attitude and poise, which can only be learned by example. Today, I am a police officer for the Indianapolis Police Department. I deal with society and the problems it creates as a result of individuals trying to find the easy way to succeed. My experience in the majority of my runs as a policeman is that people make bad decisions because they lack the ability to think for themselves. When I approach a difficult situation, I often think back to my coach. The proper state of mind, the ability to overcome an opponent, and the heart to live with one's decision have helped me be successful in school, with my career, and especially with my family."

Judge Robert Lipo Jr. pays tribute to Dick Basham, Marquette University High School (Milwaukee, Wisconsin):

"When I was 11 years old, I suffered a catastrophic spinal cord injury that did two things: it cut short my dreams of being an athlete and, more importantly, it made me realize I needed to get the best education possible. When we met, I was an angry and disappointed young man given the recent events in my life. I believe you saw this and encouraged me that even though I could not be an 'athlete,' I could participate in sports in a different role. You suggested being a team manager. As I now recall our initial conversation about being a team manager and what transpired thereafter, I will forever be grateful. You pushed me to get involved, insisted I move forward, never giving me time or reason to look back and dwell on what had happened to me. You gave me the confidence to participate in athletics, even though I was not able to compete. That confidence has stayed with me. After college, I went to law school and graduated, worked for a federal judge in Washington, D.C., and worked as a prosecutor in Texas for twelve years. I was a criminal attorney for ten years, and I am now a judge for the city of San Antonio municipal court."

Serving Branson High School (Branson, Missouri), Coach Steve Hancock has been a true influence for his community as well as the football team. Derek Alms verifies that

"Some truly defined and difficult men (friends of mine), who wouldn't listen to authority and could really care less about their future or their education, played football for Coach Hancock. They were willing to change for the sake of the team, and I believe their lives were impacted by that experience. Coach Hancock didn't give up on difficult guys. If they were willing to work and try, he was willing to stick his neck out for them. He showed them the respect that other adults had not shown them. That influenced not only those boys, but those of us in the community watching from the sidelines."

Coaches sometimes never know the influence and the impact they are having until a grateful mother tells them. The mother of a player of Coach Bob Schneider (Newport Central Catholic High School, Newport, Kentucky), wrote,

"Mike's father passed away when he was in the third grade. My biggest fear was how I was going to raise two children on my own. All I kept reading in the parenting books was that the most powerful role model in any child's life is the same-sex parent. What was I going to do? How was I going to keep him on the right path? I was lucky when he became involved in football. My prayers were answered. Coach Schneider, you and your coaching staff helped me raise my son to be the man he is today. Your year-round discipline, devotion, and dedication to care for and teach the boys by example was the difference maker. The power of your influence will be everlasting."

In Praise of A Coach's Influence

Former football players from high school, college, and the professional ranks have been influenced by their coaches and are very proud to tell the world what their coaches meant to them as players and now as men.

Clinton Holmes, who played for Tim Teykl at B.F. Terry High School in Rosenberg, Texas, shares his story:

"As a young teenager I was lost in the weeds of high school. As a sophomore in 1992, when Coach T took over at B.F. Terry High School, I was barely a starter on a sophomore team. I was drinking and partying with other students. I pretty much entered the life of debauchery. I had a smart mouth, and I thought I had all the answers. I thought I had everyone fooled, that I could just coast along and good things would just fall my way. Coach T pulled me aside at the end of my sophomore year and told me he saw me as a pillar of the Ranger football program, a starter and eventually a team captain. He said my after-school activities and partying were a problem. If I would just straighten up and follow his lead, he would mold me into something that I and the town could be proud of. I was astonished. How did this man see a bright future in me? I had average grades, a smart mouth, and a propensity to party. The bottom line was that Coach Teykl gave me a vision. He told me in a few simple words that I had a gift and it was criminal to waste it. Because of Coach Teykl, I am now a captain in the Army, graduated from West Point in 2000, and played four years of football for the Army team. I have served overseas and have led soldiers for the past six years. I am very proud of my service. Coach T created an environment and personally gave me guidance that allowed me to make changes in my life and be a successful person. Coach T helped me to act and play like a champion. Coach Teykl is still my mentor, and he is still my coach. I know if I need a shoulder to cry on, he is still there in my corner."

Frank Kush, the great football coach of Arizona State, had the reputation of being a real taskmaster, yet was deeply loved and appreciated by his players. This note verifies his influence over his players and the insight into the difference he made:

"I arrived at Arizona State. I was not the best kid. I had social deficiencies and issues. I had a lot of talent, but I didn't focus and had some off-field problems. Coach Kush knew that I had talent, and he also knew about my problems. Coach talked to my mother and really went to bat for me, even though I had to leave Arizona State and sit out a year because of my problems. Coach Kush continued to work with me, even though I was out of school. One thing he did was have me work with disadvantaged kids to help build them up at the same time I was rebuilding my own credibility and restoring my character and integrity. Some on the team didn't want me back because of my off-field antics. Coach Kush called me into his office and said, "I am gonna go to bat for you. I believe you deserve a second chance. What you do with this opportunity will determine what happens with other players who might have some problems and need a second chance." In other words he said, "If you blow this opportunity, you may well eliminate an opportunity for another young man." I was determined not to let him down, and I didn't. I loved Coach Kush. He is one of my best friends. We talk often, and I still go to him for advice. People still identify me with Coach Kush at Arizona State University, and I wouldn't have it any other way."

As the head coach of the Minnesota Vikings, Leslie Frazier says,

"I am faced with tough decisions every day. There is no doubt in my mind that if it were not for the influence of Coach Marino Casem and his staff, I would not be where I am today."

Coach Frazier describes his first meeting with Marino Casem and his staff:

"I was thrilled to meet the coach and decided to follow him to Alcorn State to play football. Coach Casem immediately began to influence my thinking. First of all, he was very confident in

his team and his staff. He instilled in me and my teammates a
pride about wearing the Alcorn State uniform. We won a lot of
games at Alcorn State, and I earned my college degree while I
was there, but without a doubt the most influential part of my
stay was Coach Casem. I learned mental toughness from him,
as well as the importance of playing with passion and how that
translates to life. I can remember Coach Casem would bring
us together after each practice and share a few words with us,
not about football, but about life. He not only wanted us to be
good football players, but he wanted us to be great men. Coach
would challenge us to be men of integrity and to represent
our families and hometowns in a way that would make everyone proud. He challenged us to never let the circumstances of
life define us. He would say, 'I know where you've come from,
where you live, how you were brought up, so never let that
define you either. I expect greatness from each of you.' Those
words still resonate with me today in my everyday life. Coach
Casem's approach to coaching and influencing people is still a
part of my life."

Melvin Simmons arrived on the campus of the University of
Georgia having lived through life without the presence of a mother
or a father, yet he persevered and became one of the top high school
fullbacks in the nation, out of tiny Williston, Florida. Simmons
loved football and played it with a passion. He burned out a lot
of lights and scoreboards, because by the end of his senior year,
he had amassed more than 80 touchdowns and 3,500 yards rushing. Out of 75 scholarship offers, Simmons narrowed the choices to
Ohio State, Florida State, and Georgia. He chose the Georgia Bulldogs and became a member of the 1980 recruiting class. There was
another freshman running back in that same class who happened
to be the country's top-rated running back that year, Herschel
Walker. During Simmons' freshman year, he was having grade
problems and got in a little trouble. Simmons said,

> "Coach Dooley called me into his office and told me if I wanted
> to make something of myself, I needed to go to class and do all
> the things it would take to succeed in life."

Simmons said that even though he continued to have problems, his head coach became a father figure to him, as Coach
Dooley would not relent. Coach Dooley punished Simmons

several times but chose to give him the opportunity to get back up again and learn from his mistakes. Simmons said,

> "By my junior year, I finally got it right. Coach Dooley taught me about being a man and standing up when you're wrong. If you do something wrong, take your punishment like a man. Finally, Coach Dooley taught me about responsibility. He taught me to stand up for my own mistakes, but keep pushing hard."

In 1985, Simmons joined the U.S. military and spent twenty years as a military police officer. He now works for the DeKalb police department in Georgia.

On not having a family when he came to Georgia, Simmons says, "The Georgia football team and coaches were my family and they helped raise me into a good man." Melvin Simmons stood the test of adversity and has become a man full of courage, discipline, and perseverance. This is thanks in part to Coach Dooley's time with him in college. Simmons has harvested lessons of strength and overcoming obstacles that will last a lifetime.

Paul Thomas, in September 1995, walked on at Rice University under head coach Ken Hatfield.

> "Of course, I didn't play in the fall as a walk-on, but after going through spring training, I decided that I would go up to Coach Hatfield's office and lay out what I was thinking, then quit the team. On my way up to his office, I ran into him as he was coming in. I said, 'Coach Hatfield, do you have a minute to talk?' He stopped what he was doing and immediately walked into the locker room with me, then proceeded to spend the next 45 minutes sharing with me about football and, more importantly, about life. He talked about what it means to persevere, to fight through and stick with what you're committed to. It wasn't what Coach Hatfield had to say, it was the fact that he had a busy morning and took 45 minutes out of his schedule to sit down with a 19-year-old walk-on simply because he cared about him. Because of Coach Hatfield's encouragement, I continued to play. Eventually, I ended up on scholarship becoming an academic all-conference player. Remaining at Rice, playing under Coach Hatfield, and being directly under his influence had a big impact on my life. Coach continued to teach about perseverance and living a life of integrity. After leaving Rice

and entering the work world, I began to see how the principles that Coach taught weren't just about football, they were about life. I have since gone on and started my own company and have become involved with churches taking students on mission trips around the world, developing their leadership skills and giving of themselves to those across the world who are less fortunate. Coach Hatfield had a personal commitment to develop leaders, who were men of character and integrity. Ultimately, his goal was to develop men who would be great husbands, fathers, and leaders. Coach spoke often of the importance of developing values in our lives, but more importantly, he taught those values by the way he lived his life."

Paul White, former player at Hampton University under Coach Joe Taylor, wrote,

"Before coming under Coach Taylor's influence, I was actually incarcerated. I was a bit poor in decision-making. That's a lighter way of putting it. I had no accountability for myself, no respect, no pride, and was not the kind of person I could be. I thought I could get through life on my athletic ability alone. Until Coach Taylor, most of my shortcomings had been swept under the rug because I was a good athlete. Everything changed with Coach Taylor. He helped us to set personal goals for ourselves. His expectations for us were probably higher than ours. He expected the best of you on and off the football field. He always said we should respect ourselves and respect others. Coach Taylor expected his players to give total effort in athletics and in academics. I got in some serious trouble and was incarcerated. When I got out, Coach Taylor met with me and my parents. He decided that I had what it took to be successful. He believed that I had character, but made bad decisions that had been influenced by those who did not care about me as a person. Coach showed me my potential. I made the honor roll and graduated. I am currently pursuing a doctorate in political science at the University of South Carolina. My goal is to become an educator and influence others as Coach Taylor influenced me."

Scott Parsons played high school football for Ron Stolski at Brainerd High School (Brainerd, Minnesota) in the early 1970s. Coach Stolski said that Scott was a fiery, tough, young kid who had a lot of passion for everything he did.

He was undersized and was a two-way player for us on a great high school football team, but you could see that he needed someone or something to rein him in. He was fearless, but probably wasn't mature enough at the time to understand the path you choose may be the wrong path. Scott chose the right path, and later I had the opportunity to have him join me as a coach on my staff. We have worked together for twenty-eight years. Scott also owns his own successful business. He is a leader in his church and our community, and he is also an incredible linebacker coach. A recent addition to our staff was a hall of famer who had coached for years and years. He said about Scott, "I have never seen a better linebacker coach on any level."

Scott Parsons describes himself as a shaggy-haired teen who could have gone either way:

> "I had a reactionary personality where I could have snapped quite quickly at things. I also hung around some kids who were much the same way. When I came under the influence of Coach Stolski, he took that personality of mine and refined it and showed me a better way to deal with situations. He showed all of my teammates a better way to handle ourselves. When that team gets together, we talk about how Coach Stolski impacted all of our lives. There has been much in successful achievement among my teammates. Much credit goes to Coach Stolski."

A coach's positive influence can extend beyond his own players. In 1974, the TCU Horned Frogs were playing the University of Alabama in Tuscaloosa. Kent Waldrep, a running back, was involved in contact with an Alabama player that left him paralyzed from the waist down. When the TCU team flew home, they had to leave their teammate, as Kent went through a bevy of tests that drained him physically and psychologically. He would drift off to sleep.

In Kent's book, *Fourth and Long*, he describes one particular occasion while he was still in Alabama and awoke to the unmistakable presence of Coach Bear Bryant. Coach Bryant had with him two special visitors: George Steinbrenner of the New York Yankees and Charlie Finley of the world champion Oakland A's. Through his awe, Kent thought, "I must look like absolute hell, and in front of these guys, too."

Coach Bryant broke the ice. "Kent, you know we've enjoyed you hanging around here. It's time for you to quit lying around loafing and get back to TCU." A trace of a grin graced his grisly face. With as strong a voice as he could muster, Kent answered, "That's my plan, Coach."

Steinbrenner and Finley each presented Kent with an autographed baseball. They wished him a speedy recovery, then left Kent and Coach Bryant alone. Again, Coach Bryant spoke first. "I want you to know, Kent, you've already made all of us proud."

"Sir," Kent began, "it was a privilege to have played against your team."

Coach Bryant nodded. "You touched a lot of folks here in Alabama. Everyone appreciates your spirit and wants to help. I want you to know I'll always be here for you. You're one of my boys now, and together we'll beat this thing and get you back on your feet." Swallowing hard to choke down the tears, Kent put on his best game face, "Coach," he began, paused, and then said with all the strength he could muster, "I promise you I'll always give it 100%." "I know, son, I know," a gruff voice responded, "but you call me when you ever need to talk to a friend. Anytime, home or office. You tell the doctors to fix you up so you can get home, and I'll be back to see you." Coach Bryant did stay in touch with Kent. He meant what he said, "I will always be there for you."

My high school coaches, Speedy Moffat and Mule Kayser, followed me as a player throughout college and into my coaching career. As they had in high school, they always encouraged me. Coach Moffat and Coach Kayser attended my last game in college. The following Monday, I received a letter. Here is an excerpt:

"Dear Grant, we sure enjoyed the game, it was a fine game. You did a really good job. We are mighty proud of you, Grant. We couldn't have been more proud if it were one of our sons out there. I just hope they make the fine citizen, football player, and most of all man that you have made. Someone will get a good coach, if you still want to be one when you finish. Remember what I told you, though, all boys don't have the desire and enthusiasm for the game that you have [we were Snyder Tigers]. You can't make Tigers out of pussycats."

During college and after graduating, I would, of course, go see my mom and dad first, then I would go see my coaches. They were always there for me. Two of my most treasured honors were to have been asked to speak at each of my coaches' funerals. Interestingly enough, I did not talk about what really great football coaches they were. Rather, I talked about the impact that each had on me as a young boy and as a man. Because they inspired me to become a football coach, their influence continues.

Teaching and coaching as a profession provide the opportunity to have lasting influence. The dictionary says this about influence: "To have an effect on the condition and the development of." That definition is left incomplete: "of what?" It is then left up to us as husbands, fathers, teachers, and coaches to affect the condition of a young person's life and the development of their personal capabilities. The dictionary also defines influence as "an emanation of spiritual and moral force." To emanate means to "come out from a source." So there it is in a nutshell. The coaches and teachers are the source, and that which emanates from the source will be influence. However, it is up to the source to make sure that the influence is positive.

The coach's power of influence is very important in playing the game, but more important, "beyond the game."

Part II

Personal Development

— 4 —

The Key to Success

The last chapter, "The Power of Influence," was a difficult chapter to write because I had to choose between hundreds of coaches and their players' tributes. The fact is, all teachers and coaches who have spent a good portion of their lives positively influencing and leading would have enough thank you messages to fill an entire book. All coaches receive letters, phone calls, and emails from former players years removed from their participation. Many players sooner or later realize some of the success they have enjoyed in their lives can be traced back to the positive influence of their coach. Positive influence is like the pebble dropped in a smooth body of water, causing ripples that emanate from the impact. The ripple becomes enlarged as an ever-expanding circle, and in many cases it becomes a tidal wave of influence impacting those in its path.

The Pebble

Coach J. M. "Mule" Kayser, my high school defensive coach, came to Snyder between my freshman and sophomore year. His physical presence was an attention-getter: tall and muscular, he was extremely articulate but, as his nickname indicated, not particularly handsome. Coach played football at Texas Tech University, giving him instant credibility with me and my teammates as someone who knew the game of football. I was also impressed by the life that Coach Kayser led. He loved classical music, wrote poetry and prose, climbed mountains, and was an intellectual.

On a test in Coach's math class, I failed to complete one of the ten math problems he had given us. When the class was over, he called me up to his desk. I expected Coach's wrath, because I had not finished the test. Instead he gave me a gift of immense value. His demeanor was very serious as he said, "Grant, your greatest asset is not your physical skills, but your mind." After a slight hesitation he continued, "If you learn to control your mind, you will also control your will, your emotions, and your actions." Referring to the unfinished math problem, Coach said, "You can actually train your mind so that it will not allow you to give up on anything you start." He reminded me of words I had heard my father speak: "If you start it, finish it." The advice was excellent, but my motivation came from seeing Coach Kayser's disappointment in me and my lack of commitment to finish the job. Coach had just dropped a pebble into my smooth water, and I was feeling the ripples. Coach most likely saw me as a piece of clay ready to be molded, or possibly as an unfinished painting needing to be completed.

Observing Coach Kayser's life taught me that it is possible to be both a tough, hard-nosed, intense football player and at the same time a sensitive, caring person. Coach Kayser was all about living life to the fullest while becoming a total person, doing everything the right way. For me, at that stage of life, the coach's pebble started a ripple that soon turned into a wave impacting me with its full force. I saw his nameless theory regarding mind control lived out in his daily actions. His life was a testimony to his beliefs.

For me to implement the theory of mind control in my life, I first needed to discover exactly what I needed to control. Coach did not give me a definition of the human mind or explain exactly how it works. The dictionary provided a definition: the mind is the element or complex element in an individual that feels, perceives, thinks, wills, and reasons. Many outstanding men and women throughout history have been quoted about the human mind, and all came to a similar conclusion: "What the mind can conceive, it can achieve."

Another affirmation for me regarding the value of mind control was found in the Bible. Reading Romans 12:2, the words had a strong impact on me: "Let your mind be remade, then your whole nature will be transformed." In the school library, I found a book written by Napoleon Hill. He brought out another important point about mind control. Mr. Hill said, "To be successful, we must master our own tongue." A clear message from Mr. Hill, because what comes out of the mouth first is formulated within the mind. How we communicate with others has a lot to do with our success as leaders. Mr. Hill also said, "Think before you talk, and listen carefully before you speak." Then he added this, "With your mind, control your emotions: love, hate, fear, sex drive, and what you put into your body." It made sense to me that if through our minds we can control our bodily intake, then we should control what enters our minds. Who we spend time with is important, because they are the people to whom we will most likely be listening. Other control points are what we read, listen to, and watch. Finally, for me, Mr. Hill made a strong point about using our minds to stick to the straight and narrow. He said, "The line of least resistance makes all rivers and some men crooked." Rivers have no will determining the direction they go. Water follows the line of least resistance. The human mind can adhere to a value system with the capacity to keep a man following the shortest route to a destination. A straight line is the shortest route. For me, the value system taught me as a child by my family became my personal guide for staying on the straight and narrow.

I began to understand that first I should control my thoughts, as my thoughts are the point where action is initiated. Lewis A. Allen, a noted expert in business management, made an important point with this statement: "The greatest potential for control tends to exist at the point where action takes place." Therefore, the confluence of our thoughts and our ability to speak would clearly indicate that we should make sure our minds are in the proper gear before we engage our mouths. Stated another way, we should think before we speak, because our words plant the seeds of success or failure in the minds of others.

Coach Kayser may have had a name for his theory, but he never mentioned it to me, so I thought of it in this way: "Controlling my mind will be the key to my success."

My burning desire was to live in a house of success. If mind control was to be the foundation of my house of success, then I needed a strong foundation for the four corners of my future house of success. I envisioned four pillars of support, as was the system in ancient times. Great stone structures were supported by massive columns called pillars. The pillar on each corner of the structure provided balanced support.

The First Pillar—Attitude

Successful people who I knew in my community, which included my teachers and coaches, all had a positive attitude. They seemed to start each day looking for the best in that day. Growing up, the most positive person I knew was my mom. She is now 97 years old, lives by herself in Snyder, Texas, and if you ask her today how she is feeling, the answer will be the same as it was when I was a little boy, "Mighty fine." She has never admitted to a negative day nor does she possess a negative outlook on life. She always expected positive outcomes in life situations. She possessed positive expectations. Even though she didn't know that much about football, every game I played or coached, she was positive I would win.

I remember asking my mom, "How do you always have a positive attitude even when bad things are happening?" She sort of flippantly said, "I put on my happy face every morning when I wake up and refuse to take it off during the day."

In a similar approach, I start each day with an "all things are possible" attitude. Attitude control is definitely the first step in achieving success. I came to believe that an attitude to be successful must be positive. A negative attitude is a loser. William J. Bennett, noted CNN contributor and author, said, "There are no menial jobs, only menial attitudes." William James, a noted American psychologist, said, "The greatest discovery of my generation is that a human can, after he has begun life, alter it by altering his attitude." Winston Churchill said, "Attitude is a little thing that makes a big difference." Big dreams and what some of my classmates surely thought were ridiculous goals forced me to hang on to my attitude like a lifeline. By the time I was a senior in high school, with limited talents, I needed to put on my happy face at the beginning of each day. In English class, I read a poem by Edward Everett Hale entitled "I Am Only One." I liked the premise of the poem but could not remember the words, so I made up my own phrases. I started repeating these words in front of my mirror every morning in order to set my attitude as positive. Recently, I looked up Edward Everett Hale's poem: "I am only one, but still I am one. I cannot do everything, but still I can do something; and because I cannot do everything, I will not refuse to do the something that I can do." In more modern language, this would read as follows:

> I am only one, but I am one.
> I can't do everything, but I can do something.
> That which I can do, I ought to do.
> That which I ought to do, by God's grace, I will do.

I often tell audiences that those words to this very day still make the hair stand up on the back of my neck. By repeating those words each morning, I set my attitude for the day as I go out into a negative world, facing negative problems yet keeping a positive attitude.

"I am only one" is a cleansing admission that I am only one in an overpopulated world, but I am one of God's creations given the ability to think and to act.

"I can't do everything" is one more admission that I am limited in my abilities. For football, I was not gifted with speed or size. Though I loved music, I couldn't carry a tune in a bushel basket. Since I was limited in what I could do, I committed to the things I could do. Therefore, the second part of that sentence— "but I can do something"—reminds me that I have special gifts and talents of my own that can be used to help others, thus achieving a measure of success in my life.

Then comes the challenge: "That which I can do, I ought to do." That sentence reminds me that it is up to me to take the talents and abilities that I do have and develop them to the fullest. For a lot of people a high pain threshold and mental toughness are not notable abilities. However, those two attributes got me an education and an opportunity to reach my goals.

Most individuals are motivated by challenges. Therefore, the next sentence is motivational; "That which I ought to do, by

God's grace, I will do" stands as a challenge. In other words, "If I have the talent, abilities, and intellect to become an A student, it is incumbent upon me to be that A student." On the other hand, if my attributes fall short and all I can be is a C student, then it is my challenge to be the best C student who ever came down the pike. My positive attitude injects me with energy and a sense of positive expectations.

In 1972 I accepted the position of head football coach at Baylor University. After accepting the job, reality set in when I found the environment to be extremely negative: Baylor had won only a handful of games in the previous few years and had no weight room, no practice fields, a terrible dressing room, and a stadium with worn-out wooden seating and not a blade of grass on the field. I interviewed members of Baylor's football staff and to my amazement found some to be extremely negative. In fact, one who had graduated from Baylor said, "Coach, let me be frank with you. It is impossible for Baylor to win in the Southwest Conference." He went on to say, "Baylor football is in a negative environment; few of the Baylor alumni, students, and community supporters believe that Baylor can win." I paused for a moment, looked directly at the coach, and said, "I believe we can win or I would not have come." That coach was not retained. A negative environment produces more negativism and is a deterrent to achieving success. Negative thoughts are the enemy of a victorious football team and a victorious life. Because our lives are controlled by our mind, our thoughts will help us succeed or fail. Negative thoughts have a way of distracting us from doing what needs to be done to achieve success. Negative thoughts drain our energy and sap our physical strength, but eliminating them helps control negative habits.

Thoroughly convinced a war had to be waged against Baylor's negative environment, I realized it had to be done from the inside out. I felt confident that Baylor people could easily switch from negative to positive when they could see positive results on the football field and in the behavior and conduct of the players.

During my first team meeting, I spoke about my passion for coming to Baylor to help turn a great university into a winner on the football field. In doing so, we would change the way Baylor was perceived by recruits, the student body, alumni, and, most importantly, the city of Waco.

Finally, I said, "From this moment forward, we build on positive expectations for ourselves and ultimately for the team. In order to help you do that, take this card, read it every day and follow the instructions."

---

10 Steps to a Positive Attitude

- Repulse negative thoughts as they come up in your mind.
- Like my mom, put on your happy face and don't take it off.
- Look in the mirror and repeat words that will help reinforce your new positive approach to life, such as, "I'm a winner and I will succeed."
- Fill your mind with positive thoughts through repeating positive quotes and associating with positive people.
- Commit yourself: never utter negative words.
- Be proud. Keep your head up, shoulders back, and walk with confidence.
- Every day find a way to help someone.
- Do not associate with negatives, do not listen to negatives, and do not read negatives.
- Spend a few moments every day thinking about and being grateful.
- Visualize yourself successful and celebrating with your team after a great victory.

The Power of Belief

Spring practice was hard yet gratifying because of the effort and the attitude of our new team. A simple coaching staff believed in the players and believed we could actually turn Baylor into a winner on the football field. Our staff agreed that a private declaration of our intentions, objectives, and beliefs would motivate us. The next day I presented our staff with the declaration that I was convinced was necessary to create a winning environment and ultimately a winning team. "The power of our belief will bring us together, and together we will create something special through the power of our belief in each other, our coaches, and our purpose. If we create something special, Baylor alumni, students, and the city of Waco will join us in our belief that we can and will succeed. Positive expectations will be the foundation on which we build our team. We guarantee we will be the best conditioned, hardest working, best prepared football team in the Southwest Conference. The reason I believe it, is because I am going to see to it personally. Being the best conditioned, hardest working, best prepared football team in the Southwest Conference will bring us Baylor's first championship in decades." Our staff and our team bought in 100 percent.

An example of positive expectations and confident belief was personified in Baylor senior quarterback Neal Jeffrey. Neal had been the Baylor quarterback since he was a sophomore, and though he was not blessed with speed, he was smart, tough, and a natural leader. Our players appreciated his talent, but they appreciated his tenacity and the way he overcame a speech impediment even more. Neal had been a stutterer since childhood and still is. Through it, he has become one of the great Christian ministers to men across America.

In mid-season 1974, Baylor and Texas were playing in Waco. Before a sellout crowd, the University of Texas took a 24-7 halftime lead. With what appeared to be the same old, same old for Baylor and Texas in the last nineteen years, about a third of the fans from both sides of the field left the stadium. The Texas fans did not believe a comeback for Baylor was imminent, and the Baylor fans just knew there would not be a comeback, based on history.

Whether the fans stayed or left was not my immediate concern. Walking up the steps leading to the Baylor dressing room, I was thinking about important halftime adjustments. Then I looked to my left, and there alongside me was Neal Jeffrey. When I turned my head to look at him, I was surprised to see a big smile on his face. I reached over with my left hand, stopped him, and turned him so I could look directly into his face. I asked, "Neal, what do you find funny about a 24-7 halftime deficit?" In typical Neal fashion and only stuttering just a little bit, he said, "Coach, we've got Texas where we want them." The puzzled look on my face caused him to explain further. "Texas got the breaks the first half, but we moved the ball extremely well, and Coach, I guarantee we're going to win this game in the second half." Pausing for just a moment, I looked at Neal and said, "Neal, you are absolutely right. When we get into the dressing room, you go to the left and I'll go to the right; shake each player's hand, look them in the eyes, and tell them just what you said to me."

The players sitting on the benches with their heads down all got a determined look on their faces and started yelling at their teammates, "We will win!" The dressing room became electric. Honestly, we made no adjustments. When we took the field in the third quarter, Baylor was a new team. Texas took the opening possession, and we held them for three downs, blocked the punt, took it in to score, and the rest is history. Baylor won 34-24 and went on to win Baylor's first Southwest Conference championship since 1924.

That game has been designated by many historians as the most significant game in Baylor and the Southwest Conference's history. Neal's positive affirmation when relayed to each of his teammates renewed the belief "we are going to win." What the mind can conceive, a positive attitude can achieve. Oh the power of belief and positive expectations.

The Second Pillar—Effort

Once I set my goal to become a football coach and teacher like my high school coaches, I boldly announced that my goal was to become a head football coach in the Southwest Conference. If you lived in the state of Texas, the Southwest Conference was as big, strong, and highly recognized as any conference in the nation. I had never seen a Southwest Conference game, but I had listened on the radio. There were folks in Snyder who had actually been educated in a Southwest Conference school.

A couple of days after my bold announcement, I was summoned to Coach Speedy Moffat's office in the old gymnasium. The building was built by the Works Progress Administration during the Depression and was an unattractive cavern where Snyder High School basketball was played. The building housed the offices of the coaches as well, and Coach Moffat's office was a nondescript eight-foot by eight-foot dark hole with a door. I knocked on that door, and he told me to come in. I stepped into his office not knowing what to expect. I sat in a cane-bottom chair in front of his rather beat up oak desk, waiting for his words. I didn't think I had done anything wrong, but I was a little nervous about being called to the head coach's office.

Coach Moffat had this way about him, and you knew that he really cared. He looked across the desk at me and said, "I heard about your goals, and I respect your boldness in setting such a lofty goal. Grant, you have two years to prepare yourself academically and physically. I know you are going to need financial help in order to attend college, and of course I am aware of your physical strengths and weaknesses. Physically you are limited in size and speed; however, you have a great attitude, you are a very determined person, and you have a very strong work ethic. I want very much for you to be able to reach your goals, and that's why I called you here today. I want you to succeed, and I am going to tell you how you can reach every goal you've set." As he paused, my heart started beating rapidly. Someone I deeply respected was going to tell me how I could make my dreams come true.

I leaned forward, waiting for his words of wisdom. Coach looked directly into my eyes and initially only one word rolled from his lips. "Effort," he said. Letting the word sink in, I repeated it. "Effort." He nodded his head and then said, "Total effort. If you are willing to give total effort every day, in every way, on every play, you will reach your goals."

Sitting back in the cane-bottom chair, my mind was racing to comprehend what he was saying to me. I repeated the words back to him slowly, "Total effort, every day on every play?" "Can you do it?" he asked. Motionless for a moment, trying to comprehend, it seemed like an impossible task. In truth, I was determined to reach my goals and if that's what it took, then it seemed like so little to ask.

"Coach, I commit to you that I will try to give total effort every day, every way on every play." I rose from the chair, took two steps to the door, and just as I reached for the handle, Coach asked, "Grant, are you thinking I'm talking about the football field only?" Before I could answer, he said, "I am talking in the hallway, in the classroom, on the city streets, in your home, on the football field, as a husband, as a father, and as a coach." As I closed the door behind me, a great burden had been lifted from me as I realized I had just received the second pillar that would support my house of success. I rationalized that a positive attitude would help me achieve total effort in everything I did.

Effort defined: the conscious exertion of power; hard work; serious attempt to produce by exertion of trying. Success comes from knowing that you did your best to become the best you are capable of being. A great coach in another sport, John Wooten, said, "All the secrets to success will not work, unless you do." One of our Founding Fathers, Thomas Jefferson, once said, "I am a great believer in luck, and the harder I work, the more I have of it." Many people have taken that statement and claimed it as their own, but he was the first to say it.

Coach Moffat's gift on that fateful day was the realization that my personal total effort will forever be one of my four pillars to be controlled by my mind. A positive attitude and willingness to give total effort will contribute greatly to any success I have in the future. I knew Coach Moffat's challenge to me regarding total effort was not totally foreign, as I had observed it daily in the work ethic of my parents. It was especially vivid to me after having watched my father work ten- to twelve-hour days, six days a week, year after year, while somehow squeezing in time to be a real father to me and my sister. My dad was a total effort guy but also extremely balanced. Years later, shortly after he passed away, I had numerous individuals in Snyder, Texas, write, telephone, or tell me personally of many things my father had done for them in their time of need. He never talked about the extra effort that he gave to those in need, but looking back, I am sure that was part of the contentment he found in his life, by giving total effort to his job, his family, and those in need.

The Total Effort Guide

Through the years, I have found these truths to be self-evident regarding total effort:

- There are only 24 hours in a day.
- The day must be planned and prioritized to be maximized.
- Effort should not be wasted on unworthy projects.
- Keep unimportant issues from stealing your time.

- Take care of yourself physically.
- Appropriate amount of rest
- Nutrition
- Exercise
- Timely medical check-ups
- Take Care of Business (TCB).
- Family
- Find a way to spend quality time with family.
- Create a date night with your wife (even if it is just riding around for an hour talking).
- Leave your problems on the front doorstep.
- Always ask your wife how her day went and tell her the good part of yours.
- Spend quality time with your own children.
- When you are with your children, concentrate on them (they'll feel you've been there a lot more than you have if you really concentrate on them).
- Take time to be interested in what their day was like.
- Take some time each week to find out how your staff and their families are doing.
- Take time to ask your players about their families and schoolwork.
- Never be out-worked, out-thought, or out-given.
- Condition your team and staff so total effort can be given in the fourth quarter (Vince Lombardi once said, "Fatigue makes cowards of us all").

Mahatma Gandhi said, "Satisfaction lies in the effort, not in the attainment; full effort is full victory." Or as Coach Moffat said, "Total effort ensures total success." As you have probably surmised by now, one of my all-time favorite leaders is Winston Churchill and I quote him quite often. In this case regarding effort, he said, "Continuous effort—not strength or intelligence— is the key to unlocking our potential." Another coach at another time, Vince Lombardi, said it this way: "Leaders are made, they are not born. They are made by hard effort, which is the price all of us must pay to achieve any goal that is worthwhile." Ralph Waldo Emerson has pinpointed what he refers to as the mother of effort in this statement, "Enthusiasm is the mother of effort, and without it nothing great was ever achieved." Theodore Roosevelt, a man of great passion, energy, and intellect, pretty well nailed how hard it is to hour after hour, day after day, month after month, and year after year give total effort "every day, in every way on every play," when he said, "It is only through labor and painful effort, by grim energy and resolute courage that we move on to better things." Total effort is hard to accomplish, but the willingness to try is essential.

Example of Total Effort

The formula for winning on the football field is somewhat complex, but in its simplest form, the team with the most players giving total effort for the entire game will win. Leaving Texas Tech and taking the head football job at Angelo State College was an opportunity to do something for another one of my alma maters. I started my college education at San Angelo College before it became a four-year institution called Angelo State College. Of course, now it is Angelo State University. The football program, as a four-year institution, had never accomplished a winning season. I was challenged by that and put together a coaching staff that included Bill Lane, who had been a teammate at San Angelo College. I knew the kind of effort Bill gave as a player, and his success as a high school coach had validated my desire to bring him on as an assistant coach. My coaching staff, with an obvious work ethic setting the example for our football team, realized as a team we might lose a game, but we would never be out-worked or out-played.

Jerry Austin, a running back who played for Angelo State teams, was a major force in turning the Angelo State program into a winner. The plan I brought to Angelo State to win was simple but extremely effective. The plan: play great defense and control the football. Controlling the ball simply means making first downs, using the clock, and scoring points on those long drives. This plan required tough, hard-nosed young men who would give sixty minutes of total effort to win a game. When I asked for total effort from the team, the player setting the pace was Jerry Austin. If we needed a first down or a touchdown, Jerry would get the football and would not stop until he got one or the other. If we needed ball control, I called on Jerry. In one game, he carried the ball 33 straight times. Jerry's style of running caused the media to name him the "Hookin' Bull," because as he ran, he moved his head from left to right, destroying everything in his path.

Against Texas A&I in 1969, the defending national champion, Angelo State was ahead with six minutes to go. Of course, the national champion Texas A&I wanted to get the ball back with time enough to score and win. With Jerry Austin carrying on every down, A&I never got their hands on the ball again. When the game was over, I put my arm around Jerry's neck and thanked him for his effort. In typical Austin fashion, he looked me in the eye and said, "Coach, I could've carried it a lot more." Jerry Austin has remained a special friend. He has given that same total effort he gave on the football field to his family, his faith, his business, and his community.

The Third Pillar—Self-Discipline

Wikipedia defines self-discipline in this way: self-discipline can be defined as the ability to motivate oneself in spite of a negative emotional state. Qualities associated with self-discipline include willpower, hard work, and persistence.

Self-discipline is the product of persistent willpower. Willpower is the strength and ability to carry out certain tasks. Self-control is the ability to use willpower routinely and automatically. An analogy for the relationship between the two might be as follows: where willpower is the muscle, self-discipline is the structured thought that controls that muscle.

There have been more football games lost, more marriages destroyed, more jobs lost, and more people jailed for lack of self-discipline than for almost any other reason. Self-discipline is the assertion of willpower over base desires, and the same applies for self-control. One should act according to what one thinks, not what one feels. To be self-disciplined, you must control your emotions: love, hate, fear, sex. H. A. Dorfman, who wrote *The Mental ABC's of Pitching*, communicated through his writings about playing baseball very important words concerning self-discipline. He wrote,

> Self-discipline is a form of freedom, freedom from laziness and
> lethargy. Freedom from the expectations and the demands of

others. Freedom from weakness, fear, and doubt. Self-discipline allows the baseball pitcher to feel his individuality, his inner strength and talent. He is a master of, rather than a slave to, his thoughts and emotions.

Even though Mr. Dorfman wrote those words specifically about playing baseball, his words can be applied to every sport and to everyday life as well.

The first time self-discipline was really pointed out to me in a dramatic way was by Coach Kayser. The event to remember took place on a Wednesday afternoon prior to a Friday high school game. We were inside the ten-yard line in a contact scrimmage. On that particular day, I was playing offensive right tackle. Max Coffee, our quarterback, and I had played together all year. Part of the time I was the offensive center and learned to anticipate his snap count. I had mastered his cadence and was able to anticipate the snap of the ball, making me appear faster than I was. For some reason, on that particular day, the whistle blew and I turned back to go huddle again, making sure that my head dropped forward just enough so that the helmet covered my eyes and protected me from the dreaded eye contact with Coach Kayser. Just before I stepped into the huddle, curiosity got the best of me and I peeped out. Our eyes met as he stood there with arms folded and his whistle still in the corner of his mouth. He lifted his right hand, curled his index finger, and indicated for me to come to him. When I tell this story, I always say that it must have been a very windy day, because Coach Kayser reached down, grabbed the front of my jersey in his big hand, lifted me off the ground, and pulled me close to his face; I'm sure I could hear him in spite of the wind. Loudly he said, "Do you know what you just did?"

I said, "Yes sir, I jumped offsides."

"Do you know what that means?"

I replied, "Of course, Coach, it means a five-yard penalty."

He continued, "Let me ask you another question. Do you in your wildest imagination think that because of your lack of self-discipline the officials are going to penalize you five yards?"

"Well, no sir, they penalize . . . the whole team," I said hesitantly.

"That's my point," he scolded. "Your lack of discipline has just cost your team five yards inside the ten-yard line. Your five-yard penalty cost your team a touchdown. Failure to score a touch-down could cost your team the district championship. Because of you and your lack of discipline, this team will not play in the state championship."

His lesson was clear: a lack of self-control or self-discipline in the real world can cost you a lot more than a five-yard penalty and the state championship.

I was embarrassed and humiliated. It was a great lesson for me and my teammates, and thankfully it did not cost us a game or the state championship. The truth was, we were not a good enough team to win a state championship, but that football field lesson caused many of us to understand our responsibility to control our own actions on and off the field. If we fail to apply self-control and self-discipline in our own lives, the world will surely do it for us.

Self-discipline refers to the training that one gives oneself to accomplish a certain task or to adapt a particular pattern of behavior, even if one would rather be doing something else. For example, denying oneself an extravagant pleasure in order to accomplish a more demanding charitable deed is a display of self-discipline; thus, self-discipline is the assertion of willpower over more base desires and is usually understood to be synonymous with self-control. Self-discipline is to some extent a substitute for motivation, when one uses reason to determine a best course of action that opposes one's desires. Virtuous behavior is when one's motivations are aligned with one's reasoned aims. To do what one knows is best and to do it gladly, tells others you are happy with your value system

The Fourth Pillar—The Capacity to Care

"I feel the capacity to care is the thing which gives life its deepest significance."

—Pablo Casals, cellist and conductor

Those of us in education have always been told, "Children don't care how much you know until they know how much you care." I phrase the concept this way, "It's like mind over matter. If you don't mind, it won't matter." William Penn, the founder of Penn-sylvania, said in the 1600s, "I expect to pass through this life, but once. If therefore, there be any kindness I can show, or any good thing that I can do to any fellow being, let me do it now, not defer or neglect it, as I shall not pass this way again." A profound truth is that we all have but one life, and as we come to the end of that life, what is it that is really going to matter?

One other quote by Leo Buscaglia, an author and professor, said, "Too often we underestimate the power of a touch, a smile, a kind word, a listening ear, an honest compliment, or the smallest act of caring, all of which have the potential to turn a life around." An extremely large majority of teachers and coaches are in the education business in order to have opportunities positively to affect lives of those they teach and coach. The capacity to care is a human emotion. It is a focus that allows individuals to place a great importance on certain things. The capacity to care can be one of life's greatest motivators. The capacity to care is the pillar that probably can bear the most weight and create maximum stability for the building that the four pillars support.

In 1992 I was coaching my last football game at Baylor University. I had stepped down to become the athletic director. This final game was very important to me, because it was my last regular season game and the opponent was the University of Texas. Although we were the underdogs, if we were to win, my teams would have ten victories over the University of Texas. The Baylor team was a very young team and surprised a lot of people by being in the position to go to a bowl game if they were able to beat Texas. The national media was in attendance, and the game was to be nationally televised. It was a rather dark, misty day. During warm-ups I was standing on the north end of the field watching my team warm up for the last time. Suddenly, I felt a presence beside me. It was a fifth-year senior who because of an injury did not play during the year. But there he was, all 5'10" and 175 pounds in full uniform with a worried look on his face. It was Trooper Taylor, a red-shirt senior from Cuero, Texas. He was a relatively small defensive back who had not been heavily recruited. But when I first met him, I knew I was going to give him a scholarship, as he had such a passion to get an education. I felt like his positive personality and mental toughness would be an asset to our team, while allowing Trooper to reach his educational goals.

Trooper hesitatingly said, "Coach, I need to talk to you about something very important."

I said, "Go ahead."

So he continued, "I didn't sleep any last night. I came in early, got my equipment, and put it on. I know this is your last game, Coach, but it's my last game as well. My injury last year didn't heal as quickly as we thought it would, so I was unable to play this year. Coach, the doctors released me on Wednesday and said I could play if you would allow it. I would like to play today," he said. "Coach, I'm 18 yards short of breaking the school record in kickoff returns, so please allow me to return one kickoff? Then just one play on defense, so when I come back years from now to watch Baylor play with children of my own, I can say to them, 'It was Coach Teaff's last game and my last game, and we beat the University of Texas.'"

My reaction was probably typical of what any coach would feel under such circumstances. First, he had a severe knee injury and he would play in a tough, physical game without any prior preparation. Not good. He might fumble and cost us the game. So I said to him, "Do you honestly think I'm going to take a chance on your knee and the possibility of a fumble that could cost us the game?"

"I will not fumble, Coach!" Trooper pleaded. "Coach, I care so much about playing, will you care enough to let me have two plays, please?"

I said, "Look, Trooper, the best I can do for you right now is to tell you that I'm going to think about it."

Trooper quickly said, "Thank you, but please, Coach, I care about it, would you please care about it?"

Four times during the first half, Trooper mustered up enough courage to ask me, "Coach, have you thought about it yet?" My first half responses were, "I'll think about it at halftime." During the halftime, I actually thought about Trooper's request. I had been impressed with his persistence and his expressed desire to get in the game. I knew how much he cared about it, and I realized that I really cared about it as well. A lead of 14-7 was certainly not comfortable against a team like the University of Texas. Just before we were to take the field in the third quarter, I gave in. I waved for Trooper and Scott to come to me, so I could talk to both of them. Scott Smith was in charge of kickoffs and coached Trooper in the secondary, prior to his injury. I turned to Scott and said, "What I'm going to say to you is not up for discussion. Let Trooper return a kickoff. It is important to him, and he cares deeply about it. I want you to know I care about it as well, therefore I expect you to get it done." I went on to say, "Scott, somewhere in the second half, get Trooper in on one play on defense. He cares about it, I care about it, and I expect you to care about it as well."

As fate would have it, Trooper returned the kickoff close to midfield and gave the Baylor Bears the opportunity to score on the first drive and take a lead of 21-7. We had two turnovers that led to two field goals, and Texas had a drive for another seven points, so with two minutes to go, the score was Baylor 21, Texas 20.

Texas had the ball on the Baylor 38-yard line, fourth and two to go with no timeouts. If the Baylor defense could rise to the occasion, the game would belong to the Bears, but if Texas made the first down, they would likely kick a field goal and win the game.

Texas came to the line of scrimmage in an I formation, and everyone in the stands knew they were going to give the ball to the tailback, which they did, and he drove hard to the line of scrimmage. But just before he got to the line of scrimmage, he was forced airborne by our defensive tackle, who had penetrated the Texas backfield. I was standing on the 38-yard line looking directly at the ball carrier as he was airborne. To me, he looked as though he would make the first down. All of a sudden, out of the corner of my right eye, I saw a green jersey literally flying through the air, hitting the ball carrier straight on; both stopped in mid-air and fell directly to the turf. The ball was spotted, and I could tell it was going to be very close. The officials brought the chains in to measure. Texas' ball was three inches short of a first down. All that was left of the game was for Baylor to take care of the football and run the clock out. Just before I sent the quarterback in with his final instructions, this green jersey appeared in front of me, jumping up and down and screaming, "I made the tackle, I made the tackle!" As I focused in on the individual, it was Trooper Taylor. Trooper had made the tackle that won the game.

Of course, we ran the clock out and won the game. The players carried me out onto the field in celebration, where the student body took over and carried me around the field. Finally, I got down off the shoulders of students, found my family so we could walk off the north end zone together, as we had planned. As we approached the end zone, the media was waiting. The cameras were rolling, and they immediately began to interview my wife, Donell, and our girls. I quickly looked around and saw Scott Smith standing with the other coaches close to the north end zone facility. I took about four strides toward him and yelled out, "Scott, come here. What was Trooper doing in on that last play?"

He said, "Oh my word, Coach, you had made it very clear to me that Trooper cared, you cared about it, and I should care about it as well. The problem was that if our defense held on that last play, there would not be another chance to get him in on defense, so I made the decision to send him in."

I looked directly at Scott and said, "Thank you, Scott, for doing that."

Scott's reply was, "Coach, I might as well go ahead and tell you, you'll see it on the film anyway; Trooper didn't line up in the right spot."

I looked back at Scott Smith, smiling, and said, "It's okay, Scott, he ended up in the right spot."

I returned to where my family was being interviewed. As the media turned to me, I was asked, "To what do you owe this, your last victory over the University of Texas?" Without hesitation, I said, "I owe it to caring." With puzzled looks they said, "What do you mean?" I said, "One young man who has not played in a year, cared so much about the opportunity to play, he came to me and asked if he could get in this game. Because he cared so deeply, at halftime I began to care, too. I gave the responsibility of putting him in the game to an assistant coach who cared enough to put Trooper in at the most critical stage of the game. Doing so allowed Trooper to make the play that won the game. Yes, you can chalk up this last victory over Texas to caring." Trooper Taylor joined the coaching profession and has proven over and over to be a coach of influence who shares his capacity to care with those he coaches.

Conclusion

The influence of a coach, in this case Coach Mule Kayser, continues. He gave the gift of knowledge that influenced me to use, magnify, perfect, and pass on the "key to success." Through the years, family members, friends, coaching staffs, players, and, most importantly, children and grandchildren have used "the key to success." Two derivatives, motivation and leadership, will be addressed in the next two chapters. Both had their genesis in the key to success. To consistently control your mind is hard work and takes motivation. Self-motivation became my closest companion, and interestingly enough, self-motivation led me to a burning desire to lead and set me on a path of lifelong study of leadership.

At the conclusion of the math class, the pebble of influence created a ripple that turned into a wave, and the wave continues, *as does a coach's influence.*

— 5 —

Motivation

Personal motivation is in fact one more essential function of our mind. Internal and external images and facts must be processed by our mind before triggering our actions. Animals are much more instinctive than human beings. In humans, the thought process controls the action, good or bad. Fear and reward motivation seem to be prominent in animals. Positive reinforcement used by animal trainers is reward motivation—a pat on the head, an encouraging word, or a bite of a desired food. Fear motivation is called positive punishment or negative reinforcement (withdrawing an undesired stimulus when the animal performs the desired behavior). Research and most experts downplay the value of fear and reward motivation in human beings. Most of us have experienced personally the effect of fear and reward motivation.

Fear Motivation

Fear motivation is created by a threat, concern for reprisal, or fear of failure. Through the years, I have come in contact with many successful individuals in all walks of life. When the opportunity presented itself, I would ask them about the motivation behind their success. Many said, "The fear of failure motivates

me to work harder than those around me. I am afraid I will fail."
The fear of penalties or loss of privileges motivates certain individuals. I think it can be said that fear motivation is not the most
productive type of motivation.

My first experience with fear motivation occurred one Saturday night in Snyder, Texas, when I was twelve years old. I worked
every Saturday at a grocery store until 10:30 p.m. After work, I
was allowed to go to a movie with my friends and actually come
home by myself after midnight (it was a really small town). One
Saturday, my friends and I saw a scary movie, and though we
never spoke of it, we were all probably a little afraid to go home
by ourselves after the movie. My house was about six blocks
straight north on Avenue S. One block off the square there were
no street lights, just big cottonwood trees in the dark. The wind
was blowing so the limbs of the trees were rubbing against each
other, making strange noises. About a half block off the square,
fear motivation set in. If I had been clocked that night on a 100-
yard dash, I might have been close to a world record. I know for
sure it was the fastest of my life. I was motivated to get past those
trees and to my house, knowing it was safe there with my mom
and dad.

Reward Motivation

As a child, I saw a picture that made me laugh, although I did not
understand what the picture meant. The picture was of a donkey
pulling a cart with a long stick tied to the harness. The stick
protruded out about a foot in front of the donkey's head. A juicy
carrot dangled from the stick, just out of reach of the donkey. As
the donkey stepped toward the carrot, the cart moved forward.
The donkey was motivated by the juicy carrot, just one step away;
however, as with most physical rewards, the carrot was out of
reach. A cruel act, one might say, although not so different from
other forms of incentive motivation to which we all respond—the
job advancement, the house, the free summer trips for reaching
certain goals, bonuses, and even the adulation of superiors. Athletes are motivated by financial status in the professional ranks:
the Final Four, the National Championships, the Crystal Ball—
all appropriate incentives for motivation. However, the question

remains, what motivates you in your own responsibilities when there is no carrot in front of you or the carrot is just out of reach?

Homer Rice, a brilliant and innovative head football coach who achieved success on the high school, college, and professional levels has given our profession his leadership secrets over the years. He says, "You can motivate by fear and you can motivate by reward, but both those methods are only temporary. The only lasting method is self-motivation."

Reaching the same conclusion early in life, I stated in my book *Coaching in the Classroom* that "I believe the truest form of motivation, the most lasting and best, is self-motivation."

The Hot Button Theory

When gasoline engines were developed, they were magnificent pieces of early engineering. However, they would not start or run until a supply of gasoline reached the engine and an electrical charge ignited the gasoline, starting the engine. The engine could not start until someone pushed the starter button, which completed the contact between the electrical source and the engine. The electrical charge released into the piston caused the engine to run. Through the years, the starter button became known as the "hot button." Self-motivation could easily be characterized as "finding and pressing your own hot button." Self-motivation is propelling ourselves into action, not depending on external forces offering rewards or putting fear in us. The first step in self-motivation is discovering your own hot buttons.

In order to understand our own self-motivation, we must first understand motivation. In 1943, Dr. Abraham Maslow defined motivation in an article entitled "A Theory of Human Motivation." His definition explained it as self-actualization. According to his definition, it simply means "the full realization of one's potential." Maslow uses the terms psychological, safety, belongingness, love, esteem, and self-actualization. Self-actualization describes the pattern that human motivations generally move through. In Maslow's work, he studied who he called extraordinary people, such as Albert Einstein, Jane Addams, Eleanor Roosevelt, and Frederick Douglas, rather than the neurotic. Maslow's theory suggests that the most basic level of needs must be met before the individual will strongly desire (or focus motivation upon) second-ary or higher level needs. With all due respect to Dr. Maslow, I found early in life what of course may be looked at by some as an oversimplified theory of motivation.

From my personal experience growing up, playing high school and college football with a minimum of talents and tools needed to successfully play the game, I found personal motivation to be essential.

Looking back at thirty-seven years of coaching, with thirty of those years serving as a head football coach on the college level, and for the last nineteen serving as executive director of the American Football Coaches Association, self-motivation has been a necessity.

Self-Motivation

What I learned from my personal experiences has been verified over the years by such experts as Paul Meyer, the founder of Success Motivation Institute (SMI). I met Paul in 1973 while coaching at Baylor University. Paul's international headquarters was located in Waco, Texas. In conversations, he and I discovered that we were both heavily involved in the same concepts and theories about motivation and leadership. We became very close friends, and a couple of years before he passed away, I invited Paul to speak to our coaches on leadership. In typical Paul fashion, he responded and actually wrote a book for the membership of our Association called *The Coach I Always Wanted to Be*. I highly recommend the book to coaches of any sport.

In the book, Paul asked the coaches a question, then answered it: "Who motivates the motivator? He must motivate himself." Paul says,

> The coach can no longer look to the upper echelon for outside inspiration. He is the upper echelon. Once the coach realizes the motivation for his continued success must come from himself, he can proceed with the proper steps to achieve it. He can build a comprehensive program of personal motivation that will keep him moving steadily forward. He can and must 'press on.' He cannot stand still.

You will find in self-motivation a recognition that Maslow's theory of motivation incorporates the "hot button theory," and he believes that man is individually motivated by personal needs. I could not agree more. However, I also believe that a "need to succeed" is the king of personal needs.

Dr. Maslow points out the following areas of personal need:

- *Esteem needs*—self-respect, personal achievement, and self-esteem
- *Social needs*—in today's world, social media has become dominant, which incorporates all social needs, including friendship, belonging to a group, giving and receiving love, as noted by Dr. Maslow
- *Safety needs*—again, a reflection of today's society, living in a safe area, medical insurance, job security, retirement, police protection
- *Psychological needs*—the needs required to sustain life, such as air, water, food, sleep.

Dr. Maslow's motivation concept based on need has more applications to adults in the workplace, whereas coaches and teachers are dealing with students and athletes on the high school and college levels. Though many in today's society unfortunately face the same needs that adults face, there are those in the educational system who are confronted with what I refer to as the "journey needs." The journey is becoming an educated individual and responsible, successful adult while developing self-motivation, leadership skills, and techniques to achieve success.

The journey needs are basic: the need for physical development, the need for maturity, the need for continuing eligibility, and the need to understand the rules of the school, the NCAA, and the laws of the land. We need the tools to make the journey successful and the tools to become self-motivated. Self-motivation is embodied in finding your own hot button and pushing it at the appropriate time, thus starting your engine and propelling yourself into action.

In order to find one's hot button, one must master the basics.

Know Thyself

Ultimately, in order to set goals that are realistic and reachable, one must know oneself. Years ago, I developed a simple method for an individual to analyze his or her strengths and weaknesses and honestly recognize positive abilities and talents as well as negatives.

Self-Evaluation

On a sheet of paper, draw a line across the top with another down the middle. On the top left side, write the word "Assets" and on the top right side, write the word "Liabilities." Assets are your strengths, and liabilities are your weaknesses. Under Assets and Liabilities, draw five lines. Now, on the left side list your five best assets, and on the right side list your five greatest liabilities. Examples of an asset might be your attitude, work ethic, integrity, or loyalty. The liabilities list could include descriptions such as negative attitude, lazy, lack of confidence, or put things off.

The objective is simple for your listed assets and liabilities. Like the lyrics to an old song, "accentuate the positive and eliminate the negative." Build on and increase the good, the assets. Evaluate each negative and try to understand where you developed the negative, as it will help you as you strive to eliminate those listed negatives. Eliminating your liabilities and accentuating your assets is step one to becoming a self-motivated person.

How Do You See Yourself?

Asking the question, "How do you see yourself?" is the use of your ability to create mental pictures based on your heart's desire. No goal-oriented or ambitious person should ever see himself in a negative light ten years down the road. Knowing where you want to go is the first step in successful goal setting.

Once when Donell and I were leading a marriage improvement seminar, I asked that same question to the group in attendance: "How do you see yourself ten years from now?" I had not been told there were two couples in the audience who had been married more than seventy years. One of the husbands was 96 years old. At a break following the session on self-motivation, he gingerly made his way to the stage and tapped on my shoulder. I turned around to face head-on the 96 year old. His voice shaky, he posed this question: "Coach Teaff, would you like to know what I wrote down on the question 'How do I see myself ten years from now?'" I replied in the affirmative, excited to hear what a 96 year old's goals might be for the future. With a big smile on his face, his raspy old voice made it clear that he was a gentleman of humor and insight. He said, "I wrote down 'I just hope I can see myself ten years from now.'" Humor aside, the idea is to visualize your heart's desires, then make them come true.

Using Mental Pictures

After mastering Coach Mule Kayser's theory of mind control, I found another perfect mental tool for my overinflated goals, though some might refer to it as daydreaming. I created mental pictures of myself being successful and used my imagination pre-emptively to see my dreams and goals becoming a reality. I found that creative visualization had what I thought was almost mystical results. In the 1960s, I read a book called *Psycho-cybernetics*, written by Dr. Maxwell Maltz. The book introduced Dr. Maltz's analogy of the brain as a cybernetic "servo-mechanism." This is similar to a computer on a guided missile designed to find automatically a path to the target (self-image). Dr. Maltz's book turned me on to the subject of self-image psychology and goal visualization. The following statement had a huge impact on me: "the mind cannot differentiate between that which is vividly imagined and that which is performed."

Successful golfers picture their most difficult shots before they hit them. Watch on television, and you will see the golfer step away from the ball, swing through the stroke he wants to use, and watch the imaginary ball land in the perfect spot. Babe Ruth almost certainly visualized home runs going over the fence. On one occasion, he confidently pointed to the area where the ball would go over the fence. The average football player can become better by picturing himself in situations that will occur during the game and imagining himself successful.

A football team can vicariously experience the invigorating feeling of victory even before the game starts. That feeling is a second best to actually winning the game; however, the imagined feeling adds to the confidence already attained by knowledge and great preparation for the game. Personally as a coach, I employed the concept of psycho-cybernetics in my own life and with my teams. During the week, as a part of the regular routine in preparation for a game, our team members were encouraged to spend quiet time visualizing their responsibilities and actions on every play in which they would be involved, so that when it was time for the game, they would have rehearsed their responsibilities many times more than allowed on the practice field because of time constraints. We found our players to be better prepared, as they had played the game many times before kickoff.

On game day, during our devotional time, I asked players to close their eyes, and visualize successful execution of what they perceived to be their most difficult job in the upcoming game. The players were then asked to visualize their teammates and coaches in the dressing room after the game high-fiving and enjoying the victory.

Unbeknownst to the players, this was a method of having them relax before the game. I remember one specific time playing Auburn University on the road before a sellout crowd. Knowing we were in for a difficult game on the road, I did something a bit unusual. During our visualization time, I asked them to imagine themselves with only a few minutes to go, down to Auburn by less than a field goal. I asked the defense to visualize what each of them would have to do to stop an offensive drive by Auburn and get the ball back for our offense in order to win the game. I told the offense to visualize taking over with only a few minutes left in the game and executing what they would have to do to drive the length of the field, kick a field goal, and win the game.

As though scripted by a mysterious force, with only a few minutes left our defense had to stop a drive and get our offense the ball in order to have a chance to win the game on a field goal. Amazingly, that is exactly what happened. After the game, many players asked me how I knew we would find ourselves in that circumstance. My honest answer was, "I didn't know, but I know football. I know when you're playing a good team on foreign soil, if you are to win, the odds are the victory will come through having to do it the hard way. I can't think of a harder way than to stop a strong offensive team with a lead and then have your offense execute a flawless drive in order to take a shot at winning the game with a field goal." Which is exactly what we did on that day in Auburn, Alabama.

Mental Preparation

Mental preparation for a game is equal to the physical preparation. On Sunday, our staff would meet to determine a psychological theme for the upcoming game. We would use the theme to prepare our team to win. Using the theme of the week as a catalyst for all preparation, the staff determined what needed to be emphasized for the rest of the week.

As an example, we might be playing an extraordinarily tough opponent on the road, forcing us to the underdog position and creating the need to have the theme "Whatever it takes." That theme would be posted in the dressing room on Sunday afternoon and remain there the entire week, so the players would see it every day. The trainers and equipment people would have matching signs in their respective areas. The assistant coaches would be assigned responsibilities each day in their meetings to emphasize from their own vantage point what they believed it would take for their individual players to understand the theme "Whatever it takes." Coordinators came at it from their perspective, and at the end of each day of practice I would add a thought or idea using an example or story related to "Whatever it takes."

In 1978 we had a tough season because of some early injuries, and we were fighting back. At the end of the season, we were playing a particularly tough team. The theme of that week was "Whatever it takes." On Thursday afternoon, I remember emphasizing the theme by telling the players a story of two Eskimos fishing on the ice, each with the same equipment and bait. One of them was catching fish, while the other was not. The unsuccessful fisherman said to the successful fisherman, "We're using the same bait, the same equipment, the same size hole in the ice, so what is the secret to your success?" The one catching the fish said, "You gotta keep the worms warm," indicating he kept his bait in his mouth, so he would not be presenting a frozen worm to the fish. I said to the players, "Now that's doing whatever it takes. Remember, it may be distasteful or painful, but each of you needs to do whatever it takes. If you do, collectively, we will win the game." We did.

Again, in 1985, I remember using the same phrase, "Whatever it takes." We were playing Southern Cal—at that time the number two team in the nation—in their coliseum, and at half-time we were leading. I vividly remember the players in their excitement walking up to each other, screaming, "Whatever it takes!" In the fourth quarter, our defense had to hold the top running team in the nation to four plays inside the five-yard line in order to win, and we did.

The Secret Society of the Gold Dot

In the spring of 1979, the Baylor team was coming off a very tough 1978 season that was littered with injuries and losses. Though we had beaten the ninth-ranked team in the nation in the last game of the season, 1979 needed to be an outstanding year.

In those years we did not have the luxury of having our players in summer school, so when the spring was over they went to their respective parts of Texas to work in summer jobs and to follow a workout plan presented to them by our staff before they left. We were not around them, and they were not together, so they had individually to be self-motivated to do the work that would help them reach their individual and team goals. Being concerned about this particular summer, I had an idea that I thought would serve as a visual reminder of our commitment to each other, to Baylor, and to winning in 1979.

Without telling any of my staff members, following spring practice I invited the freshman players who were to be the rising sophomores to come to my house to talk about the 1979 season. It was a great time of fellowship. When it was time for them to go, I gathered them together, asking them to sit on the floor in my den. I had previously prepared for this moment; secretly taking helmet tape, I chose gold, took a hole punch, and created a couple hundred gold dots. I put the gold dots in my pocket in a small container and told no one what I was doing. That night, as the freshmen gathered around me, I said, "To commemorate our excellent spring and to allow all of us the opportunity to be together and to be encouraged to reach our individual goals throughout the summer, I formed an organization. I would like this freshman class to be the first members inducted into it."

The guys' eyes widened as I held up a tiny gold dot. Peeling off the back, I placed the dot over the six at the bottom of my watch. I turned my wrist to the group so they could see where I had placed the gold dot. I said, "Tonight, as I place this gold dot personally on your watch, you will officially become a member of The Secret Society of the Gold Dot. The Secret Society of the Gold Dot means you cannot tell anyone what this dot means. Only you and your teammates will know, once they have been told by me. You cannot tell your coaches, you cannot tell the upperclassmen, you cannot tell anyone on campus. You cannot even tell your mom or dad. You will be asked many times, 'What is that gold dot on your watch?' You are simply to say, 'I am a member of The Secret Society of the Gold Dot.'" I then placed a dot on the six of each freshman's watch. Of course, now I guess it would have to be done on their cell phones. Then I said, "Now, as you look at your watch during the day to determine the time, you will see the gold dot, reminding you of the goals you will set personally and as a team. It will remind you to do things on a daily basis that will allow you to be successful."

"The color of the dot is gold. Each letter in G-O-L-D stands for something very significant. The 'G' stands for the Goals you have set, individually, collectively. Write your goals down for yourself and for the team, carry them with you, and look at them each day to remind yourself of your responsibility."

"The 'O' stands for Oneness. Many times I have seen teams overcome a great adversity and go on to become successful because the individuals on the team were close and cared for each other, creating the oneness some opponents do not have. That oneness must be created for our team for the 1979 season—a oneness that only a cohesive, caring group of team members can create."

"The 'L' stands for Loyalty. Loyalty is the foundation of success. Be loyal to your goals, personal and team. Be loyal to your teammates. Though you are many miles apart, your loyalty will have you all doing the same thing at the appropriate time each day. Be loyal to your coaches and expect loyalty in return from them. Be loyal to our philosophy offensively and defensively, and to those who support us."

"The 'D' stands for Determination. It is an intangible we all possess, and when used properly it brings success to our doorstep.

Be determined to do the things on a daily basis that will allow you to come back in the fall properly prepared, so that this team can reach its goals. G-O-L-D: The Secret Society of the Gold Dot."

The next day, the freshmen walked around the campus. Both upperclassmen and coaches kept asking, "What's that gold dot?" The freshmen would smile and say, "I'm a member of The Secret Society of the Gold Dot." Of course, the more they refused to talk, the more interest was generated. The next two nights, I had the incoming juniors and seniors, and I repeated the same procedure.

Finally, in a staff meeting, I informed the coaches. They proudly began to wear their gold dots, and soon everyone on campus was asking the question, "What do the gold dots on the football players' watches mean?" An article appeared in the school paper asking the same question. The gold dot started a tradition at Baylor based on its perceived success. The '79 team was a champion of the Peach Bowl and played Alabama in the Cotton Bowl after becoming the undefeated Southwest Conference champions in 1980.

A banner with a gold dot hung in the Baylor dressing room and was carried on road trips to remind those who followed the '79 and '80 seasons that Goals, Oneness, Loyalty, and Determination would forever be the fabric of Baylor's future successes.

Goal Setting

Self-motivation has been around since our early ancestors were pursued by hungry animals. Sometimes there can be more than one form of motivation used by an individual, as in the case I just described—fear and self-preservation. In order to activate self-motivation, one needs to set goals physically, mentally, and spiritually.

Think of these three goals as a three-legged stool upon which your life sits. Failure to develop in any of the three areas creates a weakness in one of the legs of the stool. A two-legged stool will collapse. Using the stool as a metaphor, it is obvious that we must set and reach goals in those three areas of our lives.

There is a proven yet simple method of setting and reaching goals. First, determine the goal you want to reach, then make a judgment on the time it will take to reach it. Secondly, analyze what it will take to reach the goal and break that category into two sections. One—immediate goals, or the goals you can reach on a daily basis. Two—intermediate goals, or the goals that fall in between the immediate goal and the ultimate goal.

It is a proven fact that when our goals are written down and we proclaim them to those around us, we make a personal commitment. To solidify the commitment further, those goals should be written and proclaimed orally.

Each year, our players were given a new goal card to update. They had a copy and gave me a copy, so I could know their goals and we, as a staff, could help them reach those goals.

In training our freshmen in goal setting, I would always personally ask them what their major goal was as a freshman at Baylor. You would be surprised at some of the answers I received. On several occasions, I was told flat out, "I want to win the Heisman Trophy." My answer was, "A good goal for a freshman is to try to make the travel squad." One answer was so profound that I continue to use it as an ultimate example of goal setting.

Mike Singletary, a freshman from Houston, Texas, and a potential linebacker, when asked my freshman year question, responded, "My goal is to make a positive contribution to our football team this year." Wow. What a goal. If every freshman had set the same goal, we probably would have had the best football team in the history of Baylor University. By the way, that freshman class did become the best in Baylor's history. In 1980, they won the Southwest Conference championship by three games.

Mike's attitude and quick adaption to goal setting put him in a position to fulfill his first-year goal. During the eighth game of Mike's freshman year in 1977, we changed defenses because of an injury with the nose guard position. The change created a need for a middle linebacker, we changed our defense to a four-man front. Mike played his first game as a starting middle linebacker against the Arkansas offense. Mike's preparation for making a positive contribution as a freshman returned great dividends. He had 28 unassisted tackles and helped to hold Lou Holtz' offense to one of its lowest outputs of the season. From that moment forward, history in the Southwest Conference was to be rewritten. Mike went on to become a three-time All-Southwest Conference player, three-time All-American, three-time captain of the team, and a two-time winner of the Davey O'Brien Award. I would say that was a positive contribution to his team.

Self-motivation was a key for our freshmen academically. Playing football while maintaining eligibility and progressing toward graduation was a big job and a challenging one. Therefore, one of the examples I liked to use regarding goal setting and understanding the immediate and intermediate goals was to lay out a plan for success in the classroom.

If your goal was to receive an *A* in a particular class, your immediate goals would read like this:

- Take precise notes in class.
- Do not procrastinate on daily assignments.
- Approach each class period with a positive attitude.
- Commit the appropriate time daily for study.
- Sit on the front row, listen, and take notes on every word.

A player was always asked to prioritize these five steps and make them their own goals.

Goals can serve as guidelines and direction finders in our lives. Sometimes when we lose sight of our ultimate goals, they can be used to get us back on the right path.

Aubrey Schulz was a junior college transfer who came into our program as an upperclassman never having been a goal setter. Aubrey took to the idea because he was driven to get an education. His ultimate goal was to be a head coach on the highest high school level in the state of Texas, at that time called Division 5-A. Aubrey also had goals to become our starting center and gain thirty-five pounds in less than one year.

In the spring of Aubrey's first year at Baylor, he did become the starting center, but at 190 pounds. His announced goal was to report in the fall at 235. Living daily to reach that goal, his workout regimen and eating habits were all directed by his immediate goal. The next fall when Aubrey and his team weighed in, he had hit a solid 245 pounds and went on to become a first team All-American center for Baylor.

In the spring of his junior year, the director of the dormitory where Aubrey lived rang with a disturbing call. He informed me that Aubrey had had a problem in the dorm the night before, and also said there was no proof that Aubrey had been the instigator of other events but that he might be kicked out of the dorm if he made one more mistake. Being kicked out of the dorm would probably cause me to suspend him from the football program, and thus he would lose his opportunity to finish his education.

I sent out the word for Aubrey to come to my office, and shortly after noon, he walked in. Aubrey sat down in the chair in front of my desk and obviously did not know I had been informed about the incident. The dorm director informed me that someone from an upper floor in the dormitory had dropped a trash bag full of water on a passerby. Everyone had been laughing and having fun about it, but the dorm director had thought it was dangerous, inappropriate, and serious grounds for probation. Without saying a word, I reached into my desk and pulled out a copy of Aubrey's goal card. I handed it across the desk and said, "Read this out loud." "My ultimate goal professionally is to be a Division 5-A head coach in the state of Texas." A clear, concise goal. I said, "Aubrey, your behavioral patterns in the dormitory are not conducive with reaching your ultimate goal. Your conduct has put you in a position for a possible suspension from the dorm and ultimately from our football program. How do you think you will reach your goal of being a high school head football coach if you are no longer at Baylor, no longer on this team?" "Coach, I was just having fun. I didn't mean any harm," he replied. I said, "Aubrey, your actions must reflect your goals, even on a daily basis. A lack of attention to what it takes to get where you want to go can ultimately lead to failure." Aubrey's head dropped, and his eyes turned up toward me. "Coach, I understand exactly what you're saying. I promise you will never have another problem with me. I want to reach my goals."

I never had another problem with Aubrey. He went on to reach his goal as a head coach in a 5-A high school in the state of Texas, very successfully.

Who Motivates the Motivator?

I would be remiss in my love for and my commitment to our profession if I failed to address self-motivation and goal setting for our teachers and coaches. I have always held to the belief that if leaders, coaches, teachers, fathers, and parents give a sermon on life, they should live it. If we are teaching others through motivation of goal setting, we must ourselves be competent and successful in that arena. Setting a goal is like the rudder on a boat. If a boat has no rudder, it cannot be guided. The rudder is the goal that sets the direction you want the ship to sail. A beacon on the shore is like a visualized goal; I can see the beacon, so I set my rudder (goals) to go to the beacon. If I do this, I will become a goal-oriented, self-motivated leader.

My first year out of college, while coaching at Lubbock High School, I met and married Donell Phillips, a cheerleader from Texas Tech. Amazingly, we moved into an apartment on Baylor Street.

Shortly after we were married, Donell and I sat down at our little kitchen table to talk about my dream and who I wanted to become. I thought it was important for her to know these things, because I wanted and needed her support. If she was unable to support my dream and my goal, I needed to know, so I could change direction; however, she was excited about my plans, so I began to talk to her about setting goals in three-year increments. On that night, we became a family of goal setters. It is amazing how we reached goals year after year and continue to this day, setting goals and planning to reach them.

We decided to use three-year increments to reach what we thought at the time would be our ultimate goal. It was truly amazing how, planning and working together, we clicked off those goals year after year. I shared all my goals with Donell, and she particularly liked the one concerning my becoming a head football coach in the Southwest Conference. We expanded our goals by including physical, mental, and spiritual goals. We determined our home would be a Christian home, and we would raise our children in that environment. That decision was by far the most important one we made.

As a high school coach, I was making $3,000 a year, so we set a goal to make someday $1,000 a month. No matter what we made, we would give 10% to the church as a minimum and save another 10%. We would buy a home as soon as we could to build equity, and three years later in Abilene, Texas we were able to do so. A brand new $13,000 three-bedroom home. It stretched our budget, but we were building equity. We knew our life in coaching would be busy and intertwined with other lives, so we set aside time for just the two of us. We committed Thursday night to be date night, and we still claim Thursday as "our time." Donell worked the first few years of our marriage to help us achieve a solid financial foundation. Her goal was to be involved in my profession, and especially with coaches' wives. To this very day, she is heavily involved with the American Football Coaches Wives Association, which she helped start several years ago.

An unintended consequence of family goal setting is that it works just like it does with a team. It brings a family together with a common purpose.

Challenges that Motivate—"Take Care of Business"

In order to teach accountability to my football teams, I used four little words that became ingrained as a part of our team mentality. The four words were "Take Care of Business." The players on my respective teams at McMurry, Texas Tech, Angelo State, and Baylor always responded positively to the emphasis I placed on their personal accountability in doing the things that would make them winners on the field and off the field. The first step was carefully to explain to the team the meaning of accountability: "You are responsible for your attitude and your approach to life, as well as your action and behavior, and your academic progress toward eligibility and graduation. You are also responsible for your effort, your discipline, and to care about your team, your teammates, your coaches, your family, and collectively, our team goals." Finally, I would challenge the teams by saying, "We all have business for which we are accountable, so each of you individually must take care of your business. The challenge is 'TCB: Take Care of Business.'" After Baylor's Sun Bowl victory over the University of Arizona in 1992, I designed a ring to be given to every coach, team member, doctor, trainer, and as a matter of fact, to everyone who played any role in that special last year of my coaching. The ring had several significant reminders. One statement was used as the theme of the dinner that the city of Waco and the Texas Sports Hall of Fame gave Donell and me after the bowl game. The theme was "From Pride to Excellence." Because it was significant, I had the words placed on the outer top of the ring. The first thing we did upon taking the Baylor job was to instill pride in the football program and the university, and that foundation of pride helped us over 21 years to gain what others claimed was excellence.

On one side of the ring was a replica of Floyd Casey Stadium. On the other side, the initials "TCB." Baylor was an underdog to the great Dick Tomey's Arizona team. We trailed for most of the ball game. Late in the fourth quarter everyone on the sidelines was yelling to the players on the field. When I finally realized what they were chanting, a smile creased my face. They were admonishing their teammates to "TCB." Take care of business they did, and we all enjoyed the victory in the last football game I ever coached.

Players were not the only ones to take care of business. My football staff, in my opinion, did the best job of coaching imaginable. The coach who was to follow me was on my staff, and he had already determined who he would retain and who he would dismiss. The new coach kept only a couple of coaches, so there was an uneasy feeling because the bowl game brought us all together to work toward one last victory. Throughout the preparation and the game, the staff had committed themselves to take care of business. They did, working together smoothly to help our team to victory.

My first year at Angelo State University, I asked each of our players to add to their goals the concept of "TCB." You can reach your goals successfully by making sure you take care of business on a daily basis, doing the things you are asked to do and the things you need to do. I made the statement that on the football field there would be occasions when individuals, by taking care of their business related to the position they played and their role on the team, could actually win a game for us. It just so happened that in the fourth game of that season we were playing my alma mater, McMurry College. The previous week I had lost three running backs and several defensive players to injuries while playing on the road against a strong defense. We were going to have a hard time scoring.

As the week went on, I realized that our offense had to be our kicking game. Bobby Manchaca, a defensive back, returned all of our kicks. He was small but very good. At a team meeting earlier that week, I singled Bobby out and said, "Bobby, I'm putting the whole offensive load on you." I did not smile, nor did he. I went on, "Take care of our business on defense by forcing kicks, and we will then rely on you, Bobby, for the yardage that will put us in a position to score points. Offense must take care of business by being penalty-free with no turnovers."

The first punt of the game by Bobby was very high. As he caught the ball, the McMurry team was right on top of him. Bobby turned 360 degrees toward the goal line to get away from his pursuers. When he did so, two McMurry guys hit him head-on, making the ball squirt free into the end zone where McMurry recovered it for a touchdown. "So much for winning this game with our specialty teams." Bobby came to the sideline, head down. As he approached me, however, his head came up. He looked me right in the eye and said, "Coach, I will take care of business. I will run the next punt back for a touchdown."

Our defense held for the second time. As McMurry punted the ball, Bobby was waiting on our 30-yard line. He softly caught the ball, retreated about five yards, then straight back up the field, quickly cutting to his left and down the sideline eighty-five yards into the end zone. He came to the sideline with the biggest grin I have ever seen on anybody's face and yelled, "Coach, I told you I'd take care of business and I did." That day, Bobby Manchaca became the face of self-motivation.

Bobby scored three times that day, amassing over 250 yards of returns. Angelo State University won a game with the special teams, just "taking care of business."

The 1980 football season was the best in Baylor history with a 10-2 record. It would not have been if one of our players had not risen to the occasion and clearly taken care of business. Jay Jeffrey was the younger brother of Neal Jeffrey, who had led us to the championship in 1974 as a quarterback.

During the championship drive, we played an outstanding SMU team at home. The winner had a good shot at becoming the Southwest Conference champion. At halftime we were down four-teen points. We came out in the third quarter and Jay sprinted to his left and threw the ball back to his right directly into the arms of a defensive back, who waltzed into the end zone untouched to score. Now Baylor was down twenty-one points. Jay walked to the sideline, went directly to the bench, and sat down with his head in his hands. "Send someone to get Jay," I said. As he approached me, before I could say a word, he quickly asked, "Am I going back in the game, Coach?" I immediately said, "Of course you are, you're our quarterback and we can't win this game without you. You will be the one who makes the difference in this game. And remember, Jay, we believe in you." Jay went back into the game, and the rest is history. After the game, a sportswriter marveled at the come-from-behind victory for Baylor, asking Jay, "What motivated you so much in the second half?" Without hesitation, Jay responded, "Coach's faith and confidence in me, my personal commitment to my team, and my determination to take care of my business on the field and let my teammates take care of theirs."

Believing that self-motivation is the ultimate key to individual progress and achievement, I find validity in part of Abraham Maslow's theory of self-actualization. Maslow recognizes the importance of goals in leading one to full potential as a person. Only a small percentage of the population reaches a high level of self-actualization. Using the power of the mind, which responds to that inner "want-to" and quest to fulfill one's needs, ignites in each of us a capacity to be self-motivated.

My personal motivation is striving to be better tomorrow than I am today. Meaning, I want to develop every asset I have to the fullest. I am motivated to learn a new word every day, both the definition and how to use it, so I can be a better communicator. In my car, I listen to CDs of books that I otherwise would not have time to read. My goal is to remain a highly motivated leader for my family, for my staff, and for the members of the American Football Coaches Association. As such, I am motivated to ask you as an individual to become self-motivated and teach the fundamentals of self-motivation. Then you will live it as an example to those you teach.

Leaders who are highly motivated will make the time to study great leaders who have been successful in other areas as well as coaching.

— 6 —

Leadership

Leadership is defined as a method by which a person or group influences others to obtain certain goals and objectives. Wikipedia begins with this description: "a process of social influence in which one person can enlist the aid and support of others in the accomplishment of a common task" (from Martin Chemers, *An Integrative Theory of Leadership*).

When man started walking the face of the earth, two things were necessary to sustain life—fire and leadership. As a human race, we are way past rubbing two sticks together to create friction hot enough to ignite a little clump of dead grass; however, the need for leadership continues to increase. Nomadic family groups searching for shelter and food were led by the most dominant male. Family groups banded together to become tribes, then nations. Nation building created a need for political leaders and military leaders to protect their subjects/citizens or to conquer other nations. A new type of leader, above and beyond the dominant male, was needed. Written history has given us example after example of leaders, some very good and some very bad.

Military leadership in America has been critical since the Pilgrims landed on Plymouth Rock. In the last century and a half, sports have been a vital part of the growth and development of military leaders, as well as of thousands of leaders in every segment of American society. The lessons taught and learned on the friendly "field of strife" have been responsible for thousands of leaders who learned never to give in and never to quit. General Douglas MacArthur spoke the words that are now inscribed on a plaque at the United States Military Academy's Michie Stadium. MacArthur said, "On these fields of friendly strife are sown the seeds that on other fields on other days will bear the fruits of victory." General George C. Marshall, another World War II leader, said this about the United States Military Academy: "When I want an officer for a secret and dangerous mission, I want a West Point football player."

General Colin Powell describes leadership this way: "Leadership is the art of getting people to do more than the science of management says is possible." The United States Military Academy and other colleges and universities have served as the cradle of leadership decade after decade.

The United States military, for over two hundred years, has developed leaders from the lowest to the highest military ranks. In battle, the leader may fall, but the chain of command designates the next to lead. In many cases, leaders emerge to take charge and accomplish what seems to be an unattainable goal.

Jack Lummus Jr., a native of Ennis, Texas, and a baseball and football star at Baylor University, signed with the New York Giants football team in 1941. Lummus played both offense and defense as an end when the Giants reached the NFL championship game that was played two weeks after the Japanese bombed Pearl Harbor.

One month after the game, Lummus joined the United States Marine Corps and rose quickly to Company Commander. His unit landed on the beaches of Iwo Jima in February 1945, where seven thousand Americans were killed on that bloody island. Jack Lummus was one of those who died, exhibiting stunning bravery for which he was awarded the Congressional Medal of Honor.

This description of Jack Lummus' death was created by the Committee on Veterans' Affairs of the United States Senate, recognizing him as a recipient of the Medal of Honor.

March 8, 1945, after having fought without rest for two days and nights, Jack Lummus was leading a rifle platoon attached to the 2nd Battalion, 27th Marines, 5th Marine Division. The Marines were in action against Japanese forces that were deeply entrenched. Advancing into the face of a concentration of hostile fire, Lummus was knocked down by a grenade explosion. Recovering he moved forward and single-handedly attacked and destroyed the occupied placement. Under fire, from a supporting emplacement he fell from the impact of a second grenade, sustaining painful shoulder wounds. Disregarding his injuries, Lummus continued his one-man assault by charging another pillbox, killing all the occupants. He then returned to his platoon position and encouraged his men to advance. While moving forward under fire, he rushed to a third fortified installation and killed its defending troops. He continued to lead his men, personally attacking foxholes and spider traps, systematically reducing the opposition until he stepped on a land mine that took his life.

Richard Newcomb, in a book written in 1946, *Iwo Jima*, described Lummus' last action:

> Suddenly Lummus was at the center of a powerful explosion, obscured by flying rock and dirt. As it cleared, his men saw him rising as if in a hole. A land mine had blown off both his legs that had carried him to football honors at Baylor University. His men watched in horror as he stood on bloody stumps, calling them on. Several men, crying now, ran to him and for a moment, talked of shooting him to stop the agony. But he was still shouting for his men to move out, "Move out," and the platoon scrambled forward. Their tears turned to rage; they swept an incredible 300 yards over the impossible ground and at nightfall were on the ridge, overlooking the sea. There was no question that the dirty, tired men, cursing, crying and fighting, had done it for Jack Lummus, their leader.

Are Leaders Born?

"Leaders are born not created," someone once stated. Of course that statement has been argued both ways. Vince Lombardi made his case very emphatically when he said, "Leaders are made, they are not born. Period. They are made by hard effort, which is the price all of us pay to achieve any goal that is worthwhile."

From a practical standpoint, I believe that certain individuals are born with an innate desire to lead. That innate desire could emanate from our DNA, some might say our destiny, or more specifically defined "a quality that arises from within, versus something learned or experienced."

Innate Desire or a Calling?

What is the difference between an innate desire and a calling? My attraction to the game of football and coaching, and my innate desire to make a difference, turned into what I eventually came to believe was a calling.

Reading the Bible, verse after verse indicated that there was a plan and a purpose and a will for my life. I never heard an audible voice or saw a fiery message in the sky proclaiming what I should choose for my life's work, so I relied heavily on personal motivation to fuel my desire to reach my goals.

Oswald Chambers states his opinion about a calling from God with these words: "The realization of [the call of God] in a man's life may come with a sudden thunderclap or with a gradual dawning, but in whatever way it comes, it comes with the undercurrent of the supernatural, something that cannot be put into words."

In the mid-1960s, a young black minister from Montgomery, Alabama, Martin Luther King Jr., burst onto the national scene as a courageous, inspirational, and spiritual leader. National attention was focused on Martin Luther King Jr. as he led three marches in March 1965 from Selma, Alabama to Montgomery, marking the political and emotional peak of the American Civil Rights Movement. The marches grew out of the "right to vote" movement in Selma, Alabama.

My deep feeling that God had called me to the coaching profession and into leadership was boosted one night when I heard a radio broadcast of Martin Luther King Jr. saying, "I could hear an inner voice saying to me, 'Martin Luther, stand for righteousness. Stand up for justice. Stand for truth. And lo, I will be with you.'" Dr. King wept when he said, "I can't stop now. History has thrust upon me that which I cannot turn away from." It was clear that Martin Luther King Jr. felt "the sudden thunderclap" as well as the "gradual dawning"; whether he wanted it or not, he was called.

A few years earlier, in 1960, as a 26-year-old head football coach at McMurry College, I offered a football/track scholarship to a black athlete, Kenneth Decker, from Kermit, Texas. Unlike Martin Luther King Jr., it was not a conscious effort on my part to integrate McMurry College or college football in the state of Texas. I recruited Kenneth based solely on the fact that he fit the criteria by which I measured every prospective athlete. Kenneth was a fine young man with an engaging personality and a deep desire to become educated.

Qualifying Criteria for a Scholarship

- Core values—positive character traits
- Intellectual capacity to graduate—a passion to get an education
- Athletic skills, but with an up-side for development
- Exhibits a desire to learn and work to get better every day.

The criteria used to determine Kenneth Decker's qualification for a scholarship at McMurry College remained the same through my thirty-seven years of coaching.

Kenneth quickly adjusted to college life and began to make headway and improve as a freshman football player. I must admit that I was oblivious to what we would encounter in the next two or three years. I had supposed that Kenneth would be accepted as a member of our team and of the Abilene, Texas community. I was right about that, as our players, student body, and the city of Abilene readily accepted Kenneth as part of the McMurry football team. However, I found out that the world outside of Abilene was not quite ready to accept Kenneth.

Through Kenneth I learned a lot about the real world in which I was living. The first football game of Kenneth's freshman year, we were playing Austin College in Sherman, Texas. We, of course, bused from Abilene to Sherman, going through the outer edge of Fort Worth. We stopped at a café in the northern part of Fort Worth and ordered chicken fried steak with all the trimmings for an after-game dinner on our way back to Abilene. After the game, we arrived at the café, unloaded the bus, and walked to the porch of the café. I could see through the front door that the steaks were already on the tables. Kenneth happened to be to my right and a little behind as we stepped onto the porch. The café owner and cook, wearing a stained white apron around his waist and a cigarette behind his right ear, said in a very loud voice, "Is he with you?" pointing to Kenneth.

I responded, "Yes, he is a member of our team." The "N" word rushed from the proprietor's mouth as he informed me that Kenneth would not be allowed to eat in the dining room but could eat in the kitchen. I was stunned, and silence fell over the team as the confrontation continued. I said loudly, "Kenneth is a member of our team, and our team eats together."

Without using profanity but very emphatic, the proprietor said flatly, "He eats in the kitchen."

I responded with one final desperate question: "Are you telling me one of my players cannot eat with his teammates and coaches?"

He replied, "He eats in the kitchen!"

I looked directly into the man's eyes for a few seconds, then said loud enough that the players behind me and to either side could hear, "Okay, if Kenneth doesn't eat, none of us will eat. I hope you enjoy your steaks." With that, I turned and walked briskly back to the bus. The team and coaches silently loaded the bus, and we drove west to Abilene with not one complaint from the players or coaches. That night, we all experienced hunger pangs from a lack of food and the painful reality of America in 1960.

Prior to the next road trip, Kenneth came to my office and said we needed to talk. He said, "Coach, we can't go through the season refusing to eat our meals. I'll be more than happy to eat in the kitchen on the next trip. Trust me, I'll be fed real good back there."

The next year things began to change, and by the time Kenneth graduated, it was clear that America was changing for the better. Through Kenneth's years at McMurry, he opened many doors for those who would follow. Kenneth's fantastic attitude, as well as his understanding that he was actually blazing a new trail, encouraged his coaches, teammates, and others in our community. Everyone appreciated his class and the dignity with which he handled himself. His resolve to be a part of facilitating the changes motivated all of us.

Because of Martin Luther King Jr., young men like Kenneth Decker, and thousands of others both black and white, America and sports were changed forever.

Leadership—A Lifetime Journey

Thousands of individuals throughout history have risen to a place of leadership in their families, nations, businesses, armies, and sports. Aspiring leaders must learn from the leaders who have gone before, emulating the best of their leadership skills and eliminating styles and techniques that fail to fit their own philosophies. All great, positive leaders have core values and positive character traits. Some leaders have more natural talent and skill than others. Natural talent is a gift, but leadership skills, such as communication, can be developed. Communication is the foundation on which all successful leaders begin. You can be a visionary with the greatest of plans, but if your vision and those plans are not communicated effectively, failure is imminent.

As a sophomore in high school, when offered the opportunity to lead I became an enthusiastic and willing participant. Early on, opportunities arose: drama club, student government, the role of captain of football and basketball teams, as well as a two-year captain position in Junior College football and a three-year captain position at McMurry College. After one year of high school coaching, meeting and marrying my lifetime co-coach, Donell, staggering responsibilities of leadership were thrust upon me. I became head track coach and assistant football coach at age 23, was elected a deacon of the Southwest Park Baptist Church, and—maybe the toughest job of all—became co-director with Donell of the athletic dormitory at McMurry. When Donell and I were married, I understood clearly my responsibility as the leader in our home. I immediately designated Donell as a co-leader and partner as we began to set goals for our marriage, our life's work, and eventually our children. While holding our firstborn in my arms, I realized this new life was a part of me, and my responsibility was to become the best father and leader of our home possible. Unequipped and untrained, embracing the responsibility of leadership created a new level of motivation to learn to lead. So began a lifetime study of great leaders in all fields.

At a very early age, after realizing my family played roles in three great wars, I became intrigued with military leadership. My father was a sergeant in the Texas National Guard when World War II began, and my great-grandfather, William Jefferson Teaff, was a Captain in the Confederate Army. Henry Teaff, my great-great-great-grandfather, served in the American Revolution and with General Washington at Valley Forge. Studying the great generals of those wars led me to several conclusions about leadership.

Conclusions

Leaders Never Stop Learning

The truth is leaders should continue to learn and lead simultaneously. Don Faurot, former head football coach at Missouri, was known for his innovations in offensive football and as a respected leader in our Association. Coach Faurot was a great leader in our profession and for years was also recognized as one of the most innovative offensive minds to have ever coached the game. A few years ago, at age 92, Don was attending the AFCA convention and I was lecturing on short yardage offense. I noticed Don was sitting on the front row and scribbling in a small book. After the session, Coach Faurot sought me out, asking for details on my lecture. After answering his questions, I asked, "Coach, you have been retired for over twenty-five years, so why do you still attend lectures and keep extensive notes?" Coach Faurot said without hesitation, "Never stop learning."

Leaders Serve

For over twenty-five years, Coach Tom Landry of the Dallas Cowboys and I crisscrossed the nation raising money for the Fellowship of Christian Athletes (FCA). During that time, I served two terms as the national chairman of the board, and I have continued to help raise money nationwide and in Central Texas to help send coaches, their families, and athletes to FCA summer conferences and camps. Coach Landry and I talked often about the importance of serving others through our leadership. After Coach Landry's passing, in order to honor him and the passion he felt for serving others, I along with hundreds of others continue to serve as a tribute to Coach Landry.

Leaders Create

My interest through the years included national issues affecting our profession, our game, and those who play it. Mike Cleary, visionary executive director of the National Association of Collegiate Directors of Athletics (NACDA), and I felt there was a need for positive promotion of the game of football. No organization had taken on that responsibility, so the AFCA and NACDA started an organization we named College Football USA. We asked the collegiate commissioners and the National Collegiate Athletic Association (NCAA) to join us and help create an even more powerful organization to promote college football's positive contributions. NCAA Football, as an organization, has shared millions of dollars with universities, conferences, and other stakeholders in college football. It has been a pleasure to serve as a part of NCAA Football.

Leaders Lead through Tough Times

Being a leader has a lot of positives that accompany the role. However, nothing is guaranteed, and sometimes extremely bad things happen and the leader ultimately is responsible. Two of my darkest and most painful times as a leader occurred while serving Baylor University as the head football coach. In 1979 Kyle Woods, a sophomore defensive back from Dallas, Texas, had a head-to-head collision with a running back during a scrimmage, fracturing his neck. His spinal cord was damaged, and in an instant, the 19-year-old was a quadriplegic. Out of sheer necessity, I grew dramatically as a leader through that period of time, because the buck had to stop with me. The responsibility was mine, and as painful and arduous as the experience was, it turned out to be a unifying, uplifting, and motivational thirty years for Kyle's teammates, his coaches, and hundreds of others who came alongside us to be a part of whatever future Kyle Woods would have. In those years, the university had only $60,000 in insurance and that barely paid our way out of the hospital. Three days after the injury, I started a trust fund for Kyle and his future needs. That experience proved over and over again the goodness of people and how much they care about others. Kyle inspired us all with his courage and positive attitude. He had a huge impact on everyone who met him. He was an inspiration to his teammates. Kyle was injured in August of 1979, and the team, at the end of the year, was selected to play Clemson in the Peach Bowl. On their own, the team dedicated the game to Kyle and in a dramatic way won it for him. Seeing to Kyle's needs over a thirty-year period created a bond between his teammates and his coaches. Even though Kyle passed away recently, he continues to be the glue that holds us all together.

Leading for a Safer Game

First as a football coach and in recent years as the executive director of the AFCA, my commitment has been to work with the National Athletic Trainers' Association, creating videos and DVDs on proper tackling fundamentals and approving a book of tackling drills that stresses the safety of proper tackling fundamentals. Working with head coaches and the NCAA to change contact rules in spring practice and during fall training camps has had a positive effect on the physical well-being of our athletes. Understanding the impact that an injury like Kyle's has on an entire family, we encourage and support those who try to help football players and their families who have suffered catastrophic neck and head injuries. For the last few years we have worked with stakeholders in college football regarding concussions, sickle-cell anemia, heat strokes, and improved protective equipment. The NCAA, football coaches, and administrators in the game of football care for the safety and well-being of our athletes more diligently by providing a safer game.

Broken-Hearted Leader

In late September of 1990, Baylor University was playing Arizona State in Tempe. Our offensive right guard sustained a knee injury, which created an opportunity for a red-shirt freshman, John Karkoska. With excitement, John stepped into the starting role of the right offensive guard. With an open date, we had two weeks to prepare for our next opponent. Late in the week, on a normal day for late September, John suffered a heat stroke. As the head coach and leader, I was responsible for everything and everyone connected to our football program. While John gallantly fought for his life, my responsibility was leadership. John's family, his coaches, his teammates, and his friends prayed diligently for him daily. Ten days later, a few minutes before game time, John passed away.

John and his mother, Dolores, were extremely close. During the time John was in the hospital, prior to his death, my responsibility included dealing with the trauma our team and coaches were going through. The media had endless questions about the workout and John's health prior to the heat stroke. However, my toughest moments were spent with John's mother, trying to be a comfort for her but feeling so helpless because I could not step into his hospital room and fix it. We all believed that somehow John would make it through. Unable to sleep at night, my refuge was the bedroom closet and my Bible. Searching the Bible from cover to cover looking for answers, I found many verses and words of comfort, but John's reality brought no comfort. John's teammates were distraught because he was so highly respected and had had a huge impact on all of them as well as his coaches.

A Mother's Leadership

After the funeral, John's mother felt strongly that Baylor University should take the lead in a concerted effort to create a safer environment in which football players could play the game, by stressing the importance of hydration and making sure players felt comfortable in telling a trainer or coach if they did not feel well. Dolores Karkoska's challenge to all of us at Baylor was received positively, and Baylor University worked with an outstanding video producer to create an appealing video with the two strong messages Mrs. Karkoska had recommended.

Every high school and college in America received the video. The response was very positive. I am so grateful and indebted to John's mom for her leadership in creating the video. For all who worked on the video, it was our tribute to John's memory and to the mother who lost her only child. At that time, I committed myself, as a coach and a national leader, to be involved every day in making the game safer to play. For twenty years now, here at the AFCA we have joined with the NCAA, the National Athletic Trainers' Association, high school associations, the National Football League (NFL), equipment manufacturers, and the NCAA Football playing rules committee to make the game safer. Dolores Karkoska's leadership helped create an awareness across

America that has undoubtedly saved lives. There is no way to know how many, but what I do know is that, as long as I live, I will be involved in making our game safer to play.

Leaders Share Experiences

Since 1979 my heartfelt intentions have been to make myself available to coaches on all levels who are dealing with a catastrophic injury or death. Coaches have few people to whom they can relate under those circumstances. My willingness to share my experiences has always been received with open arms. The ultimate goal is to help others deal with the myriad of issues they will face during these tough times.

Since 1994 our membership has been reminded of the following: it is imperative that those of us with responsibility for the safety and well-being of our athletes "practice good medicine." That phrase simply means that we do everything in our power as coaches to help provide the safest equipment, while using the safest drills to teach the contact of football. Most importantly, all medical decisions should be made by the medical staff.

Leaders Negotiate

In the mid-1980s, the AFCA and the NFL saw eye-to-eye on very few situations. The NFL and the AFCA created a committee to attempt to solve the myriad of issues between college and professional football. For an eight-year period things were about as bad as they could get. There was little trust and great anger and resentment from the college coaches, because there were no regulations on NFL franchises as they encroached on campuses during the spring meeting and tested players. NFL teams tested players physically, psychologically, and individually. This constant encroachment became a burden and a problem. In 1994, during the AFCA convention in Anaheim, California, I met with Paul Tagliabue, the commissioner of the NFL. We discussed the previous committee system used by both the AFCA and the NFL, and it was determined that it was no longer viable. As issues between the college coaches and the NFL continued to escalate, Mr. Tagliabue and I decided that he would provide someone in his office with authority, and the two of us could solve the existing problems between the NFL and college football. Bill Polian, who later became the general manager of the Indianapolis Colts, was the man. Bill had the authority, so we started to work. By the end of 1994, a smooth working relationship had developed, and it continues to this day.

Leaders by Any Other Name

For a high percentage of the leadership tasks to which I have committed myself over my lifetime, ultimately I had to figure out how to succeed. Leading while learning at the same time was the catalyst for becoming a planner. Planning to lead successfully, I believe, is a responsibility of leaders.

The following is the basic plan for my personal leadership:

- Become the leader I need to be
- A vision will become a plan, the plan a goal, the goal a purpose, and the purpose our motivation
- Live my values and strive to make a difference
- Challenge and encourage
- Be transparent—trustworthiness will be a fertile field for success
- Care not who gets the credit as long as the job gets done
- Motivate by teaching self-motivation
- Become a role model and an example
- Teach those being led to lead
- Together-we-can attitude
- Believe.

Transforming Leadership

In 1978 I read for the first time that my style of leadership should be called "Transforming Leadership." James MacGregor Burns, Pulitzer Prize-winning historian and authority in leadership studies, in his descriptive research on political leaders, identified what he called Transforming Leadership, which was a process in which "leaders and followers help each other advance to a higher level of morale and motivation." Burns went on to say that the "transforming approach to leadership creates significant change in the life of the people and the organization."[18]

In 1985, Bernard M. Bass, professor emeritus of the school of management at Binghamton University, New York, extended the work of Burns by explaining the psychological mechanism that underlies transforming leadership. Bass introduced the term "transformational" in place of "transforming." Bass said, "The extent to which a leader is transformational, is measured first in the terms of his influence on his followers. The followers of such a leader feel trust, admiration, loyalty, and respect for the leader, and a willingness to work harder than originally expected. Transformational leaders offer the followers something more than just working for self-gain: they provide followers with an inspiring mission and vision and give them an identity."[19]

Leadership Requirements

After years of leadership, study, observation, and exposure to great leaders, identifiable requirements of leadership began to emerge. In my book *Coaching in the Classroom*, six requirements were defined:

1. *Knowledge*—have a thorough knowledge of your task and those who could oppose your successful completion of the task. Know your staff, team, employees, and associates. Know their talents, their strengths, their weaknesses.
2. *Courage*—it takes courage to create a plan and stick with it—courage to give others credit and take the blame if the plan fails.
3. *Communication*—"Failure or success of a well-conceived plan rests solely on the shoulders of communication." Clearly define the plan, the ultimate goals, and individual responsibilities in order to achieve the goal. A leader must communicate his or her own passion and confidence, as well as express appreciation.
4. *Character*—in order to succeed, a positive leader must possess and live a value system. Positive character traits such as integrity, trust, accountability, and faithfulness are essential to the leader. Leaders are judged by their personal actions and words.
5. *Decisiveness*—a leader must be able to make decisions with confidence after studying the options. Being indecisive is a ticket straight to failure.

6. *Decision-making*—a leader can easily possess all of the previously mentioned leadership requirements and end up a poor and ineffective leader by making bad decisions.

Examples of Bad Decisions

A poignant reminder of the importance of decision-making took place in the fall of 2011, following a summer filled with football programs and major institutions having to respond to a myriad of allegations. Then in late summer, the scandal at Penn State swept across a horrified America. College football was inundated with negative press. A sportswriter from Cleveland called me to ask, "Do you think that big-time football, big salaries, big budgets, grandiose facilities, television coverage, and big paychecks to universities from conferences have negatively affected leadership in these institutions?"

My answer was quick, as I responded, "No, not at all." I went on to say, "Leadership is leadership. Honesty is honesty. Integrity is integrity, and wisdom is wisdom. Great leadership is the same under all circumstances and all vocations, including politics, the corporate world, and sports. The success of a leader is ultimately based on the decisions made. Each leader must make decisions based on their moral and ethical compass, wisely using the facts available."

Leadership Lesson

In the wake of a grand jury indicting a former Penn State assistant coach on charges of sexual abuse, the president of the university and other high-ranking officials were fired. Ultimately, Joe Paterno was relieved of his coaching duties by the Penn State University Board. After Coach Paterno was fired, Joe evidently felt the decision he had made at the time fell short. Coach Paterno's statement was a flashing red light for all in positions of leadership: "I wish I had done more," Coach Paterno said. Eight months later, a scathing report issued by an independent investigation headed by former FBI director Louis Freeh said, "The most powerful men at Penn State failed to take any steps for 14 years to protect the children who were victimized."

The Lesson

As coaches we have an obligation to take appropriate action at the appropriate time. I once described leadership as a lonely job, and it certainly can be when bad things happen. If we make decisions to do the right thing at the right time, seldom will we have to look back and say, "I wish I had done more."

Joe Ehrmann of the Coach for America organization clearly describes a leader's responsibility: "It's not enough to be just a 'good man'—you have to engage in what is around you and become a man of action. An involved man's voice and actions are in alignment with his moral and ethical beliefs. Moral courage enables us to stand up for what is right even if it means standing alone or risking rejection or negative consequence."[20]

The Actions of a Leader

The givens for leadership are integrity, wisdom, and trust. However, a leader must also be a person of action. The following actions are essential to successful leadership:

- *Ask others for their opinion*—asking for an opinion denotes respect for the individual being asked. It says to others, "Your opinion is important and will be considered." It also gives the leader insight that he might not otherwise have.

- *Set an example*—never ask anyone to do anything that you are not willing to do; the flipside of that is, it is okay to ask someone to do something you have already done. As an athlete running wind sprints, it always comforted me to know that my coach had run those same wind sprints in another time and another place. The example of the leader sets the tone for everyone.

- *Take responsibility for failed efforts*—leaders who point fingers and place blame publicly will not remain in a position of leadership very long. As a leader, you do everything in your power to achieve success, remembering success is not always possible. Taking responsibility for that failure without playing the martyr will enhance your chance for success at the next attempt.

- *Give others the credit*—when achieving success, point out the efforts and contributions of others. Everyone knows that you are the leader and you had a part in the success, but there are many within the group who will be recognized only if you acknowledge them. The basic philosophy I adhere to is very simple: it doesn't matter who gets the credit as long as the job gets done.
- *Make sound decisions*—substitute the word "solid" for "sound" and making such a decision will produce the exact same results. "Solid" and "sound" denote "factual" and "basic," and those types of decisions can be made only with the proper information concerning the issues and the problems related to them.
- *Listen*—listen to others' ideas. Many times a leader's responsibility is that of broadly outlining objectives. After setting broad objectives and directing discussions about them, if you listen to and generate the ideas of others about the broad objectives, you add a "we" flavor to what you are trying to accomplish.
- *Have a written plan*—like the rudder on a ship, written plans keep you on course. You can also use them as a yardstick with which to measure your progress and get feedback on your performance. Written plans keep you from putting off action and becoming stagnant. A plan keeps you focused on your goals and not on the doubts that always occur.
- *Visualize the end result*—visualizing a successful end result creates positive expectations of your stated goals.
- *Solve problems*—anticipating that there will be problems allows the leader to have a predetermined back-up plan and a procedure to follow. Approach each problem with individuality, apply the win-win-win theory to each problem, and don't jump to conclusions. It is a fact that problems and setbacks will occur, but the quicker they are solved, the better.

- *Make accountability a top priority*—accountability according to Wikipedia is a concept in ethics and governance with several meanings, such as the acknowledgment and assumption of responsibility for actions, decisions, and policies, including administration, governance, and implementation.

Leadership Character Traits

Leaders I have studied and observed over the years have possessed most of the positive character traits listed. As you read through these character traits, do a mental checklist for your own qualifications to lead. If you find yourself wanting in any of these positive character traits, the good news is that they can be developed.

- *Sincerity*—if you are a good actor and can fake sincerity, then I suggest you go into the movies and do not consider yourself a candidate for leadership. Sincerity can be faked for only a short period of time, and leadership demands consistency over the long haul. Either you are a sincere person or you are not.
- *Caring*—those being led don't care what you know until they know how much you care.
- *Emotion*—emotion means you are able to show sincerity and caring in your demeanor. Although emotions must be controlled, those you are trying to lead must know that you have a fire and intensity within you that burns with an emotional zeal.
- *Loyalty*—I could write an entire book on loyalty as a character trait. Loyalty is a two-way street: loyalty to the leader, and the leader's loyalty to those within the group or organization. There can be disagreements or opposite opinions, but when a final decision is made, it must become "our" decision.
- *Diplomacy*—the adage says, "Discretion is the better part of valor." The same should apply to diplomacy. A diplomatic leader should be wise and have a broad view. He should be able to join two separate opinions into one powerful force by finding agreement

on certain issues. Being a peacemaker is a role of the diplomat.

- *Dependability*—"solid," "steadfast," and "accountable" are descriptions of a person who is dependable. If a leader lacks this trait, even though he or she may be strong in other areas, that lack will keep him or her from achieving the goals set for the group. Being dependable includes being on time and consistent in terms of both your personality and your rhetoric.
- *Judgment*—growing up in a small West Texas town, the definition of good judgment was "horse sense." Some may call it common sense. Translated, this means using your basic instincts of justice and fairness in the decision-making process.
- *Enthusiasm*—there is a time and a place for everything, especially for a leader's enthusiasm. A positive attitude creates strong enthusiasm and excitement in the leader, generating enthusiasm within a group.
- *Fairness*—over the years I have developed a basic rule for progress in a business deal or major goal. It must be a win-win situation. Looking at every situation under the microscope of fairness, you can create plans in which the outcome is fair to all.
- *Endurance*—the runner with endurance always finishes the race. A leader without endurance will literally be worn down and will have a tendency to retreat from his intended goals. Leadership is physically and mentally tiring, and most of the time, worthwhile goals are the hardest to attain and take the longest time. Endurance, both mental and physical, is essential to being a successful leader.

Two Examples of Transformational Leadership

Baylor University Transformation

Having no interest in Baylor University's football job, I was as shocked as everyone else when I actually took it. Having been an assistant at Texas Tech, then the head coach at Angelo State, my goal was clearly to be the head football coach at Texas Tech. After agreeing to coach at Baylor, the reality set in quickly. I found the following:

- Historical losing football program in the Southwest Conference
- Terrible facilities
- A loss of faith in the football program
- Players who overall were not typical Southwest Conference athletes

The Facts

- Reality: we came because we felt called
- Ignore the negatives
- Roll up our sleeves and get to work

The Plan to Transform

- Surround myself with a staff that believes
- Build a positive environment
- Never mention the negatives
- Preach positive expectations
- Hire several high school coaches
- Speak positive expectations where two or more are gathered
- Engage the faculty and students in the plan
- Create a partnership with the Baylor band and cheerleaders
- Start a physical development program
- Find a way to build a weight room

Players and staff needed to understand and accept the following:

- We will win with defense and a running game.
- We will be better conditioned.
- We will play smarter and tougher.
- We will become a family.
- We will win.
- We will be loyal to each other.
- We will protect our teammates.
- We will be a credit to our program.

- We will be a credit to our university.
- We will be leaders.
- We will be an example to other students.
- We will be an example in our community.
- We will attend class.
- We will graduate.

The Facts

- Every position on the football team is open.
- The best players will play.
- Our scout team will be the best in the Southwest Conference.

Recruiting Plan

- Be humble and appreciative.
- We build trust through honesty.
- We treat high school coaches with respect, appreciation, and as equals.
- Recruiting will be our lifeline and will sustain our program.

Qualifying Criteria for a Scholarship

- Core values—positive character traits
- Intellectual capacity to graduate—a passion to get an education
- Athletic skills, but with an open up-side for development as an athlete
- Exhibits a desire to learn, work, and get better every day

Recruiting Strategy

We will recruit players with character and the academic capability to graduate and thus we will always have strong junior and senior classes. Players with those characteristics will be in the program through years four and five to develop physically and graduate.

Development of Freshmen

When the freshmen arrive on campus, we will meticulously prepare them for what they will face as students and intently develop their character and their leadership traits. We will weld the freshman class together by having them sit with someone different at each meal and purposefully get to know members of their class. They will be taught the fundamentals of leadership as well as leadership traits and leadership action. At the end of the first week, the freshmen will pick their own leaders, who will join the upperclassmen in a leadership council. The leadership council will be given great responsibility. They will serve as a conduit, relaying information back and forth between the council and their teammates. For any success we achieve at Baylor, our team leaders will play a great role in that success.

In three years, Baylor University football was transformed from last place in the Southwest Conference to first place.

The American Football Coaches Association's Transition

In 1992 the Board of Trustees of the AFCA appointed a search committee to identify a leader to succeed Charlie McClendon, who was formally ending his twelve-year tenure as the executive director. My last year at Baylor was in 1992, so during the season, the search committee informed me that I was the person they wanted to head the AFCA. At the time, my goal was to remain at Baylor as athletic director and hopefully to usher the university into a new conference. However, in July of 1993, Donell and I made the decision that our profession, the Association, and the game needed us. The news release of August 22, 1993, announced, "Grant Teaff will become the executive director of the American Football Coaches Association."

Mel Pulliam, the public relations director of the AFCA at the time, inserted a quote from me into the press release. Nearly twenty years later, I look at what I had to say and realize nothing has changed:

> I am excited about the challenge of serving the AFCA membership and leading our Association through the challenges of the future. I look forward to the support of the AFCA membership and others who love the game. Thousands of coaches

across this nation teach more than just how to play the game. The same coaches serve as role models, not only to the student athletes they coach, but to their communities and to our nation. The opportunity to work with them was an important factor in my decision.

Every day I wake up driven by the same passion and challenge. I ask myself these three questions: (1) What can I do today for our game? (2) What can I do today for those who play the game? and (3) What can I do today to help our coaches be better tomorrow than they are today?

Coaches are leaders who play an influential role in the lives of those they teach and coach. Each year it becomes more and more important for our coaches to accept the role of mentor and father figure. Strong leadership leads to essential influences "beyond the game."

A Plan for Transforming the AFCA

My goal was to develop the vision of what the AFCA could and needed to be. I then had to turn that vision into a plan that would create ownership in every member of the Association. The vision would not be "my" vision, but "our" vision.

Proverbs 29:18 says, "Where there is no vision, the people will perish." AFCA needed a continually changing vision that our membership could buy into, be proud of, and work to accomplish.

Eric Hoffer's sage advice is as follows—"The leader has to be practical and a realist yet must talk the language of the visionary and the idealist"—and following Mr. Hoffer's advice has paid big dividends for me and the American Football Coaches Association.

All segments of the coaching profession were to be included when developing a vision. The AFCA was to be an inclusive organization that listened to all voices; assistant coaches, minorities, NCAA divisions, the National Association of Intercollegiate Athletics, and high school coaches would have representation through the Board of Trustees. Each board member would be a conduit of information to the board and back to their constituent groups.

After five months of study, I developed twenty major goals and presented them to the board during the January meeting in 1994. In six years, with the help of my staff, the board, and our volunteers, we reached all twenty goals, with the final goal being the building of the national headquarters in Waco, Texas.

> My goal was to lock arms with our membership, taking our Association to new heights, and as I said in the news release quote, "I am excited about the challenge of serving the AFCA membership and leading our Association through the challenges of the future." There have been many challenges, and we have stood up to all of them.

Admiral Arleigh A. Burke describes leadership in this way: "Leadership is understanding people and involving them to help you do a job. That takes all the good characteristics like integrity, dedication of purpose, selflessness, knowledge, and skill, as well as the determination not to accept failure."[21] Martin Luther King Jr. gave a great definition of a leader: "A genuine leader is not a searcher for consensus, but a molder of consensus."[22]

The important role of a leader is to create a culture in which a team, an organization, or a business can flourish. Feeling and exhibiting pride is a foundation on which excellence can be built. Both Baylor University and the AFCA needed to believe in their potential excellence, then embrace the plan and execute it. For the AFCA, there was a need for a culture of inclusion, professionalism, and an understanding of the responsibilities that come with having influence "beyond the game."

In summation, there are four personal traits in which I believe. All of these traits can be developed and perfected. They have, in fact, impacted everything I have done and every action taken as a leader.

1. Care deeply and strive each day to make a difference.
2. Readily accept challenges and readily extend challenges to those you lead.
3. Be self-motivated and passionate about motivating others.
4. Be a positive influence, within the game and beyond.

Part III

Coaches' Generosity

A Coach's Wisdom

If I made a list of my most-admired leaders in football, Homer Rice would be close to the top. Homer was a successful coach on all three levels: high school, college, and the professional ranks. Following his coaching career, he became an outstanding leader as an athletic director. As an author, he has written two books of exceeding value to coaches and athletes, *Leadership for Leaders* and *Leadership Fitness*. Rice developed the attitude technique philosophy and the total person–total success program.

In 2011, I wrote a letter to over 700 head football coaches asking them to share their successful solutions to the AFCA-defined six social issues.

Like hundreds of other college head coaches and former head coaches, Dr. Rice thanked me for taking on "the most significant problem this country has ever faced." To emphasize his point, he quoted from the book *Failing Liberty 101* by William Damon, professor of education at Stanford University and a Senior Fellow at the Hoover Institute. Dr. Damon wrote, "The most serious danger the United States faces today is not that of a foreign enemy, but that our country's future may end up in the hands of a citizenry incapable of sustaining the liberty that has been America's most precious legacy." He adds, "We are failing to prepare today's young people to be responsible American citizens—to the detriment of their life prospects and those of liberty in the USA of the future." He identifies the problems—decline in civic purpose and patriotism, crises of faith, cynicism, self-absorption, ignorance, indifference to the common good—and shows that our disregard of civic and moral virtues as an educational priority is having a tangible effect on the attitudes, understanding, and behavior of a large portion of the youth in our country today. Damon explains, "Unless we begin to pay attention and meet our challenges as stewards of a priceless heritage, our nation and the future prospects of all individuals dwelling here in years to come will suffer, moving away from liberty and toward despotism. This movement will be both inevitable and astonishingly quick."

Wow! Talking about upping the value of what coaches and teachers do on a daily basis, Mr. Damon could not have made it more emphatic or clear. We are as coaches and teachers teaching and influencing far beyond the game. Practices and the game are the great classrooms for influence and change.

Dr. Rice, whom I prefer to call Coach, along with other coaches, responded positively to my request for them to share their successful solutions to social issues, and over 100 replied, adding their wisdom gained from their own experiences.

Coach Rice said, "In order to cope with the social issues of peer pressure, drug and alcohol, criminal activities, negative attitudes, premarital sex and so forth, the program I developed brought in speakers on each subject to explain the pitfalls of falling into any of the social issue categories. When a player did fall into any of these situations, it was handled by a medical team with the solutions for the young men to be cleared of chemical substance abuse and other personal problems. A sports psychologist was on our staff to meet with each individual."

Coach Rice continued, "One of the toughest issues to deal with is the negative home situation, whether it be no positive male role model, lack of discipline, or negative attitudes. The athlete coming out of this situation most often believes he will never make it in the real world and often follows the negative side of life. KIPP (Knowledge is Power Program) charter schools have proven an individual can come out of any home condition and learn. This school sends over 80 percent of its students to college. They can learn and do, and most become outstanding citizens through the educational programs. This model should be a copy for every public school in America that is not producing these types of results. "Finally," he said, "America has spent billions and billions of dollars for so-called 'entitlement programs' and they have yet to work. What will work is a sports program that contains the total person program, which addresses all of the social issues that are affecting today's youth."

Coach Rice's response was no different from hundreds of other coaches. All were thoughtful and willing to share their wisdom, methods, and techniques in order to help fellow coaches and the coaches of the future deal with today's social issues. These selfless acts of giving and sharing are typical of the coaching profession.

Wisdom is much more than accumulated knowledge or enlightenment. The definition of wisdom I like best is "the ability or the results of the ability to think and act utilizing knowledge, experience, understanding, common sense, and insight." In coaching, knowledge, insight, and wisdom come from those who coach us. Where did our coaches receive their empowerment of knowledge and wisdom? From their coaches. Coaching is one of the most generous professions, because every coach is grateful for the generosity of the coaches who preceded him. Today's coaches know they must bestow their knowledge and wisdom on those they coach and be willing to share that wisdom with coaches yet to join our profession. Coaching is all about giving back and teaching. Ibn Gabirol (b. 1020 A.D.) said, "In seeking wisdom, the first step is silence, the second listening, the third remembering, the fourth practicing, the fifth—teaching others."

My passion for the AFCA has been to capitalize on the generosity and willingness of coaches and encourage them to share their knowledge and expertise with other coaches. Football coaching is one of the few professions in which knowledge and wisdom are happily handed down from generation to generation. Year after year, at the AFCA national convention, over one hundred coaches unselfishly share the secrets of their success, technical expertise, and philosophy. The hunger to seek knowledge and wisdom regarding social issues and other important aspects "beyond the game" convinced me that today's coaches realize, as

William Damon expressed it, that "unless we begin to pay attention and meet our challenges as stewards of a priceless heritage, our nation and our liberty are at risk."

Coaches face young people each and every day, entering the educational system in America, who are misguided by negative peer pressure, lacking accountability, and in many cases filled with disrespect. Some families, from the highest socio-economic levels to the very lowest, allow their children to develop an attitude of entitlement. Fatherless homes, negative male role models in the home, and dysfunctional parents add up to the large numbers of young people with multiple social issues.

Head coaches from high schools, colleges, and universities, when asked to help other coaches with solutions to the myriad of social issues, responded with an astonishing outpouring of wisdom.

Coaching Wisdom

Mike London
University of Virginia (Virginia)

We have two themes for our program here at Virginia. The themes or messages begin in the recruiting process as far back as the sophomore and junior year in high school, during unofficial visits to campus. All my decisions related to the team are based on these three priorities: faith, family, football. The day-to-day team rules are very simple: (1) Go to class. (2) Show class. (3) Treat people with dignity and respect. All players should follow these rules and base their behavior on these rules when faced with a decision.

We meet with our players once per week on academic achievement and anything else that may need to be discussed (not football related). This constant line of communication is very helpful in preventing problems before they occur or having a good history when it happens. Constant communication is the key.

Our coaches must all be prepared to live as we speak. This is not a program of "do as I say, not as I do." We are all role models for our players. This is the only way they can respect your word.

Kirk Talley
Northwestern College (Minnesota)

Check my heart!

Must weed my own garden and remove me, my agenda, and my
need to fight for my rights before getting in a teaching or coaching
environment. If this is not a genuine humility, these kids can smell it
and will only do just enough work to keep a coach quiet or to make
us "happy" and give the perception of ownership and care for their
careers.

Proverbs 27:17 says, "Iron sharpens iron; so a man sharpeneth the countenance of his friends."

If, as coaches, we fail to be transparent in our humility, the kids will sense it and only do just enough work to keep the coach quiet and happy. This example sends the message to the players that they should take ownership of their own lives and their careers. As stated above, "weed our own garden" may be the place to start if we are to have the greatest impact on our players. A great example of this is Joe Ehrmann. In his book, *InSideOut Coaching*, Coach Ehrmann states, "Being introspective and listening to my wife, allows me to have greater influence with my players." Our staff listens to Joe and implements his solutions for peer pressure all the way through character development.

From a practical aspect, one of the things that we do is two-fold. First, we take practice time and have the men discuss life questions and scenarios that may come up, in their classes or at home. We do this to help prepare them as they leave college and move into the "real world." The other aspect of this two-fold relationship is working with men on a one-on-one basis. This has been the most effective method I have found in twenty-nine years of coaching.

When I have a young man in my office telling me his life struggles, one may see why he may be struggling on the field, in the dorm, or in his social life. One of the things that can benefit them as young men is a listening ear and someone to speak life into them. We can do that in the office or out on the field, before or after practice (I believe all coaches are capable of relating to players this way after hearing Ehrmann's story). We have a great staff here, and we do our best to speak life into players and challenge them. We make our share of mistakes; however, because we are vulnerable with them these men benefit both concurrently and in the future.

There are no easy answers, and as our world continues to produce young people with social issues, as coaches we need to be more aware of their need for us to be in touch with them in their lives.

Frank Beamer
Virginia Tech (Virginia)

Each day in preseason practice, we have a fifteen-minute Team Educate session. During that time, we invite different speakers to talk briefly about many of the social issues. For example, last year we had a gentleman whose wife and son were killed by a drunk driver. His message was strong and powerful. I believe if you attack these social issues by the people who have been affected by them, that it's the best message you can get out. Another belief here is that it is our responsibility to educate the student-athletes concerning these different social issues and then it's up to the student-athlete to take responsibility for their actions.

Fisher DeBerry
Former Head Coach
USAF Academy

Peer Pressure—I always approached things with our players as "Don't do something just to do it, but be the best in doing it" (tackling, etc.). Do it better than anyone on our team, in our conference, or in America. This supported one of the three Core Values of the Academy: "Excellence in All We Do." The others are "integrity above all" and "service before self."

Every season I brought someone in to talk to our team who had experienced a negative with alcohol or drugs. I spent a lot of money, but I felt the players would listen to someone who had been there and had bad experiences. They then could get the inside and true story from someone who had been "down that road." I felt that I had no credibility in this area; therefore, I felt they would listen, respect, and respond much better to someone else.

We had only one RULE in our program! That was *"DO WHAT'S RIGHT."* If you make bad choices you must be accountable, and they knew it would be in a BIG WAY (5:30 a.m. with me, suspension, or off the team). The hardest thing I ever had to do in my career was to suspend twelve players for the last game. It was Senior Day, and eight of those players were seniors. I felt that I had to do this to make a point of the responsibility that they were going to have for the lives of others in their future officer and leadership positions.

I constantly reminded the players about profanity and sex, asking them, "Is this what you would want for your sister?" That hit pretty close to home for them.

Finally, I constantly reminded them to *"REMEMBER WHO YOU ARE."* I wanted them to take ownership of our family, the team, and do nothing to bring it discredit.

Home—I constantly reminded our staff that we might be the only father figures to some of their position players. I encouraged them to show their players that they cared for them in all areas of their lives and to work them extremely hard, and to love them.

I used to tell the team after every game win or lose: (1) I expect you to go to church tomorrow. (2) I expect you to call your Mama tonight and tell her you love her and thank her. (3) I would remind them, "Remember who you are." I am confident this was ingrained as several former players have indicated that they found their wives in church. My wife and I started a foundation to send single-parent kids to summer FCA camps in hopes that they would have a life-changing experience.

Entitlement—I told the team the only entitlement they have is to protect the legacy of previous teams and they are entitled to give their best in everything they do for the opportunities and abilities that God had given them.

Lack of Respect—When a player "let his brother down," he knew that in order to stay on the team he would have to pay a big price and look his brothers in their eyes, ask their forgiveness, and state what belonging to the team meant to them.

Accountability—"Be your brother's keeper." The team is yours. What do you want it to be? The team does not belong to the head coach, but it belongs to the players.

James Mitchell
Director of Football Development
Duke University (North Carolina)

Peer Pressure, Respect, Fatherless Homes, and *Entitlement* are four of the most important ones that we deal with on our teams today because they also affect how a young man adjusts to his new environment of campus, city, and coaches. Here at Duke we have established a Directory of Football Development position that deals with the athlete on a one-on-one basis. We have programs with our freshmen that we tailored from the NFL rookie symposium. We also work closely with our student-athlete development staff on campus for profile testing and other resources to help in their adjustments.

We have a Big Brother program that involves training and a workshop before they become Big Brothers; then they teach the program to the freshmen. We have an eight-week leadership class with players whom the head coach selects. The purpose of this program is not only to ask them to be team captains but also to teach them how to lead with their own personalities and to hold their teammates accountable as well as themselves. We do profile testing and some exercises from a book called *Habitudes.*

There are also job-shadowing and internship programs that we implemented to help them adjust to life outside of football. The program consists of resume building, interviewing skills, and networking. These programs are done in cooperation with a professor on campus. There are numerous chances for community service opportunities as well.

We do this because it is important to our head coach and his vision for boys to become men regardless of their background. It would be beneficial if you could create a generic program on the four issues that will give schools a reference point to start with their young men. We have a responsibility to produce young men who will be great husbands, fathers, and leaders regardless of where they are from or what they have or don't have in life. We are very fortunate that this area is a priority in our head coach's philosophy.

John McKissick
Summerville High School (South Carolina)

I've been the athletic director and football coach at Summerville High School in South Carolina for sixty years, and we have always run what I call a "tight ship." We have about 85 players on the varsity football team, 60 on the junior varsity team, and 50 on the B-team. We think that if you take care of the small distractions, you won't have any large distractions or problems. We don't allow long hair or earrings (male students) on any of our teams. We keep an eye open for drugs, alcohol, and gangs. If they can't sacrifice and abide by our rules, then we remove them from the team. We haven't had a big problem with this because they know beforehand what to expect. I think, as coaches, we should put character first. We try to teach self-discipline and to believe in yourself, to have dedication and pride. If you can get your teams to be self-disciplined without being forced to do what's right, then they will never quit and you'll have a winner.

If a student-athlete is having parental pressure then we will have a meeting with the athlete and his parent to talk about the problem and this generally takes care of it.

One thing I know about our kids is that they will do whatever we demand of them if they know we are about them and are treating them fairly.

Bill Snyder
Kansas State (Kansas)

Lay out guidelines centered on each young man's faith, family, personal life, academics, and his role as a football student-athlete.

They then complete a form to identify their goals in each of these priorities in their lives and a tentative projected plan to achieve each of these goals.

I then meet with each player to discuss their priorities/goals and the plan for successful achievement. We then address intermediate goals (steps in the plan) to prevent them from being overwhelmed with large distant goals. Next we mutually identify people whom they can bring into their lives who genuinely care and who have the capacity to assist them with developing their plan and monitoring its progress. Bringing people into their lives who want to, can, and will help make their lives better, is a very special choice for them to make and pursue.

We also have in place a "Transition Class," an accredited college class with credit in which all our incoming players are enrolled that addresses all the issues a young college student encounters as he transitions from high school, which includes all six of the social issues. We have daily "Unity" periods after workouts in which the team breaks down into small groups to discuss the "Topic of the Day."

Tom Landry
Former Head Coach
Dallas Cowboys

Discipline and Morale—I always believed if you're going to have good morale on a team, you have to have one set of rules, one standard for everyone. Most successful players not only accept rules and limitations, I believe they need them. In fact, I believe players are free to perform at their best only when they know what the expectations are, where the limits stand.

I see this as a biblical principle that also applies to life, a principle our society as a whole has forgotten: you can't enjoy true freedom without limits.

We often resent rules because they limit what we can do. Yet without the rules that define a football game, you can't play the game, let alone enjoy it. The same thing is true in life. To live and enjoy the freedom we have in America, we have to live by the rules of society. To live life to its fullest and truly enjoy it, we need to understand and abide by the rules God spells out in the Bible. God isn't out to spoil our fun; he knows that life without limits results in anarchy and misery. It's only when we have absolute limits that we can be truly free to enjoy the best life has to offer.

Mark McQuade
Shenendehowa Central High School (New York)

I have been a line coach now for the last twenty years. In the early years just after my playing days, I was the single, high energy, my way or the highway guy. Now, I am married with five kids, seeing things in a whole different perspective. Throughout all of this, I have always provided a time for me to *lower the line*. This means giving my players the opportunity not to be in a coach/player role all of the time. I have them see me as something other than a coach. This is essential in knowing how your players interact, what makes them tick, who's in love and who's out of love, etc. Many different topics are discussed by the players at dinner. Now as a father I bring my boys with me to dinner. My players now get to see me and how I am as a parent instead of a coach. Sometimes conversation turns to my boys and what their dreams are when they get bigger, what was it like when I was younger, and so on. My kids are starting to get attached to some of the linemen, because they get to eat with them every week. Another important part of this is if I got on a kid that week or even that day, I would make an effort in talking with that player about why I got mad at him. By the end of dinner, before the end of the night we would usually make fun of it. If I let that go until the next day, then he would have to sleep on it and wait until we would see each other that next afternoon. That could provide some tension. Remember, *"Kids don't care how much you know . . . until they know how much you care."* That quote speaks volumes to me. Another intangible I get out of *knowing* my kids is I get a sense of knowing which kids I can go up one side and down the other and which kids will not respond to that. Personality traits are exposed, and I get a real good sense of how to read them.

Each kid I coach is still held to the same standard as far as accountability. However, I approach things differently with each one. The only way truly to do that is to get to know them in a very real way. I have been going out to dinner with my linemen now for the better part of twenty years. It is in those moments when I think I tap into something that other coaches don't experience.

John Magistro
Westerville High School (Ohio)

As the football coach at Westerville High School for the past three years, I have encountered all six of the social issues.

After my first two years as head coach, I realized the reason the football program had not experienced any success was not their physical skills, but a lack of discipline and love for one another, selfishness, and many other character flaws. As a coaching staff and with the input of our seniors, we decided to address these past problems with leadership meetings every month, where we would bring in someone who touched upon all of the above. Players were also encouraged to bring with them quotes from famous athletes, writers, etc., and they had to translate it into what it meant to them. We would spend ten minutes before every off-season workout discussing why these famous people achieved success. We also started a monthly team activity. We went bowling, did community service, and incorporated various competitions after and even during our workouts. We had to learn to love one another instead of putting one another down all the time.

This past January was our second off-season with this, and we are seeing big improvement. Also, this past season we went 8-3, the most wins in school history, won our conference, and made the Ohio Division I playoffs for the first time in school history. This season, our players and coaches are even more determined to take this to another level.

Kyle Whittingham
University of Utah (Utah)

Our efforts to address these important issues begin with our recruiting process. We clearly communicate to our recruiting prospects the Principles, Fundamental Philosophies, and Core Values of our program. A crucial component of our evaluation and assessment of a recruiting prospect is how they fit in these key areas, and an observation of how they react and embrace them when they are communicated to them. In short, we place as much weight on our evaluation of a prospect's character traits as we do his football skills.

Program Based on Two Principles: Honesty and Accountability

The University of Utah football program is based on two key Principles: Honesty and Accountability. Plain, clear, direct, and honest communication is expected within the entire organization. We have an open-door policy with all coaches, starting with the head coach. With honest communication comes much responsibility, and this is something we stress with our coaches, staff, and players. All communication, especially difficult conversations, will be respectful.

Each member of our organization has clearly defined roles and expectations. Accountability for performing the role to the best of one's ability is based on our "5 C's of Accountability":

- Character—it fits with the Core Values of the team
- Competent—there is the mental and physical ability to get the job done
- Consistent—every day, every play
- Committed—full buy-in, without question
- Cohesive—a team first mentality

Three Fundamental Philosophies: Trust, Decision-Making, and Core Values

Trust is the single most important ingredient for our football team to be successful. Players must trust the coaches that they have their best interest in mind, and will put them in the best possible position to succeed. Coaches must trust players that they will give 100 percent effort, make good decisions that are in the best interest of the program, and will follow all team rules at all times, whether in the presence of their coaches or not.

Combined with the foundation of our Principles and Fundamental Philosophies, our Core Values are a set of behavioral guidelines that help address social issues our players face. Our Core Values are:

- Honesty
- Service leadership
- Treating women with respect
- Abstaining from illegal drugs
- No underage drinking and zero tolerance for DUIs
- No stealing

Mistakes are correctable; however, decisions that breach our Core Values are dealt with in a very serious manner.

Courtney Wash
Del Valle ISD (Texas)

Peer Pressure—We continually talk to the athletes about how this is the greatest pressure they will face. If they can resist pressure from their friends and in some cases their own families, they will have the ability to say no to any negative situation. Because our athletes tend to live in the moment, we talk about visualizing into the future: where do you want to be in 1, 5, and 10 years?

Disrespect—The biggest issue with our athletes is a lack of self-confidence which leads to a lack of respect for themselves and authority (parents, teachers, and other). We work hard on building their self-image and self-confidence. They will try to mask their lack of confidence through presenting an "I don't care attitude." We work with them and hold them accountable for their actions, whether it is on the field, in the weight room, in the classroom or hallway, or in the community. Once the boundaries are set they will hold you accountable by seeing if you will follow through; if you do you will begin to change the behavior, if you don't you lose your credibility with the kids. Our biggest goal is improving how they see themselves.

We are the parents, brothers, and family. We try to walk the walk so we can talk the talk. In a nutshell, we lead through example. Sometimes we question a kid's decisions, effort, and attitude. We first must do a self-check and check our own decisions, efforts, and attitudes. We talk about putting aside anything going on in your lives for the duration of practice, off-season work, or anytime we have them, but when we are finished we will help them in any way we possibly can. As they turn into adults no one will care what is going on in their personal lives, it becomes all about production.

No one is entitled to anything but an opportunity. There are many resources to assist them, in school and in society, but it is for assistance, not to become dependent. This leads to accountability.

We talk about choices. Everyone has choices. We are all accountable for the choices we make. The athletes are no different. We have "reminders" for negative or poor decisions. There are escalating "reminders," with the ultimate being separation from the program.

We are around the athlete between 3 and 5 hours a day. That leaves 19–21 hours they may be surrounding themselves with questionable people. If we do a good enough job with peer pressure and disrespect, this should not be an issue. We talk to them about truthfulness; we give them fair and honest evaluations. It is not done to hurt feelings, but they need and deserve to know where they stand. We ask them questions about us and expect a truthful response. If a kid wants to go play college football, we talk about realistic places they may play. Sometimes no one wants to hear the answers, but we teach reality. We want them to know that character is what you do when no one is looking.

Joe Susan
Bucknell University (Pennsylvania)

Peer Pressure—Many of the young men we recruit are leaders, and we try to pair the leaders with the followers. The younger players are working to find their place on this team. They want to be like, act like, and treat others like those they perceive to be our leaders or role models. We have to work so hard at times to undo 17–18 years of development. I strongly believe that coaches need to value their roles as mentors and understand that everything that we say and do they listen to and perceive through their own filters. If we get them when they are young and are in critical periods, we must be alert to the influences on campus, off campus, and in the world. If we ignore it we condone it.

Disrespect—At many times the cultural background of an individual makes them prone to not understanding respect. They struggle with self-respect and mask this with false bravado. The basic concept we drive home is to treat others how you want to be treated: THE GOLDEN RULE. We bring in people to speak to our team regarding treatment of women. We do not tolerate swearing on our field from our team or our coaches. We do not wear hats in the building, and we make certain our players get to know their professors.

The Home—Many of our players come from single-parent families. Even those who have two parents will often have minimal contact because both work. We see our role as coaches as important in providing them a positive, male role model. It comes with resistance many times in that they are often skeptical because they have been wronged by men. They have to develop the trust and confidence that there is someone here who will listen. Many times that is what they need the most.

Entitlement—This is a spoiled generation that struggles with responsibility. This means that adversity and conflict aren't something they are used to. We try to expose them to adversity on and off the field setting. Challenging them physically, but also challenging them mentally, builds a characteristic of selflessness. It also makes them understand that to get something you must work for it.

Accountability—We impress upon them that everything they do as a part of our team impacts more than just them. All of their actions can be related to how people view "football players": how they act when times are good, how they grow when times are bad.

Character—We have a saying, *Character is who you are when no one is looking.* Our team understands this is something that goes directly back to them, that what they do wrong is a reflection upon them as much as it is a reflection on their teammates. We wear a band on our wrist that has the acronym **S.A.M.**, which stands for **Selfless, Accountable, Mentally Tough.**

Jim Slaughter
San Angelo Central High School (Texas)

Peer Pressure—The head coach and his assistants must establish a relationship with the kids. Our peer pressure has to win. It is a constant battle.

Disrespect—Talk and tell stories. Always try to pull kids aside when they show disrespect in front of other people. I was once told by a very smart person that "if you call kids out in front of their peers, you will not get the results you want." You have to show your players respect, even though at times it is not deserved.

The Home—The field house and the school are lots of times the only safe and caring places in your kids' lives. Understand that and accept it. Be there for them.

Entitlement—Deal with it. Do not try to run and hide. Those are the kids and adults who want to run your program. They must be handled in a diplomatic way.

Accountability—Lots of stories are out there for this. Look at TCU. I posted bulletin board articles all the time of athletes who thought they were bigger than the program or the team. Examples of stupidity are endless.

Character—Help your leaders. Create leaders. Don't talk about how bad they are; work to make them do the right thing. Pull them aside to teach them and congratulate them. If they appear to be sucking up, you will lose the best ones. It is a game that winning coaches play well. It depends on the group. Sometimes, but not very often, you have a group that wants to do everything right. Plan to win big! Your troubled students always seem to be your best athletes. Such is life. Deal with it by handling the challenge. That is why athletics and what we do as coaches is such a difference maker.

Rich Spisak
Ball Brothers Foundation

Peer Pressure—I have always emphasized to players that they will always be faced with choices day in and day out. The choices they make will determine how they are perceived. I would tell them to imagine a little man (me) on their shoulder, and if that little man tells them not to make a certain choice then there is probably a reason. I tried to get them to think about how the choices they make will affect their future. Most kids make immediate decisions with no regard to what could happen in the future. Most choices you make in a day have a quick and finite number of consequences. Today's athletes must understand in today's world that certain decisions they make can have long-term effects immediately. Whether it is drugs, alcohol, sex, or criminal activity, the choices they make not only affect them but also others. These athletes need to worry about only what they can control, and the only things they can control are the choices they make and their attitudes. I would constantly tell players not to worry about things they cannot control. A good teacher or coach repeats himself quite often. You just never know when some of the stuff is going to stick.

Home—Over my years of coaching, an athlete's home environment has changed dramatically. The majority of players are from single- or no-parent homes. Levels of poverty have also increased to levels that are scary. Coaches must know their players and not only be coaches but mentors. Players need strong, disciplined figures in their lives. A coach has the leverage to do this. They want someone to give them direction. I always felt that building relationships with my players was very important. Treat these athletes the way you would want your son treated—I always lived by that principle. Simple, but it works. If the players trust you and know you are consistent and fair, I believe they will respond. We cannot control what goes on at home, but we can influence and guide these athletes.

Entitlement—There is no better team sport than the game of football. The team was always first, and no individual took precedence. We developed a culture that supported this from day one. You were either on board or you were not. There were no second chances. The players knew the punishment and knew we meant it. I believe it was as simple as saying what you mean and meaning what you say. Entitlement was simply not acceptable.

Lack of Respect/Accountability—You treat people the way you want to be treated. We lived by this simple rule. The players, as well as the coaches, were held accountable and responsible for all their actions. We taught civility in everything we did on or off the field. If a situation arose, it would be dealt with and handled accordingly in a timely manner. Situations were handled immediately, and the team was always kept abreast of the matter. There were no exceptions.

Stan Laing
Former Head Coach
Northside ISD (Texas)

What I have learned in dealing with the social issues you have listed goes back to what I learned from a man you know extremely well, my college coach Hershel Kimbrell at McMurry. What I learned from him as a player has carried me through my career as a coach and administrator, both positions being the same in coming down to simply motivating people to put forth their best effort. Coach Kimbrell was a master at this, and really it came down to one very simple thing—his genuine love for what he did and the players he coached.

Great coaches over the years have expressed the importance of love and how we have to love our players unconditionally. The number one job of a coach is to love his players and to communicate the expectations of players to love one another. We all know the best thing about athletics, when it is all said and done, is the relationships that are built—love is what makes this happen.

Sometimes when we mention the word love, it is taken lightly in terms of "teddy bear love" or holding a girlfriend's hand. The kind of love great coaches instill is the kind of love that holds us accountable to making great things happen. This is the kind of love that makes us passionate for the things that are important in our lives.

In terms of dealing with the various social issues coaches as well as school administrators face, there are three words that express what has to be continually communicated to young people so that they can have a very clear understanding of the choices they need to make when dealing with very common social issues our young people face on an almost daily basis. I will simply state them, and it is up to the individual coach how they are communicated in a way that comes from the heart. Coach Kimbrell expressed these words in such a way that he never had to raise his voice, but his players always strived to put forth their best effort because they could "feel" the love and passion he had for the game and his players.

Three simple words:

1. *Actions.* Do what's right/Do your best. Most young people really do know the difference between right or wrong but have to be reminded constantly—Do What's Right. Doing your best is simply that. Nothing more, nothing less.
2. *Attitude.* We have all heard the saying, life is 10% what happens and 90% how you react to it. Coaches and administrators must express an optimistic attitude all the time—the glass is ALWAYS half full . . .
3. *Love.* This is really our Actions and Attitude combined—making this the most important word because it is the most powerful. It is the Golden Rule: treat others as you would like to be treated.

These three simple words must be expressed to our young people today, and today only.

When tomorrow arrives, they need to be expressed today, and today only. And so on . . .

Vic Wallace
Rockford College (Illinois)

Back in the late 1960s I was exposed to Paul J. Meyer and the Success Motivation Institute. I became a firm believer that a person can control their mind and therefore who they are and how their future will develop.

Social issues are of mixed environmental and cultural causes. When a player comes to my program he steps into a new environment and new culture, the one our coaches and players have created. All I have to do is convince him to leave his old environment and culture behind. Most players want to do this; the hardest thing for them is dealing with the old environment and culture trying to suck them back in.

My objective is to build their self-image, self-esteem, and standard of excellence. Once they become a new person, the battle is over. Their old friends and family will always try to pull them back, but they now see themselves as superior and don't respond.

Every person has different hot buttons and must be handled individually. I train my staff to coach more than the game, and we all learn together. We absolutely make a concerted effort to coach the person as much as we coach football.

Jim Ledford
Berkner High School (Texas)

Peer Pressure—Each spring we have educational seminars where we bring in speakers such as district attorneys, police officers, defense attorneys, probation officers, etc., who provide information to our athletes pertaining to the consequences of poor decisions that have been made in the past. We have done this for the past three years, and our athletes seem to take it to heart. It has also made them aware of such things as sexting and swapping inappropriate pictures and comments through social media such as Facebook. Also, drug testing has been a great deterrent in helping give them a reason as to why they cannot participate in the same activities as others. We can never keep them from going to parties with their friends, but we can provide them an excuse as to why they can't do some of the thing the others do. It lets them blame it on the "Coach."

Entitlement and Character—Two seasons ago our coaching staff identified those two areas as a major concern for our team. We took a totally different approach than in past seasons. We began to focus on others. We took the team to Scottish Rite hospital to see students who would love to run and play but could not for whatever reason, and we brought in a team of instructors to let our athletes participate in activities as if they did not have vision, were born without an arm, could not hear, etc. We then took our athletes to one of our tougher elementary schools that had several children with learning disabilities. They were provided the opportunity to tutor and develop relationships with those students. All of these things began to cause the focus of our athletes to come off themselves, and it made them thankful for what they did have rather than what they did not.

Accountability—The best thing I have ever done is just not let players practice. I have tried all kinds of punishment, and none have ever worked for me. But when I took away players' ability to practice with the team for being late or not communicating with our staff, it vastly improved their accountability.

Conclusion

Coaching is a multifaceted profession. The coach must become an expert in the fundamentals of the game of football, philosophy, and strategy. The coach must become a master in analysis and adjustments in real time. The coach must thoroughly understand the conditioning and safety in the rules of the game. However, I believe that the coaches' greatest responsibility is influencing and coaching "beyond the game." Man's intangibles—faith, values, and purpose—when developed fully will determine one's course in life. A truly wise coach understands this and spends purposeful time addressing the intangibles.

Part IV
Solutions

— 8 —

Peer Pressure

Peer pressure occurs when influence is exerted by peers or a group of peers in any age group. The definition of a peer is the following: one of equal standing with another; one belonging to the same societal group based on age, grade, or status. Experts agree that negative peer pressure can cause a lack of self-esteem, disregard for personal values, emotional damage, and premarital sexual activities and create an environment in which alcohol and/or drugs are used.

Peer pressure is not relegated to teenagers. Peer pressure is something with which human beings have dealt since their numbers on earth began to multiply. The Bible relates the story of Adam and Eve in the Garden of Eden. The two were very close in age and together were trying to figure out how to make it in their world. Then unexpectedly the first recorded example of peer pressure occurred. Eve convinced Adam he should eat the fruit, even though they both knew it was forbidden. Simply put, peer pressure can be defined as the influence of one friend or a group of friends. As human beings, we all desire to be accepted and appreciated by those around us. In order to secure a feeling of belonging, individuals sometimes engage in activities contrary to positive social development. Therefore, negative peer pressure can encourage engagement in activities such as smoking, drug abuse, and premarital sex. All of these activities can be detrimental to the participant.

Statistics nowadays abound in every area of interest. An amazing amount of research and information regarding peer pressure has been compiled over the last few years. However, I found four sources that give us all the information we need about peer pressure.

1. The Adolescent Substance Abuse Knowledge Base reports that around 30% of teens are offered drugs in middle school and high school.
2. According to the national household survey on drug use and health from the U.S. Department of Health and Human Services, 74.3% of high school students have tried alcohol.
3. 3.1 million teenagers smoke, according to the American Lung Association.
4. The Kaiser Family Foundation reports that about 50% of teenagers feel pressured regarding sex in relationships.[23]

In a survey of the members of the American Football Coaches Association, peer pressure was ranked number one when we asked them to prioritize six basic social issues. The coaches reported that peer pressure to use drugs and alcohol was prevalent. Next was premarital sex, and the last two negative peer pressures were gangs and criminal activities.

As a college recruiter for thirty-seven years in both track and football, I wanted to know more about an individual player than just his athletic skills and academic performance level. I wanted to know about his character and the type of individual he was. Seeking references from principals, teachers, coaches, and administrators, I gained valuable information. The technique that helped me to determine what the individual was like away from the authority figures in his life was to determine with whom the recruit spent his time. Who were his friends, or you could say, who were his peers? If you can determine who the influencers are, you will have a pretty good idea about what to expect from the person you are recruiting. Over the years, many fine athletes with great potential for success in life have lost opportunities because of those with whom they associated and those to whom they listened.

As a result of selective recruiting, the majority of my team was made up of individuals who possessed a value system, a work ethic, and a desire to become educated. I could and did create an environment of positive peer pressure.

My final test for those being recruited was important and paid big dividends through the years. When recruits would come in for a recruiting weekend, the staff would specifically assign certain individuals to the recruits. After spending Friday evening and Saturday with the recruits, I would meet with the host players on Sunday morning before I sat down with the visiting athletes. My players knew their role and that was either to reject or verify the selections that our coaching staff had made. To me, it was a fail-safe that seldom failed.

One of my defensive coaches had been recruiting the number one defensive back in the country, a young man from Dallas, Texas, for over a year. As was my custom during recruiting, early Sunday morning I met with the recruit's student athlete host to receive a very critical report. It was a simple process: the host would give me a thumbs-up or a thumbs-down on the recruit. The quote I remember from the host for this recruit was, "Coach, this is not your kind of guy."

Fast forward, if you will, to just before noon that Sunday when it was time for the athlete and the recruiting coach to come into my office to talk about a possible future at Baylor University. Before I could say anything, the visiting athlete said he had decided Baylor was his choice and he would become a Baylor Bear. I looked directly at the young man, and much to the chagrin of the recruiting coach, I told him that we did not have a scholarship for him.

The young man signed with a national power in the Southeast Conference. I remember seeing a picture in the *Dallas Morning News* of the recruit signing his letter of intent in a Jacuzzi. Later that spring, headlines proclaimed that this young man and some of his peers had been caught robbing a video store at gunpoint. The penalty for robbery was several years in the penitentiary in

Huntsville, Texas. Somehow, possibly through his words, attitude, or even actions, the Baylor players determined that he would not be a good fit for our program.

That summer, I was doing an interview with a noted sportscaster from a Dallas radio station, who knew Baylor had refused to sign the recruit. The interviewer flat-out asked me how I knew this particular young man was involved in illegal activities. The announcer also asked me why I had not offered this great player a scholarship. I said, "I did not know he was involved in illegal activities, I just knew that my players did not feel he would fit into our program."

Had the young man come to Baylor, he would have been thrust into an environment and pre-planned system of creating positive peer pressure. He might have changed; however, history told me he was more likely to influence our players negatively than the opposite. Our challenge to each incoming football player was to "always be the best you can be and set your goal to be better tomorrow than you are today." To actually live up to that pledge, to improve every day, the peer pressure, words, and support must be positive from teammates and classmates.

It should be noted that an environment of positive peer pressure does not always work. I remember one young man from Houston, Texas. I would not have given him a scholarship except one of our outstanding players and leaders knew the young man from high school and felt the environment at Baylor would turn him around. He came to Baylor on a scholarship with a lot of baggage other than his suitcase. He had great talent and could have been an All-American football player and likely would have signed with the National Football League. However, his mentality was so ingrained that it could not be changed by his coaches or his teammates. He stole from his teammates and was dismissed from his scholarship at Baylor. My hope was that someday through positive peer pressure at Baylor, he might have responded in a much different way. I learned the hard way that was not the case. The following spring, while our coaching staff and players were practicing, he came through Waco, slipped into the coaches' dressing rooms, and relieved the coaches of their cash and valuables. Not every story has a happy ending. Not every solution for overcoming negative peer pressure with your players will be absolute. However, it is imperative we use every tool available to create positive change in the lives of those we coach.

Peer Pressure Solutions

Adversity in life is a great teacher. Seeing adversity handled in a positive way among our peers has a tendency to inspire, motivate, and change us for the best. Kyle Woods is a great example of positive peer pressure.

Kyle was a Baylor defensive back who had a catastrophic injury in 1979, a redshirt freshman playing on the scout team and scrimmaging against the number two offense. Kyle, playing in the secondary, tackled a running back just as the back cleared the line of scrimmage. Kyle had his head in the wrong position. The sound of the helmets crashing together told even the casual observer that this could be very bad. It was. As Paul Harvey, the noted speaker and commentator always said, "Now, the rest of the story." Kyle broke his neck and instantly was a paraplegic. It was a stunning and sobering experience for the staff and the players to go through. A bright, healthy nineteen-year-old had his life dramatically changed in a split second. That moment ultimately changed all of his coaches, teammates, and friends.

From the time of Kyle's injury, because of the way he handled the terrible accident, he became an inspiration to our team. Throughout the fall of 1979, he was in intense rehabilitation. Partially because of his inspiration, the 1979 Baylor team was selected to play Clemson University in the Peach Bowl in Atlanta, Georgia. Clemson would be the national champions in 1980, and understandably they were an outstanding team in 1979.

There are three examples related to Kyle Woods that clearly demonstrate positive peer pressure. Two of these incidents happened prior to the Clemson/Baylor game and one in the game itself.

Example 1

The team, without my knowledge, voted to dedicate the Peach Bowl game to Kyle Woods. At a press conference the day before the game, our captains announced their plan. Though an underdog by ten points, the captains proclaimed at the press conference that they would beat Clemson and dedicate the game to their teammate, Kyle Woods. Had they asked me, I probably would have said, "Beat Clemson, then give Kyle the game ball." But no, they wanted the world to know their intentions.

Example 2

I had asked Kyle to speak to the team the morning prior to the game. The power of his influence came through in what he said to the team: "Everybody asks me how I am able to handle the fact that I am paralyzed. It goes back to two things: my deep faith and what my grandmother taught me. She was 87 and kept the children everyday while our parents worked. She had arthritis and could barely get around, but she was always there for us. I was very young, but I remember the day she called me to her side as she sat in her rocking chair. 'Kyle, I can see it in your eyes. You are concerned about me, and yes, I have a hard time getting around. I am in pain, but I want you to know how I make it through each and every day.'" Kyle continued, "She looked at me and uttered these words that I live by, 'I may give out, but I won't ever give in.'"

Kyle looked out at his teammates and said, "Always remember, if you never give in, you can never lose." Kyle went on to say, "The clock may run out while the other team is ahead, but if you never quit, you'll never be a loser."

Example 3

The Peach Bowl was a sellout. Playing in the game itself was a great way to end a season that started so disastrously with Kyle's injury, but on that afternoon, the story was fascinating. With four minutes to go, like Kyle, the team had no intentions of giving in, so the offense drove the length of the field to score and take the lead. On Clemson's next offensive series, the Baylor defense intercepted a pass that secured the victory, a 24-18 upset of Clemson University. The players made a promise to Kyle that they would win, and they did. They celebrated by carrying Kyle, wheelchair and all, around the stadium to the cheers of thousands. They were thanking him for his inspiration, for his influence as a peer and his profound lesson on "never giving in."

More Inspiration

The very next year in 1980, Baylor was experiencing an unde-feated season on the way to a possible national championship. Baylor was playing San Jose State at home on a beautiful Saturday afternoon. The unfamiliar west coast offense employed by the San Jose team kept them in the game until late in the fourth quarter on what the experts would call a fluke play. They scored and won the game. At the time we were fifth in the nation and looking at an undefeated season. I was truly amazed at how quickly it knocked our players to their knees when they realized what the loss had cost us. The following week we were to play the Uni-versity of Arkansas, a Lou Holtz team that was projected as a possible conference champion. All week long our players had the cloud of "oh, what might have been" floating above their heads. I tried to snap them out of their funk, but to no avail. The game was on national television scheduled for a 2:00 p.m. kickoff. Kyle Woods would have been a redshirt sophomore in 1980 and had yet to see a game in Baylor Stadium, where he was injured in late August 1979. Kyle wanted to come to the Arkansas game, so I made arrangements to have him present. A young baseball player from Baylor volunteered to go to Dallas to pick up Kyle and bring him to the game. That young player by the way is the current head baseball coach at Baylor, Steve Smith. Steve arrived at the stadium and rolled Kyle out in his wheelchair onto the field. Graciously, Lou Holtz came over to speak to Kyle just before both teams went into their dressing rooms.

The Baylor team assembled in the dressing room for final instructions. About that time, Steve Smith wheeled Kyle to the center of the room. Kyle and I had talked on the phone, and I had told him of my dilemma of trying to get the team past the loss to San Jose and ready for the Arkansas game. The truth was, we were still undefeated in conference play, and by beating Arkansas, we would be a step closer to winning the conference champion-ship. With time running out before we had to go back to the field, the team gathered around Kyle. I leaned down and asked him if he had anything to say to his teammates. He looked up at me with a very determined look and said, "I sure do." Kyle turned his head to the right, then moved it slowly back to the left, seemingly looking at every eye in the room. He paused for a moment, and then said, "Turn a setback into a comeback."

As the players were thinking about what he said and looking directly at Kyle, he moved his hands to the arms of the wheelchair, arched his back and somehow pushed his hips forward. Pushing off the arms of the wheelchair, he rocked forward and stood up in the middle of the room. That was the first and the last time Kyle ever stood. His message was clear. "If I can turn my setback into a comeback, surely you can do the same on the football field."

The players got the message from their peer. You can't let what happened yesterday keep you from being successful today. The truth of the matter is Coach Holtz and the Arkansas team never knew what hit them. Baylor won by a score of 42-15 and went on to win the Southwest Conference Championship, undefeated by a whopping three games.

The positive influence exerted by Kyle on his peer group of teammates impacted all of our lives for the next thirty years. Kyle's teammates and coaches formed a support group who stood by him spiritually, emotionally, and financially. Over a period of time, the group furnished Kyle with two different homes equipped to help make his life better. Kyle's transportation was financed by the gifts of Kyle's supporters, as was his college degree that allowed him to become a counselor on the collegiate level for handicapped students. What started out as a great tragedy turned into a magnificent thirty-year experience of inspiration, giving, and caring. Positive peer influence was evident from the time of Kyle's catastrophic injury to his death thirty years later.

Solutions to all social issues by coaches can come in two forms: planned and spontaneous. Events created an opportunity for spontaneous positive peer pressure when Kyle Woods was injured. Other solutions must be planned and created and not always for specific solutions; but once executed, the results seem to have a positive effect on more than one of the social issues. Sometimes spontaneous solutions have an impact equal to those that are meticulously planned and executed.

In order to combat negative teenage pressure, parents, teachers, and coaches must be open to creating a dialogue. High expectations and clear boundaries set by parents, teachers, and coaches have an unusual positive effect.

Coaches have the unique ability to create positive peer pressure through natural groups created by the game of football. These groups learn together and work together to become an essential part of the team. The small groups made up of running backs, defensive line, wide receivers, and offensive line create peer groups. The position coaches have a unique opportunity to instill camaraderie and closeness in their groups. Coaches should find a way to build confidence and self-esteem in their players who may have lost it through negative peer pressure. Teaching leadership and goal-setting is a strong enabler to overcoming negative peer pressure.

Band of Brothers
Coach J. B. Poole
Dakota Wesleyan University (South Dakota)

Our goal here at Dakota Wesleyan University, as a coaching staff, is to develop positively the young men we have the privilege of coaching. This program, entitled "The Band of Brothers," is extended over the entire four-year period of time. Essentially, the program is a four-part series that matches the four years a player is in our program.

> *Part 1.* Our freshmen and all new transfers are required to read the book *Season of Life* by Jeffrey Marx. *Season of Life* is the *New York Times* best-seller that emphasizes enhancing personal growth and fostering more meaningful relationships (positive peer pressure). As the head coach, I meet with the group four times for one hour each meeting. The meetings occur during the fall. We spend the entire time discussing the contents of the book and how they relate to each individual.

> *Part 2.* Our sophomores are required to participate in seven service projects led by our defensive coordinator over the year. Our requirements for these service projects are to do things that will "get your hands dirty."

> *Part 3.* Our juniors and third-year players are to participate in seven leadership seminars led by our

quarterback coach. We invite various successful leaders in our community to discuss topics of leadership. Our players must prepare a series of questions and discussion topics related to the speakers' presentation for the final forum.

Part 4. We require our seniors to attend a three-day senior retreat held prior to their final season. At the retreat they have to read portions of the book *Wild at Heart* by John Eldredge, which is about discovering the secret of a man's soul. The seniors then participate in discussions about team, family, faith, character, and leadership, as well as compete in a series of challenging games that include bass fishing, clay shooting, and prairie dog hunting. *Realizing those three challenge games may not be available for everyone, the games should be based on interests and availability in your area.*

Coach Poole's "Band of Brothers" creates an environment to develop a brotherhood within the team. As players learn together, they become significant, positive peer influencers of each other.

Future Tiger Football Club
Coach Rick Wimmer
Fishers High School (Indiana)

Two years ago, we started a Future Tiger Football Club for young boys in grades K–8. Those who join the club receive a Future Tiger Football Club t-shirt sporting the "Tiger Ready!" logo, a poster schedule we produce each year with a picture of our seniors, a Tiger Value Card (fundraiser card with numerous discounts from local merchants), and a season ticket (optional with a higher cost). Three activities we hold for the boys in the club help create a relationship with our players that we hope not only results in a positive experience for the young Tiger Club member but also helps our older players understand the influence they can have on those young guys who look up to them. The three activities include the following:

1. *Meet the Tigers Night*—Tiger Club members are invited to watch the end of the practice, and our older players introduce themselves and hang out with them

for awhile. Our Gridiron Club (parent boosters) supplies some drinks and snacks for the club members and players. Club members receive their t-shirts and posters on this night.

2. *Sideline privileges for home games*—Tiger Club members are allowed on the sideline during warm-ups for home games. I have a parent posted at the gate to check them in. These young guys get a kick out of high-fiving our players as they run on and off the turf during warm-ups. Again, our players get a sense of their influence with these young kids. Club members are escorted off the field when our team takes the field for the final time.

3. *Tiger Big Brother Program*—Tiger Club members are assigned to players (seniors first, then others who want to be involved). The high school players are told to write a short email or letter to the club member thanking him for being a part of the club, encouraging him to do well in school, asking him about his activities, and asking him about when he might come to see one of his junior high games.

Managers
Tom Culver
Avon High School (South Dakota)

One of the things that we have done in our program to help our players succeed is to start with the younger kids. We have high expectations of behavior for the players at all levels of our program, and so far most of our players have conducted themselves accordingly. I have noticed in our school that some of our younger kids have had more behavior and social issues.

So a few years ago I decided to try something with our student managers. I have elementary students as student managers for our program. I allow any boy who wants to be a manager to be part of the team, with the only stipulation being that they attend practice every week and keep their grades up. I do not turn down any kid who show interest in being a manager. I have been criticized for having eight or nine student managers on the sidelines, but I feel those kids are spending two-plus hours a day around some of the best kids in our school and playing football.

If there is a manager who is not behaving in a way we expect, I will assign one of our captains to spend some time with the manager during the school day or other activities to show what type of behavior is expected.

I believe this has made a real difference with some of our younger boys. Many of them look forward to being a manager and being a part of the Pirate football team. I have even gone out and asked more kids to be managers when I believe they have some problems in their lives and that being a part of a team would be beneficial.

So far, six of our student managers have gone on to become All-State football players for our program. There will be many times that varsity players will talk about experiences they had with the team as a student manager, so I feel this has helped them become fine young men in our community.

Player Meetings
Gene Chizik
Auburn University (Alabama)

We constantly have team meetings regarding social issues, as well as addressing them on an individual basis as they arise. In individual meetings, players will meet with one of the coaches or our chaplain and we will role-play with them, placing them in "what would you do?" situations, and discuss real life examples of how others' similar actions led to very negative consequences.

We also encourage our team members to lean on each other and seek out their peers for advice. Oftentimes, these young men feel more comfortable with that scenario, rather than addressing one of their coaches with a personal issue.

No matter what arises, we never let a known social issue go unaddressed. Another thing we do is call in guest speakers to talk on these social issues. We make sure any speaker we bring in is someone the team can relate to, listen to, and respect. We want our players walking away having been changed for the better and being encouraged to make better choices in their lives.

Tiger Night Lights
Rick Wimmer
Fishers High School (Indiana)

We host a Tiger Night Lights for boys in grades 1–4 in the spring. We will have 70–90 young boys there. We will use our high school players to set up eight learn-by-doing stations and will emphasize to our players that the object is: (1) keep everyone safe, (2) teach the boys some football in a way that they are having success, and (3) be sure they have fun.

Stations include passing, receiving, blocking (vs. shields), tackling (vs. bags), running back station, kicking, defensive back station, and long-snapping. Our players coach one to two drills teaching the fundamentals and making sure everyone has fun. Participants are also put on teams to play a version of touch football called Airball and given a chance to participate in an NFL Combine event complete with 40-yard dash, short shuttle, vertical jump, and obstacle course.

Our players run all of this with some supervision from coaches. The evening ends at 10:00 p.m. with players and participants eating pizza together, and oftentimes, our players are signing autographs on the participants' Tiger Night Lights t-shirts.

Some of the goals of our program are to help our players be responsible, helpful, and courteous. We want to give them opportunities to realize that they can have a positive influence on others and that young people are watching them and know who they are.

Tiger Budz
Chad Rogers, Former Head Coach
Snyder High School (Texas)

In an effort to create an environment of positive peers for our elementary students in Snyder, Texas, we designed a program for our high school football players that would let them see how the younger students looked up to them, and that, of course, encouraged them to be proper role models.

The process:

- Each elementary class adopts a player, a manager, or a cheerleader.

- The Tiger Budz become mentors to the younger students.
- Tiger Budz learn to give back to the community by giving their time and encouragement.
- Tiger Budz benefit from the adulation and recognition of the young students.
- The elementary teachers and the elementary students make the Tiger Budz feel special. The Tiger Budz then feel obligated to set a good example.

This program clearly teaches the old adage, "What we put into the lives of others comes back into our own."

Conclusion

Any initiative or effort that stresses personal accountability, positive character traits, and a value system will play a large role in helping young people overcome negative peer pressure. Finally, a reminder to peers and coaches alike who seek to influence in a positive way: the human tongue and actions are the two leading influencers for good or bad.

Power of the Human Tongue

Over the centuries, much has been written about the power of the human tongue. I particularly like the New Living Translation of James 3:2-6, which says,

> We all make mistakes, but those who control their tongues can also control themselves in every other way. We can make a large horse turn and go wherever we want by means of a small bit in his mouth. A tiny rudder makes a huge ship turn wherever the pilot wants it to go, even though the winds are strong. So also, the tongue is a small thing, but what enormous damage it can do. A tiny spark can set a great forest on fire. And the tongue is a flame of fire.

Ralph Waldo Emerson points out the good as well as the bad capabilities of our tongue: "No man has a prosperity so high or firm, but that two or three words can dishearten it; and there is no calamity which right words will not begin to redress."

— 9 —

Disrespect

The social issue classified as disrespect is extremely troublesome, because in order to be respected, one must give respect. The dictionary defines disrespect as emblematic of a lack of special or high regard, esteem or consideration.

Our policy at Baylor University as a football program placed great emphasis on preparing incoming freshmen to be knowledgeable of, and ready for, the change that would come in their lives. In August of 1978, during a meeting with the freshmen, the coach's goal for this particular day was to prepare our freshmen for all eventualities during their first year. We had maps of the campus, instructions about library use, and strict rules about class attendance, including being on time and even sitting on the front row in their classrooms. Today, of course, most colleges have a fully staffed academic team. We found that by showing a sincere interest in our players as total individuals and students, they realized that we cared about them as individuals, not just as football players. An open and honest discussion about core values usually opened a lot of eyes. Those discussions led to many private conversations with players who wanted to become the best they could become and realized they had yet to establish their own core values.

One day, I remember talking about the importance of developing a capacity internally to really care about themselves, their goals, and being a part of something very special, like the Baylor football team. I explained that developing a passion, a love, if you will, is a strong internal motivation force. I remember saying that as human beings we tend to give more effort toward that which we really care about. Concluding the discussion, I said, "As a group you have common interests and common goals, and you are going to be dependent upon one another as you move forward through these next four years. There will be down times and up times, good times and bad times, and through it all, you must remain a team, caring about each other, your coaches, and your university." Finally, I said, "Ultimately, the care must turn to love for each other."

After the meeting, a freshman linebacker lingered behind the rest and asked to speak to me. He said, "Coach, I believe in every word you spoke, however, I think you left out one thing that needs to happen so we can truly become a team that loves each other." His presentation was sincere and immediately got my attention. I said, "Tell me what I left out, Mike." The young linebacker looked me squarely in the eye and said, "Respect. For me personally to love someone, I must first have respect for them."

Mike Singletary, future Baylor All-American and three-time captain, went on to become one of the great linebackers in the history of the NFL. His statement was exactly right. When someone exhibits a lack of respect for authority, their coaches, or their team's goals, as Mike said, it would be hard to have respect for them, much less love them. From that moment forward, I added this comment to all future freshmen discussions regarding respect, "In order to get respect, you must give respect."

In order to turn disrespect into respect, teachers and coaches must show and teach respect. Confucius said it more eloquently: "Without feelings of respect, what is there to distinguish men from beasts?" In life there are so many important things that must be respected—our freedom, our flag, our leaders, and, as I was taught as a child, our elders, as shown by replying with a "yes, sir/no, sir" or "yes, ma'am/no, ma'am."

Vince Lombardi, the great Green Bay Packers coach, said, "Football is like life—it magnifies perseverance, self-denial, hard work, sacrifice, dedication, and respect for authority." I like very much what Clint Eastwood, the very successful actor, director, and movie producer, said: "Respect your effort, respect yourself. Self-respect leads to self-discipline."

As a coach responsible for the safety and well-being of my players in practice and in the game, I took that responsibility seriously. However, one of the greatest tools for developing an individual personally is creating a team environment. Football is not an individual sport, although individuals within the framework of the team can and do excel. I found that team-building creates a great environment for mental and physical growth for the individuals who are members of a team.

Coaches Teaching Respect

Through years of interviews at the AFCA convention with the Master Coaches, I learned that building respect in an individual player is a high priority for most coaches. In one of the interviews, I posed a question to Don Nehlen, former coach at West Virginia: "Don, is there something that you incorporated into your training that taught your players respect?" He said, "I made my players understand the meaning of respect by the way I respected them." Don went on to say, "The number one thing I wanted to make sure that my players understood was the fact that we as coaches had an open-door policy. They were told they could come and see me, or any of our coaches, at any time. When a player makes a trip to the football building to see one of the coaches, they usually have a problem. If the coach is not available, that problem can fester and it can hurt your football team. Respect is generated in a player when they can observe a head coach and his assistant's honesty. Your players may not always want to hear what you're telling them, but as long as you're honest, they're going to respect you. If you're honest, fair, and consistent, your players will be encouraged to use your open-door policy."

Coach R. C. Slocum of Texas A&M said, "It's important for the players to be able to come any time and have access to the coaches, to feel like they can come and talk."

Coach Bobby Bowden, alluding to the same subject, said, "I can say it in one word, availability. To make myself available for my players is probably the greatest thing I can do for them."

Coach John Gagliardi, winningest coach in college football, said, "We have an open-door policy, that's for sure. We're always available."

Coach Terry Donahue of UCLA said this about being respected by players: "First, everybody who coaches wants to be respected by their players. Being a head coach or assistant coach means that players have a certain level of respect for you. I think it's important that coaches earn the respect of their players. Coaches need to understand that players are going to respect you first because of who you are, then the rest of it you have to earn. You earn respect by your knowledge base, by the way you conduct yourself in crisis, by the way you handle yourself outside of football, and by the way you are perceived by your players as to the kind of person you are. I would much rather be respected by my players than liked by my players."

Team Building through Mutual Respect

The Formula

Remembering the training I received as a child and how effective it was, I one day found the source of my intense training by my parents. I found a neatly folded, yellowing note that was obviously given to my father by his father. The date on the note was my birth date. The note read, from Proverbs 22:6, "Train up a child in the way he should go; and when he is old, he will not depart from it." My children and grandchildren have been beneficiaries of my grandfather's note, as has every freshman class throughout my coaching career. It is, of course, a fact that as teachers and coaches, whether on the high school or college level, our freshmen may or may not have been trained up in the way they should go. As coaches, we have a responsibility to teach the newcomers to our team the game and how to play it. We teach them how to develop their technical skills at the different positions and increase their strength and speed. Ultimately, they become the best football players they can be at their positions. The game itself teaches the great lessons of handling success and adversity. Through the game and team building, we are afforded opportunity after opportunity to develop positive characteristics that will allow them to succeed in life.

Team Building

Developing mutual respect among team members is the bonding agent for that important team chemistry. In order to have a successful football team, the team must be built from the ground up. The most important part of team building is chemistry. Individuals on a team represent diverse backgrounds, income levels, attitudes, and talents. The question is how to bring all the diversity together to form a cohesive, successful team.

The Formula

1. Train up a freshman in the way he should go; and when he is a sophomore, junior, and senior, he will not depart from it. Before the NCAA changed its rule and allowed freshmen to report for football practice three days earlier than the upperclassmen, I literally delayed my upperclassmen's arrival onto campus by three days, so that our staff would have the appropriate time with our freshmen. It is of course noted now that on the college level, freshmen usually report to campus for summer school. When they come is immaterial; what is done with them when they arrive on campus is key.
2. Freshmen Rules of Engagement
    a. Never sit by the same person at any meal or meeting for the first week you are on campus.
    b. Freshman workouts allow fundamentals to be taught, and offensive and defensive philosophies to be learned.
    c. Freshman meetings
        i.   First meeting—each player describes his family
        ii. Second meeting—each player discusses his academic goals
        iii. Third meeting—each player tells something about himself that no one knows (a favorite discussion, as this session always seems to make the freshmen real to each other)

3. Freshmen are told not to let another team member outwork them (this plants a seed of mutual respect).

4. After a week, the freshman class is asked to vote on representation to the player council made up of sophomores, juniors, and seniors. The player council was a conduit between me and the coaching staff. If an issue came up, the player council would discuss it, and if they felt it was necessary, they would bring it to me. At the end of the first week together, I remind the freshmen that they are now "their brothers' keepers." If a teammate has a problem, help him. If a teammate is down, encourage him. If a teammate has that faraway look in his eyes, thinking about going home, encourage him and call me.

A strong, united freshman class would vary in its total contribution to the success of a team, but they would quickly gain the respect of the upperclassmen as a tight, hardworking, committed freshman class.

The Bonding Strength of Respect

One of the toughest football seasons of my life was 1990. I was dealing with the tragedy of the death of a team member and a teammate, struggling with the loss of a friend, while also trying to be successful on the football field. The team struggled to a 6-4-1 record, and of course, in those days winning six games did not automatically get you into a bowl game. The team, the coaching staff, and our supporters were not happy with the record. Elapsed time would help players, and it did, as we went through spring training and a summer of anticipation for the 1991 season. At the end of spring practice, I felt like this team was not a cohesive team bonded together by respect. At the end of our practice and prior to our opening game for the 1991 season, the team was called together for what I believed would be the most important meeting of the year. In preparation for the meeting I had meticulously prepared a demonstration I felt would impress our team and make them aware of just how strong a team can become when they bond together.

One of my former history teachers told me the story of an Indian Chief, who before a great battle brought the warriors of the tribe together in order to teach them a great lesson about unity. In front of the warriors he took a single one-inch limb from a tree and without saying anything, he snapped the piece of wood in two. He reached down and picked up two limbs the same size as the original limb and with more strength, snapped the two limbs. Then he picked up three, and tried with all his might, but could not break the limbs. The point my teacher made was clear: individually we are weak, but together we are strong. For my demonstration, I called a friend whose business was building church furniture. I asked for his help creating a demonstration I believed would help bring the 1991 team together. I explained what I had in mind and he verified that it could be done, and he was willing to help me.

The material was prepared, and when the team walked into our large meeting room and sat down, I immediately started the demonstration. The table in front of me had 120 paper-thin sheets of oak that had been cut from a single block. The assistant coach handed out five extra sheets of wood to five guys on the front row. The five were instructed to step forward and place all five sheets of oak on top of each other. One player was told to bend the sheets of oak. He did, and all five immediately snapped. Paper-thin sheets of oak measuring four inches by twenty-four inches were passed to every player, coach, trainer, and manager in the room. On a table in front of the players, the three captains were asked to step forward and layer their sheets of oak, one by one, on top of each other. The entire team followed suit and came forward to place their sheets of oak on top of their teammates'. Then the trainers, managers, and finally, all the coaches placed theirs.

I said, "Individually, these pieces of oak, when pressured, will snap like a twig. But when bonded together and put under pressure, these individual pieces will form a piece of solid oak that by testing, will be stronger than the same size piece of steel."

Explaining to the players, I said, "My friend will take the individual pieces, representing each member of this team, back to his plant, glue the pieces together, then put them under intense pressure where they will become one. The glue for this team to become stronger than steel is mutual respect."

Stronger Than Steel

During the week, a special piece of wood that was stronger than steel was hung in the center of the team dressing room. Then whether at home or on the road, on game day, the reminder of team unity hung in the game-day dressing room. Every member of the team, coaching staff, team doctors, trainers, and managers all had signed the piece of wood as a sign of their commitment to team unity through respect. Printed in green and gold on the top of the slab and on the four sides were these reminders: "BU 1991," "Unity," "Commitment," and "Stronger than Steel." A chain was attached to the symbol of respect and unity, in order to hang it in the center of the dressing room.

A most special memory dates back to the 1991 season in the visitor's dressing room at the University of Colorado. The previous year, Colorado tied Georgia Tech for the national championship. Both Baylor and Colorado were undefeated at the time. With three minutes to go in the game, Colorado led 14-13 on our 20-yard line, about ready to kick a field goal. That would have forced Baylor to score with less than three minutes to go.

I heard the guys on the special teams yelling to the offense as they were going in, "We're gonna block it, we're gonna block it." Sure enough, they did, and with such force, the football came back up the field and landed around the Colorado 40-yard line. The offense made a first down, then kicked a field goal and beat the undefeated 1990 national champions on their own field. After a brief interview, I arrived at the dressing room. All the players were touching, hugging, and kissing that stronger than steel piece of wood hanging in the middle of the dressing room.

The writer Richard David Bach summed up the moment with this quote: "The bond that links your true family is not one of blood but of respect and joy in each other's life." The bonding power of respect created a true Baylor family. At that moment, we were celebrating joy in each other's success and life.

Coaches Building Respect

Honoring Military
Brad Lutz
Broadway High School (Virginia)

Our football team has adopted a program that blankets so many social problems that our players face. We focus a lot of our attention and time on honoring our military, and especially the men and women who have made the ultimate sacrifice.

- Each week, we dedicate our game to a specific soldier who was killed serving in Operation Iraqi Freedom or Operation Enduring Freedom.
- Our game day compression shirts include the logo of the 10th Mountain Division; Fort Drum NY Army Spc. Brian Anderson is a Broadway High School alumnus and former all-district football player.
- Defensive Player of the Week Award: To recognize relentless work ethic and teamwork, we give an award to the top defensive performer. The award winner gets to wear a special dog tag for the following week. The dog tag includes the face and name of Army Spc. Brian Anderson.
- Soldier Tribute Game: On November 5, 2010, our team hosted our first Soldier Tribute Game. Our team played in special black Nike combat jerseys. On the back of each jersey was one of the seven core values of the Army (integrity, honor, respect, selfless service, duty, loyalty, and courage).
- Pre-Game Meal Speakers: Each Thursday, we have a big pre-game meal. I enjoy having it on Thursday because it is better for our players' performance, and it allows us to slow down and enjoy the evening together, as a family. At each pre-game meal, I invite someone with a special message to speak to our team. Their message always revolves around being a champion in life.
- Care Packages: During the off-season our team is involved in numerous community service projects. It

is a great way to help our community, while teaching our players the importance of giving. One of our projects is making care packages for our soldiers overseas.

Our program has grown into something that is bigger than football. Our players are changing the face of the program, while making a difference in the lives of many people. My point is made. These young men from the Broadway High School football program gave respect to our military, and in return gained respect, not only from those in the military, but also from other students and their community.

Post-Game Tradition
Hank Johnson
Jefferson High School (California)

Coaching in the inner city of Los Angeles, we came across many young men who were from broken homes, splintered families, abject poverty, and drug- and gang-infested neighborhoods. As a result, we instituted the Post-Game Tradition where, after the handshake, all team members headed to the visitor's exit gate. They would stand single file, remove their helmets, and win or lose, begin to clap until the last visitor had exited.

We started this tradition to emphasize and teach what we believed to be the truth about sportsmanship, character, respect, and the real meaning of winning.

The following are the cornerstone beliefs of this tradition:

- Everyone can exhibit class, and our players were expected to prove it by exemplifying the highest standards of discipline and sportsmanship.
- The scoreboard is not the only determining factor in success and winning.
- The true test of a person is how he deals with adversity.
- Our program's greatest responsibility was to develop inner city youth into proud, productive, and respectful men.

Our players began to measure success in the college degrees they obtained; became good husbands, fathers, and successful citizens;

became mentors to younger players in the program and in the community; and began to beat the odds by turning adversity into success.

Ultimately, our goal was to develop those skills that enable young students to mature into successful young men of character, thereby giving them the tools to win at the Big Game, the Game of Life.

"Real"
Keith Allen
Southwest Baptist University (Missouri)

We have a word-a-day message in fall camp to discuss what it means to be a "real" man. In addition, on Friday nights, we spend thirty minutes at the end of meetings for "real" talk topics brought up by coaches.

Every word-of-the-day corresponds with a section in the daily manual that provides quotes and thoughts from well-known coaches, players, scripture, etc. about what that word means. Some examples of the words used are attitude, caring, class, discipline, enthusiasm, and respect.

During the season, every Thursday night at 10:30 p.m., there is a team meeting to discuss a topic from camp. This also helps to keep the players from going out on Thursday nights.

M.O.M (Mom's Other Man)
Ronnie Peacock
Rogers High School (Arkansas)

We do an event with our senior players and their moms. It is a special time together. Some of the things we do:

- Private table for two (meal)
- Professional picture taken of Mom and her son
- Son presents flowers to Mom
- Hire a professional to teach them how to "Fox-trot"
- At a special time the son presents his mom a letter of appreciation, love, and thankfulness for being a good mom
- Group picture at the end of the evening.

The event helps the players respect and recognize an appreciation for what their moms contribute to their lives, and lets them convey that appreciation to them.

The Warrior Way
Ron Stolski
Brainerd High School (Minnesota)

The Warrior Way is a singular phrase that is grounded in RESPECT and has, at its base, the desire to create and maintain an environment that people want to be a part of. It operates on the premise that people will come where they are invited and stay where they are welcome. It is:

- A *philosophy* of respect for self, others, the game, officials, opponents, etc. A practice and display of that respect in all our actions and deeds.
- A *method* of teaching positive teaching principles: encouraging, not demeaning; being fundamentally sound in technique, strategy, preparation, and play.
- A *style* of play. First-class behavior on and off the field, great sportsmanship, physical preparation, and performance. Employ the power of three: preparation, passion, and poise.
- An *ideal*. A model of exceptional behavior for the program and the community. Parents, youngsters, community, and former players relate to the ideal that is the Warrior Way.
- A *goal*. A desire to achieve; to always "better your best," to do the best we can each and every day. The Warrior Way is what our teams inherit; it is what they desire to enhance.
- A *spirit*. Mostly, it is the spirit that defines the core values of the program, and that is carried by players and parents wherever they may travel in their life journeys. It is the spirit that lives in Warriors of yesterday, today, and tomorrow.

It is this philosophy that allows us to address the issues facing the student-athlete of today. It is a vital element of our school and community, and a significant reason why we have experienced success. The support of former Warriors and the community at large helps us in a myriad of ways.

Handshake Ceremony
Paul Maechtle
Southeast High School (Florida)

We usually do this on the track at the location where the 100-yard dash begins. The head coach creates a line by being the first person in the line. The head coach shakes hands with each assistant coach as they get into the line. Each player then walks past each coach and shakes hands man to man. Each player then falls into line and shakes hands with players until the entire team has shaken hands with each other, coaches and players.

Head coach and assistants go down the line and shake everyone's hands and look them in the eye. They wish them good luck on the season. They applaud their off-season workout efforts or some other accomplishments. The time can also be used to encourage where work still remains to be done.

The handshake ceremony takes place on the first day of practice in the fall and in the spring. Thursday nights prior to our Friday night football games we go to a designated spot on the field. After the head coach, or in some cases an assistant coach, gives a talk we repeat the handshake ceremony. We do this on Thursday after the final practice prior to each game.

The ceremony creates interaction between everyone on the team. Players and coaches interact with everyone, including coaches with whom they wouldn't normally interact. It can serve as a team-building experience. Over the years, some of the players have taken it upon themselves to create a snake line in the shape of an "S" with the line in honor of the Southeast Seminoles.

Twenty Questions
Brent Steuerwald
Shenendehowa High School (New York)

I start this process after the final game and finish by Christmas vacation. All returning players in 10th and 11th grade are required to meet with me for 30–45 minutes one-on-one in a private, non-threatening environment. I have done this for over forty years and consider it an absolute essential for me really to know and care about players on a personal and private basis. I cannot speak more highly about the results over these many years.

1. What did you like most about last year's season?
2. What did you like least?
3. How would you evaluate last year's senior leadership?
4. What do you think the attitude of this year's seniors will be?
5. What things did the coaching staff do that helped you the most?
6. What could you have "done without?"
7. What personal goals have you set for next season?
8. What do you think our team goals should be?
9. How are you doing academically?
10. What are your college plans?
11. Do you feel the team as a whole kept their training pledge?
12. Why were we successful last year?

13. Who, on the team, did you feel had a positive impact on our season and why?
14. What specific things in the off-season do you feel you have to work on to be an impact player?
15. How did you feel about our practice (too hard, too easy, etc.)?
16. How did you feel about our pre-game routine?
17. How did you feel about our halftime procedure?
18. Did we ever go so fast with new offense or defense that you got lost?
19. Did you feel comfortable going to your coaches for help or advice?
20. If you could change one thing in your whole football experience, what would it be?

Respect for the Disabled
Robert Lichty
Menomonie High School (Wisconsin)

Each year we team with the Menomonie Recreation Department to offer a "Super Bowl Party" for area developmentally disabled adults the week of the Super Bowl. Normally we have 40–50 who are able to volunteer. After the players share a little about themselves they are paired up with the clients.

We then share a meal, and the players assist their partners in getting their food. After the meal we play a game called "Catch Phrase" in which tables compete against each other for donated prizes. As a table wins, our players escort their partner to the prize table and help them select their prize. Menomonie Football memorabilia is always popular.

Finally, we take their pictures together, and each player and client is sent a copy. Initially, our players can be a little intimidated, because the clients can be very outgoing or have a severe disability. However, they quickly warm up and the room is filled with laughter. Seniors who participated as juniors begin asking as soon as we return from Christmas break when the party is so they make sure they are on the list.

Through this project our players learn to appreciate the many gifts they have been given, a deeper respect for all human life, and the impact they can have on others as a Menomonie player.

Affirmation
Kirk Talley
Northwestern College (Minnesota)

The greatest thing we do as coaches is live out our lives the best we can in front of the men of our team. One of the other things we do for these men is to affirm them as coaches and encourage them to affirm each other.

We start with the player and staff retreat we have together. This is a retreat where the players see we are men, and though we are there to help them be the best they can be in football, more importantly, we are there to help them be better young men.

It is a delicate balance, and it is not always easy with some of them, as they are not used to the style of transformational leadership. When they do come around, and for some it may be their freshman year and others not until they have graduated, they understand we are challenging them not only in the game of football, but also in the game of life.

We also affirm them in another way. After each game, regardless of a win or loss, we have the men individually stand up in front of their teammates and crowd and speak life into someone else on the team. Everyone hears a player speaking positively about one of their teammates. It takes the focus off the game and onto the relationships. We believe this will encourage them to encourage each other to "do the right thing."

Conclusion

Turning an attitude of disrespect into respect in itself will solve many of the social issues. Dwight D. Eisenhower put it in simple terms: "This world of ours . . . must avoid becoming a community of dreadful fear and hate and be, instead, a proud confederation of mutual trust and respect."

There is an innate desire in all human beings to be respected. Jackie Robinson, great baseball player and racial barrier-breaker, said, "I am not concerned with your liking or disliking me . . . all I ask is that you respect me as a human being." Trust is the foundation on which respect will be built.

— 10 —

Entitlement

Growing up, I never heard the word entitlement. In fact, I was an adult before reading the meaning of the word. The dictionary gave the word entitlement three definitions: the state or condition of being entitled; a right to benefits specified by law or contract; belief that one deserves an entitlement to certain privileges. That last definition is the reality that coaches and teachers face.

Entitlement has to be taught. Sometimes it is taught in the home, other times outside the home, and in worst case scenarios, both. Taught by my family and members of my community, these two basic fundamentals were my definitions: (1) there are no free lunches, and (2) you can achieve your goals, if you are willing to work to attain them.

Watching my mother and father work long, hard hours to provide for our family and to serve others in our community, I saw that my parents worked for everything they had and were not given anything. When I got out of high school, mother started working in a shoe store and continued for thirty years. My sister and I were given a small allowance for the chores we did around the house. My public working career started at age twelve at a local grocery store, then later in a tire store. During high school, my relatives owned farms and ranches, so they gave me a job driving a tractor and herding cattle. Working in oil fields around Snyder after the boom hit encouraged me to finish high school, attend college, and get an education. Earning a partial scholarship in junior college led me to work as a radio disc jockey and later as a director in television. It had now been verified—there were no free lunches, and my commitment to work hard for my goals was paying big dividends. The work done in radio and television added greatly to my ability to communicate, and that ability provided effectiveness as a leader, teacher, and coach.

Looking back, I do not believe I considered being on a partial or full scholarship as an entitlement; however, I did look at it as a wonderful place to be: "on scholarship." Interestingly, a couple of my teammates in college, and some of the players who I coached through the years, felt that a scholarship was an entitlement, and in recent years, there has been a clamor actually to pay college athletes. Overall, we in administration in college athletics have done a poor job making sure our scholarship athletes, in all sports, understand the great value in receiving a degree. National statistics are amazing as to the dollar value a degree is worth in one's lifetime.

After attending junior college on a partial scholarship, McMurry College gave me a full scholarship that included room, board, books, tuition, and fees. I could not believe it when I was told the scholarship included $10 each month for laundry. By washing my jeans and t-shirts in the shower and letting them drip dry, I had an extra $10 to spend on anything I wished. Wow! I was living the good life.

Paul Horning, the great Notre Dame All-American and Green Bay Packer who played for Vince Lombardi and went on to great success and acclaim as a broadcaster, once said, "My epitaph should read, 'He went through life on scholarship.'"

I never heard Paul explain this statement, but I think he meant that being on scholarship is a great life, and I have continued to have that great life. There is a huge difference in experiencing the great life feeling after the hard work and effort have been expended to achieve that feeling. The opposite side of that coin is entitlement, where one feels he or she is owed something and there is no price to pay for what is received.

In 2006, Sacred Heart University conducted a poll through the university's Polling Institute. They found the following: nearly 83 percent of Americans agreed that America's youth felt more entitled, compared to the last poll taken in 1996. Entitlement is in essence an attitude. The definition of an attitude is the mental position with regard to a specific fact.

The solution to the social issue of entitlement can be found in the game of football. Some would ask, "What does playing football provide?"

1. There are no free lunches—everyone pays the price to play.
2. In football and in life, one must earn playing time and accolades, as well as personal and team success.
3. Football is a goal-oriented game.
4. Teaching the importance of goal-setting and how to reach those goals will transcend an attitude of entitlement with an attitude of gratitude for an opportunity to reach goals.

In August 1980, Donell and I returned to Waco from the Texas High School Coaches Association meeting. When we got to Waco, I drove Donell home, and then proceeded to my office to work. As I started looking through my mail, I found a sealed envelope from the Athletic Department. Inside was an announcement that the athletic cafeteria was to be cancelled for the upcoming year. I was astonished beyond words. We had worked hard to recruit young men who expected an athletic cafeteria, as football players for decades at Baylor had been provided an athletic cafeteria. After slamming a few doors and letting my rage simmer down, I sat down and looked at the situation calmly. First of all, I would not follow my first instinct and slap my resignation on the table. This was one more battle I was going to fight and win. I had an obligation, not only to the coaching staff and players, but to the university as well. No matter what the adversity, I was going to find a way to get around it.

I had always been honest with my players, and this would be no exception. On the day the players reported to campus for the 1980 season, I met with our captain, Mike Singletary, a great leader and All-American on our team. Mike was revered and respected as a leader by our players. I told Mike exactly what had happened and said that it was imperative the team handle this with the proper attitude. The team that gets caught up in distractions is not a team that can concentrate on what has to be done to succeed in practice and in games.

"The only way we can make this season the kind of success that we want it to be is for the team members to make up their minds that they are not going to let this distract them," I told Mike. "From a schedule standpoint, it will be inconvenient to eat with regular students, but there will be some advantages. The students will get to know you. The food quality will be better than you expect. The problem will be the evening meal, since we get off the practice field late, and the campus cafeteria will already be closed. There will be some cold meals, and there may be some inadequate meals, but the key to the situation is how we handle it mentally."

I then asked Mike for his opinion. He looked directly in my eyes and said something that thrilled me. His words were those of a true leader. He said, "Coach Teaff, you explain it to the team as you've explained it to me, and I assure you they will do whatever it takes to handle the situation. They trust you, and if you tell them something, they know that's the way it is. I can promise, from my vantage point as captain, we will make it work." And make it work they did.

Watching the 1980 team handle the adverse situations with which they were confronted—the cafeteria bombshell, Kyle Woods' injury, and other distractions—became great lessons in the power of their attitude, mind control, and elimination of any individual feelings of entitlement. We were a Division I football team, and most likely, three days a week there would be no evening meal. I knew from the start of the season that we had a special group of young men. They won ten games while losing two, the best record in the history of Baylor University. The team won the Southwest Conference championship by a three-game margin and became one of the finest football teams ever assembled at Baylor. They were unselfish and void of any feelings of entitlement. Over the years, I have been asked many times why this team was so special. My judgment when asked that question was, and still is, leadership and a group of individuals who in 1979 bonded together through the inspiration of one of their team-mates. They remain to this day a close-knit group that still looks out for each other.

I feel very strongly that as coaches we have an obligation and a responsibility to influence our players "beyond the game." In fact, we are blessed with multiple ways of impacting our players positively: practicing to learn the fundamentals of the game and how to prepare for an opponent; classroom settings and meetings; spontaneous points to be made, as well as planned programs, activities, and created experiences that teach and mold. Some-times opportunities present themselves where we, as coaches, can teach great lessons from unplanned events that happen nationally, locally, or within the team framework.

In 1963, I stood on the tarmac of the Abilene, Texas airport, watching my McMurry team board a chartered DC-3. The con-verted World War II cargo plane held thirty-three players, three coaches, three managers, a stewardess, and two pilots. We flew to Monroe, Louisiana for a football game that night. We played well, and save for some home-cooking that I will not delve into at this point, we would have won the game. We were tired as we headed back to the airport. At that time, they did not have a tower or any other traffic, so the DC-3 was waiting on the end of the runway where we had left it earlier in the day. When we arrived at the plane, my anger about losing the game intensified because the pilots and the stewardess were not there. After about a fifteen-minute wait, they arrived in a taxi. They scrambled to get the door open and get on the plane themselves. The team and coaches loaded quickly, and the pilots started the engines.

When they received clearance from Shreveport, the plane started moving forward, straight down the runway. I was seated in the left front seat looking out the window. As we moved further down the runway without lifting off, I became a little concerned because I knew there were tall pine trees close to the end of the runway. Finally, the plane lifted off, and as I looked down, it felt as though I could literally reach down and touch the tops of the pine trees. The plane circled quickly to the left and continued to circle until it lined up with the runway again to come in for an emergency landing. Something was wrong. For some reason, they were having a hard time getting the plane down to the runway.

Finally, with time running out, the pilots let the plane drop. We hit the runway and bounced in the air, as the plane seemingly turned sideways. At that moment, I thought we would go wingtip over wingtip. The powerful engines of the DC-3 kept the plane in the air until finally we lifted above the pine trees once again. The plane again turned and circled back, lining up with the runway to make another attempted landing.

Unbeknownst to the pilots, on the first aborted landing, the plane hit the ground so hard that the left wheel and landing gear had crumpled up under the left side of the plane. We had one wheel when we set the plane down. The pilots realized we were on one wheel as the plane began to list to the left. They gave the engine full power, pulling the nose up, and we were again airborne.

The plane gained altitude, and we circled the airport again. The cockpit door opened, and the pilot stepped into the main cabin and came directly to me. He leaned over to tell me, "We have a problem." I thought that might have been the understatement of the year. There was more. He explained that the left landing gear evidently had been destroyed and now we had only one choice—fly to the Strategic Air Command base in Shreveport, Louisiana and do a belly landing. I asked, "What do we need to do back here?" He said that the stewardess would position everyone for the landing. Then he asked me if the coaches would go to the back of the plane to sit on the floor during the crash landing, as it would give more balance to the plane. The stewardess instructed the players about positioning themselves for the crash landing. It was about a forty-minute flight from Monroe to Shreveport. The electrical system had been damaged on the second aborted landing, so we had no lights in the cabin. The players and coaches alike were in total darkness waiting for the unknown. I heard a voice call out from among my players, "Coach Teaff, will you pray for us?"

I stood in the darkness of that plane and prayed one of the most fervent prayers of my life. I asked God to protect us all, and then I said, "Your scriptures tell us you have a plan, a purpose, and a will for each of our lives. My prayer tonight is that you would protect all of us that we might live to seek your plan, your purpose, and your will for each of our lives." Then I quoted

Romans 8:28, "All things work together for good for those who love God and are called according to his purpose."

I sat back down on the floor of the plane and waited for the crash landing. In those years, the Strategic Air Command was under the leadership of General Curtis LeMay, a hard-nosed, no-nonsense leader who believed he was protecting America from the Soviet Union threat during the Cold War. He would often fly around in an unmarked plane, claim distress, and land on a Strategic Air Command base, then demote everyone who let him land without authorization.

On this night, the commander of the base thought we were General LeMay claiming that his plane was in distress and asking for permission to land. Permission was granted, but the runway was not foamed down for a crash landing and the military police were waiting in full force to arrest the perpetrators.

Ten or fifteen feet over the runway, the power was shut off and the plane dropped. Immediately, the right prop flew into space and the engine exploded in flames. The cabin of the plane was engulfed with the sparks, and they illuminated the hull of the airplane. We were loaded with gas, had an engine on fire, and the plane was still skidding. Finally, we came to a stop, and one of my coaches kicked open the door. One of the players had the stewardess in his arms to bring her down the aisle. They were the first two off the plane. While the remaining players were unloading, one of the pilots came pushing his way through the players to get out the door. I thought he was going outside to cut off the gas, but I later learned that the pilots had inadvertently left the elevator locks on the tail section of the plane. He was retrieving those and eventually put them back in their rightful place in the rear closet of the plane. Everyone on the plane had four chances to die that night, but we all survived. I have had pilots who have flown the DC-3 tell me that the plane is not supposed to fly with its elevator locked, but on that night, everyone on the plane knew that the power of the engines and a power greater than the engines spared us all. We stepped away from the plane, watching it burn. I was so thankful that not one player, coach, or crew member was injured in any way.

As we watched the plane burn, we were informed that we were officially under arrest because we had illegally landed on a

Strategic Air Command base, but they quickly realized that we were not General LeMay and, of course, treated us with great concern and courtesy. We spent the night at a local hotel. Another plane picked us up the next morning to fly us back to Abilene, where it seemed as though the entire city had turned out to welcome us home. Before the flight home, one of the running backs had retrieved his helmet from the burned out plane and had it on as we were flying back to Abilene. He was not taking any chances.

As a coach, I felt compelled to seize the moment and do something so our players and coaches might remember this momentous event and especially the blessing that there were no injuries and we all lived to seek God's will, plan, and purpose for our lives. That Sunday night I called a team meeting. I told them I felt we should have a special club, only open to our coaches and teammates who had lived through the experience. It popped into my mind that we should name the club something unique, so I asked the players for suggestions. One bright young man said, "Coach, we are the McMurry Indians, so we should name our club 'The Brotherhood of the Indian Belly-Landing Experts.'" The team cheered, and I nodded my head in agreement.

The next morning, I went to a printer and ordered some calling cards, as we were forming a club called "The Brotherhood of the Indian Belly-Landing Experts." I wanted to add a special scripture to the card along with the date of the crash. Just as I walked back into my office, the telephone rang. It was the printer. He said, "'The Brotherhood of the Indian Belly-Landing Experts' is too much verbiage to put on such a small card. May I use the initials?"

I stopped by the printer late that afternoon, and he handed me the stack of cards wrapped in brown paper. I did not look at the cards, because I was rushing to the meeting. I walked in the meeting as everyone was excitedly talking. I felt so thankful that we were having a meeting to memorialize the event, and not some of the players and coaches. The room grew quiet when the players realized I had walked into the room. I began the meeting by reminding the players of a simple fact: life is a gift and not an entitlement. What we do with that gift is what is important. I reminded them of the scripture (Romans 8:28) I had quoted on the plane and asked each one of them to take the words of that scripture to heart, that we might each live our lives with an attitude of gratitude and an awareness that surely God has a plan, a purpose, and a will for each of us.

I handed the small package to one of my coaches so he could pass the cards to the players, as I explained their purpose. "This is a card commemorating our experience, joining us all together in a unique club that will be ours for as long as we live. There was not enough room for the full name of our club, so the printer abbreviated." At that point, I still had not looked at the card. Another player stood and said, "Coach, we now all belong to the B-I-B-L-E club."

Twenty-five years after the belly-landing experience, every member of the team and coaches, except one who had passed away, met in Fort Worth, Texas for one of the greatest evenings of my life. Each player related his life experiences for the last twenty-five years, and it was extremely heart-warming. One of the outstanding statistics for the group was that in twenty-five years, not one of the members of the BIBLE club had divorced. There is something to living life when you know it could have been taken away. There was no feeling of entitlement with the BIBLE club, just a profound feeling of gratitude.

Solutions to an Attitude of Entitlement

Scott Smith, a member of the Baylor team, came from an affluent neighborhood in Dallas, Texas. However, because of his parents and coaches, Scott's only feeling of entitlement was thankfulness that he was given the opportunity to prove himself on the major college level. Seizing that opportunity, he proved himself first as a quarterback, then as a defensive back on that 10-2 Southwest Conference Championship team of 1980. Scott eagerly took to the concept of setting goals to become successful, first as a player, then as a husband, father, leader, and coach.

Coach Smith teaches his players the importance of goal-setting, which, in turn, teaches the players, "Opportunity is the only entitlement." In a free society the opportunity is there, so it is incumbent on the individual athlete to seize the opportunity to set and reach goals.

Setting Goals
Scott Smith
Rockwall High School (Texas)

When an individual learns to set goals, it invariably helps alleviate many social issues, but particularly entitlement. We asked our juniors and seniors in our football program to become goal oriented and set specific goals in all areas of their life. We asked them to set goals physically, mentally, spiritually. As coaches we also ask our players to consider setting a goal of becoming a servant leader.

The method:

1. The head coach shares the importance of setting goals and working diligently to reach them.
2. Each student-athlete is given a sheet of paper with a line drawn down the middle and asked to list their personal strengths on one side and their liabilities on the other.
3. Student-athletes are asked to visualize, "How do you see yourself ten years from now?"
4. A positive vision of one's future demands that positive goals must be set and reached in order to crystallize that vision in ten years.
5. Our coaches continually asked the players this question, "How can I help you reach your goals?" (Coaches must be role models as effective servant leaders willing to help others.)

This process of goal-setting can become a solution to many of the social issues. Setting goals on a daily basis and reaching those goals encourages an athlete to set bigger and more long-range goals that will someday allow them to reach levels of success that most of them never dreamed of. By teaching our athletes to be willing to serve others by learning to set goals, individuals learn that they don't have to be given something, but they can earn it by knowing what they want and how to get there.

Community Service
Sherman Wood
Salisbury University (Maryland)

We believe one of the best ways to address many social issues is through community service. To take an active approach within our community, I first identified a community service liaison from our coaching staff. This person meets with the head coach at least once a week to discuss projects within the surrounding community.

In addition, the liaison works closely with a community service advocate from the school board. The two discuss and identify elementary and middle schools, mostly in disadvantaged neighborhoods, that are facing obvious social problems.

Each of our players (excluding freshmen) volunteers at least two hours a week in community service. Following these projects, our players are often reminded of some of their troubled years growing up at such a young age. Both player and student have a sense of respect for themselves as well as their peers and superiors.

Period 10
Brent Steuerwald
Shenendehowa High School (New York)

This procedure was initiated by the Shenendehowa Athletic Department for the development and monitoring of student-athletes in grades 9–12 for the purpose of enhancing their academic performance and college recruiting.

The Shenendehowa Central School District has allowed coaches to have the opportunity to access students' accounts, which enables them to monitor their grades, performance, attendance, homework assignments, and tardiness for overall evaluation of students' performance in grades 9–12. This has been a major boost in helping high school administration track the behavior, attendance, and academic progress of its student-athletes.

Period 10 refers to a period where teachers and coaches can monitor their athletes regardless of who they have as a teacher. Once a current sport's roster is generated through the athletic office, a teacher or coach can monitor a student-athlete's performance throughout the year. This has been influential in the overall evaluation and tracking of student-athletes at Shenendehowa.

We believe that this is another tool that teachers and coaches can have at their disposal to benefit academic and athletic success.

Character Development through Peer Discussions
Larry Kindbom
Washington University (Missouri)

When we get our players to discuss tough issues, we see the development or their value systems. We formalize the process by presenting some issues to the players for discussion in small groups.

These "issues" are presented in the form of dilemmas. We have our coaches discuss these dilemmas before we present them to the players. Then we break our team into groups by class or by position. The coaches listen to the players' discussions, but do not join in with the opinions.

When we present these dilemmas we give guidelines to the group. No one can talk for more than thirty seconds at a time. We want their ideas to be thought out and to carry a single point. We tell the group to monitor this rule. With this structure more ideas can be discussed and more people can give their opinion.

Each player learns that he is part of a greater group that also has standards that it attempts to set and keep. Coach involvement is important. I think the coaches can learn a lot about the values that our players have, as well as be the mentor when needed.

Plan for Life
Ken Sparks
Carson-Newman College (Texas)

Each incoming freshman completes a plan for life. We tell them to make goals that are specific and measurable so they can see progress and development over four years. The setting of goals in all areas of their lives helps curb the effects of social issues that can be harmful.

Categories	Goals for Each Category
Family Caring	Short Range
Spiritual/Moral	Plan to accomplish short range goals
Personal Giving	Dreams
Health/Fitness	Plan to accomplish dreams
Team and Friends	
Giving to Campus Community	
Academics Career	

Community Service Program
Hud Jackson
University of Arkansas at Monticello (Arkansas)

Our players are involved in a community service program that is second to none. We work with schools in our area in many different ways, whether it is mentoring, tutoring, physical education activities, or just talking about peer pressure.

By being involved with young people, our players see that they are not the only ones who have issues. In many cases, the kids they are working with have bigger problems than the players have.

We also started a bowling league and an ultimate Frisbee league with our players to allow them to get to know each other away from the field and in an environment that promotes fun without drugs and alcohol. A majority of players come from an environment where their childhood may have been taken away and they were forced to grow up too fast.

Conclusion

Someone once said, "Seize the moment." As coaches, we must do that. Every lesson cannot be planned, but it is up to us as influencers to take every opportunity to teach. That fateful night, and the impact it had on everyone on the plane, is still affecting lives in a positive way. In the mid-1970s, Donell and I were attending a Coach's Family Conference in Black Mountain, North Carolina. We were both thrilled to see that Dr. Billy Graham was going to speak to our group on the first night of the conference. Two years earlier, I had invited him to give the prayer prior to the Cotton Bowl and to come into the dressing room to speak to our team. The following year, Dr. Graham invited me to appear in one of his stadium crusades. So I was extremely anxious to hear him speak again. To a room full of coaches, Dr. Graham said to all of us, "A coach will impact more people in one year than the average person will in an entire lifetime." If you think about his words, he was challenging all of us as coaches to use the opportunities we have to influence those whom we coach and teach through this concept: be thankful for the talent and opportunities we have to achieve success in your life. If a young person accepts that concept, it will take them far beyond the mentality of entitlement, all the way to an attitude of gratitude.

— II —

Accountability

For centuries, people of faith have tried to pinpoint the exact age when an individual becomes accountable for their own life and their behavior. Scholars tell us that the Christian Bible does not pinpoint an exact age, though some religions designate the age of thirteen. It is obvious that this discussion will go on for years to come.

Parents eagerly await the day when their children become accountable. Certainly teachers' and coaches' lives are made incrementally better when the young people they teach and coach reach that magic age. The bad news is that the age of accountability may vary with the individual.

Developing a work ethic and adopting a value system are two of the most important actions that will ensure an individual develops to their full position and becomes a responsible person. This particular social issue has been magnified by the fatherless home. Seeing and experiencing a lack of accountability in adults has a profound effect on children as they grow. The teacher/coach is obligated to find ways to teach personal responsibility to have a transforming effect on those they teach and coach.

The definition of accountability: the quality or state of being accountable; especially, an obligation or willingness to accept responsibility or to account for one's actions. The shorter version might be: being accountable for accepted responsibilities is one of the most important things that can be taught. When it is taught and learned, accountability will eliminate most of today's social issues.

Rewarding Accountability

In 1973, I was able to hire Dal Shealy, the head coach at Carson-Newman, as an offensive coach. Our families had met through the Fellowship of Christian Athletes, and not only were we good friends, our philosophies were similar. After being a part of the 1974 Southwest Conference Championship, Dal went on to Tennessee, Auburn, and Iowa State, and to the head coach position at the University of Richmond. Dal served as president of the Fellowship of Christian Athletes for several years.

During one of our many phone conversations, while discussing how best to teach responsibility and accountability to our players, we agreed that when a player becomes accountable in one area it most often leads to accountability in all areas. Collectively, we thought the best way to teach accountability was to encourage players to be responsible members of the team and accountable to each other.

The conversation turned to comparisons of a steel chain to a team. The chain is no stronger than its weakest link, and the same can be said for the team. Like a thunderbolt, the idea came to us: create a tangible reminder of the importance of each member of the team taking full responsibility for their commitment to the team and being accountable for their own work ethic, actions, and attitude. The goal would be for each team member to commit themselves to being the most responsible and accountable member of the team, thus becoming the strongest link in the chain that represents the strength of the team.

Early the next morning, at a local hardware store, my request to be shown the steel chains was granted, and we proceeded to the back of the store where there were different sizes of chains beside a table where they could be measured and cut. I selected a chain size, so that each individual link on the chain would be large enough to recognize that it was a link, but small enough that it could be carried in a pocket. I put the links in a box and carried them back to my office.

Saving a foot-long piece of the chain, I had it mounted on an engraved plaque with this quote, "The chain is no stronger than its weakest link."

The afternoon prior to practice, I compared our team to a steel chain, challenging each player to be accountable and responsible for himself, becoming the strongest link in the chain. The strongest link would never break. If each player committed to that concept, it was obvious our team would be strong.

I carried a few of the links in my pocket to practice every day. Three days later, the awarding of the first link took place after practice. Considerations of effort on the practice field, attitude, and leadership were important; however, the accountability shown by knowing assignments on every play was one of the measures of overall accountability. Class attendance had already been checked, as well as individual responsibilities in the weight room. At the end of practice that day, I called the team together and announced I was going to award the first link. I would make the decision as to who I felt deserved the link. The link was the daily reminder of what they had committed to. After awarding the link, I told the player, "Carry this with you wherever you go, so that when you put your hand in your pocket, you will feel the link and be reminded that you are accountable to continue your effort to be the strongest link."

As practice continued, I would periodically award another link, and amazingly, the level of effort, positive attitude, and work ethic of the entire team was obviously improving.

I took very few things with me when I left Baylor University to lead the American Football Coaches Association, but I took the plaque. To this day it hangs in the staff workroom—a reminder that, as a chain is no stronger than its weakest link, the same holds true for my AFCA team. The staff is no stronger than its weakest member.

Paul J. Meyer, *New York Times* bestselling author, had a worldwide reach, as he trained hundreds of thousands of men and women in business, as well as coaches, while selling more than $2 billion worth of his programs and training methods over the years. He was a giant among men and a treasured friend. The time was approaching for an American Football Coaches Association convention in San Antonio, Texas. I wanted Paul to speak, and even though he was having some health issues, he readily accepted. He was so excited about teaching leadership to over 6,000 coaches that he actually wrote a book specifically for the coaches of the AFCA and for the convention. The book was entitled *Become the Coach You Were Meant to Be*. He not only wrote the book but gave one copy to every AFCA member. One of the great lessons in the book was about responsibility. Paul called this section of the book "The Four Elements of Responsibility." Paul said, "Taking responsibility is a trademark for every successful person alive. There are no exceptions. Those who succeed are people who have learned to take responsibility."

Paul Meyer's Four Elements of Responsibility

1. *Knowing "the buck stops here."* Harry Truman had a plaque on his desk that read "The Buck Stops Here." He understood that he carried the weight of important decisions. Today, virtually every coach shoulders some element of responsibility for outcomes. The burden you bear may not be as great as Truman's, but the same sentiment still applies. As a coach, you are the responsible party. Accept the fact that nothing—*absolutely nothing*—you do in your organization will produce the successful results you desire until you choose to accept personal responsibility for what happens to you and your team.

2. *Never blame others.* People cry "victim" all the time, blaming others for their situation, even when it is obvious that they created the entire problem themselves. Those who accept responsibility know that blaming others is a worthless expenditure of energy and effort. Blaming people leaves us with less energy for growth, improvement, and success. Great coaches don't blame others, relive failures, or repeat mistakes over and over again, they let it go. Learn from it, and then move on.

3. *Making it personal.* People who take responsibility recognize that they are responsible not only for

who they are and how they feel, but they are responsible for their own actions. They make it personal. For example, they don't quit for the day just because they have fulfilled the minimum daily requirements for keeping the door open. They go the extra mile to keep their commitments to everyone they work with. They do this even when no one else is watching. As a result, they exceed everyone's expectations . . . regularly.

4. *Being willing to change.* Personal and professional growth is always a choice. People cannot be forced to become more than they are, but those who accept responsibility are quick to change. What's more, they are willing to pay the price and accept the responsibility for personal growth. As a result, they are the first to grow, to excel, and to increase. When opportunity arises, they are the first to take advantage of it, because they are ready.

Paul Meyer, a great man who loved coaches, would be honored if we all took his four elements of responsibility and utilized them, then taught them to our players. Another great man, Winston S. Churchill, said it this way: "The price of greatness is responsibility."

Accountability is one of the most important lessons that a coach or teacher will convey. An understanding of accountability is in itself one of the foundational values of a successful and happy life. As a child, I learned early on from my parents that I was (1) responsible for all my actions, (2) accountable to tell the truth, and (3) accountable to do my best in any job given or action attempted. Accountability centers on one's discipline and a conscious decision to be responsible for one's actions, words, and attitude. Through the years, with different generations of athletes, my own children, and my grandchildren, the foundation for accountability has always been discipline. Punishment or recognition of a breach of discipline or accountability, and immediate and swift reaction to the breach, always sent a message that would sometimes last for a four-year period.

Most losing football programs demonstrate in many different ways a lack of discipline and accountability. You see it in the number of penalties that will cost a close game, you see it in the dress and behavior of the athletes, and, most frighteningly, you see a lack of resolve in the fourth quarter when the team is behind, as was expected. In order to turn around a program, an important football game must be won in the fourth quarter. When that happens, it sets a pattern for recognition of the importance of discipline and resolve.

Arriving at Baylor University in 1972, facing what most people believed was the impossible task of turning Baylor University into a winner, the foundation of our program was based on accountability, and the accountability had to be served by personal discipline. To begin the turnaround, we took drastic action toward personal development. Rest and proper eating habits were made very clear with a curfew each night, required study hall, and required class attendance. We even went so far in regard to class attendance as to require that our players sit on the front row in every class.

Being on time places the burden of responsibility and accountability on the individual. Truly being on time did not mean reporting at the mandatory posted time, but rather being in place five minutes before the mandatory time. There were physical penalties attached to many of our requirements, and some examples were psychological.

In the third year of our rebuilding program, we were playing our first conference game against a perennial power in the Southwest Conference, the University of Arkansas. We referred to road trips for football games as business trips, so we all wore coats and ties. On the day before the game, if there was something interesting around the university besides our regular walk-through, we would explore as a team. Around Fayetteville, Arkansas, there was not a lot to see, but we drove to the campus in order for our players to walk around and visit the bookstore. My wife and our team doctor's wife were also on the bus with us. Prior to unloading, as was always the case, I gave the team a specific time to be back on the bus.

The time to be on the bus came, and my trainer checked off the list of names, then turned to me and said, "Everyone is on the bus except Mrs. Teaff and Mrs. Covington." I looked at my watch and announced, "Everyone knew to be back on the bus . . . let's go to the hotel." You could hear gasps from some of the players as the bus pulled off and we left two ladies to fend for themselves.

That team of '74, eventual Southwest Conference champions, before a sellout crowd at Razorback Stadium displayed personal and team discipline when they had to drive the length of the field to score and get ahead of Arkansas to win the game. The victory was the foundation for the first Southwest Conference championship for Baylor in fifty years. There were times during the remainder of that season when the team had to come from behind to win.

In 1991, in Boulder, Colorado, we were ready to leave the team hotel to go on the bus to the stadium for an afternoon ball game with the defending national champions, the University of Colorado. We loaded the bus in front of the hotel. My trainer, Mike Sims, had the responsibility of checking off each player to make sure everyone was on the bus. One minute prior to departure time for the stadium, Mike informed me that our all-conference defensive end was nowhere to be found. We learned later that he had dropped off to sleep in his room after being taped.

Much to the dismay of my defensive coaches, I ordered the bus to the stadium. The Boulder stadium is situated in such a way that only one road goes into the stadium for parking. Even though the hotel was close, it took us about twenty minutes to arrive at the stadium. As we pulled up and unloaded the bus, there at the gate waiting for his coaches and teammates was the missing defensive end. I have no idea how he beat the bus, but it said a lot for him. And by the way, he was the leader that day on defense, blocking a last-minute field goal by the University of Colorado and, with seconds to go, setting up a field goal kick for the Baylor Bears that won the game. Discipline is always the foundation for victory and accountability.

Sending a clear message about accountability does not always mean you have to discipline your wife or your all-conference end. The message should be consistent, loud, and clear, "All are accountable for their attitude, effort, and action and for assigned responsibilities."

In 1979, while preparing to play Clemson University in the Peach Bowl, we had a great week as the players enjoyed the hospitality of the Peach Bowl representatives and the city of Atlanta. They were pleased to be receiving national recognition for having an outstanding season as a team.

As a reward for all the hard work by the players throughout the year, we took our walk-ons and our freshmen, even though they, of course, would not play or suit up for the game. The night before the game, I was having a hard time sleeping, so I went for a walk around the hotel. In the Peach Street Plaza hotel there is a long escalator going down to the lower floor. As I stepped onto the escalator going down, I saw two of our freshmen step onto the escalator coming up. They were talking and did not look up, so they did not see me coming down. When they did see me, we were seconds apart. The horror on their faces told the story. As we passed, I simply said, "You boys are out a little late, aren't you? I'll see you in the morning." The next morning, I met with the two freshmen to tell them they would not physically be going to the game, so they would not be on the sidelines with their teammates. They would remain in the hotel and watch the game on television. Word spread rapidly, and even though it was two freshmen who would not have played, the freshman classes for the next four years were the epitome of personal and team accountability. The lesson had been taught and learned at an early age. That freshman class spread the word to every freshman class during the next four years. Because accountability is such an important trait for personal and team success, coaches through the years have found many different ways to teach accountability. The following is a cross-section of those methods.

Teaching Accountability

Terry Gambill, head football coach at Midway High School in Texas, has instituted a program he calls "Question Mark T-Shirts." The use of t-shirts that send a message has been extremely effective for his program. In a few short years, he has led Midway High School consistently to compete at the highest level. A plain, simple gray t-shirt with a big question mark on it sends the right message.

Question Mark T-Shirts
Terry Gambill
Midway High School (Texas)

We give out t-shirts in our off-season program. There are three different types of t-shirts. The first shirt is a plain, simple gray t-shirt with a question mark on it. Everybody gets one of these to begin with. I ask the players, "What is the question mark?" and they respond by saying, "I don't know." That is it exactly; the question mark signifies that the person inside that shirt has a question to answer. That question is, "Will I become an accountable, consistently eligible, and positively motivated member of my team?"

The player gets out of the question mark t-shirt and will move into either a red or blue t-shirt with a white "M" on it. Each student-athlete is accountable for their academic progress and eligibility. If a player makes an A, B, or C in their classes, but misses a class or is tardy during the week, they will be in a red shirt. However, to gain blue-shirt status, their accountability is held to a maximum. They must achieve nothing below a C, with no absences, excused or unexcused, and no tardiness for the entire week.

This is an incentive for the players to take care of their responsibilities and to grow as young people. This amounts to accountability. No one likes to wear a shirt that has a question mark on it, so they are all heavily motivated to end up with that red shirt.

At Midway High School, we have had principals, teachers, and individuals from the community tell us, "Coach, you just don't know how much these players dislike having a question mark hanging over their head." It is a badge for everyone in the school to see when you wear the red jersey and everyone knows you have been accountable for your grades and your attendance. This teaches young people that they have a responsibility to be accountable in all areas of their lives.

When an individual becomes accountable, his life changes forever. An individual who is accountable to be an example to his teammates and an inspiration can become a responsible, accountable person and team member.

Life Skill Grades
Terry Jackson, Director of Player Relations
University of Florida (Florida)

Once players step onto our campus, we evaluate and monitor them in every aspect of student life. The strong support system around our student-athletes provides role models and examples of how to get it done. Strength staff are integral to discipline and respect; the Director of Player Relations, Director of Football Operations, and anyone involved with the players on a day to day basis are important to have around.

We require feedback from anyone who deals with our student-athletes. With this feedback, we in turn grade our players in the area of life skills and give them a score. Their scores will fall into the following categories: Platinum (employers excited to hire you), Yellow (you will compete for jobs, but you are not a stand-out), or Red (you need to make yourself more employable).

It is extremely important for them to see how they are perceived now and how they will be perceived in the future as it relates to jobs. Our student-athletes are provided clear and direct expectations by which they must abide if they want to be a student-athlete at the University of Florida. We don't expect perfection, but growth and personal initiative are a must to become a program guy.

Life Skills
Mike Riley
Oregon State University (Oregon)

We have a "Life Skills" program in place for all of our student-athletes. The program recognizes athletes who have performed well on the playing field, who are strong academically, and who are involved in the community of Corvallis. The recognition comes in the form of their pictures with a brief bio displayed on banners and small billboards around campus.

The program plans a series of speakers who present on the various social issues topics. These events are required throughout the year, and each topic is addressed at least every other year. We have invited former athletes, professional and college coaches, former professional gamblers and chemical abusers, and motivational speakers from the business community.

In addition, there are presentations from campus counselors who can provide on-campus help in dealing with positive self-image, anger management, chemical abuse, and developing a positive attitude and approach to dealing with fellow students and life in general.

This program has been very helpful in creating a more positive environment among our athletes and throughout the community. There is continued thought and revision as we continue to deal with these issues on a year-to-year basis.

Frank Solich
Head Coach, Ohio University (Ohio)

The Plan: to emphasize and teach Effort, Accountability, and Productivity.

1. The entire roster is drafted into eight separate teams.
2. Each player earns or loses daily based on his Effort, Accountability, and Productivity.
3. The team with the most points per player at the end of the quarter wins the competition.
4. Captains are elected.
   a. Each player on the roster votes for three captains.
   b. The top 16 votes received become captains (two per team).
5. The captains draft the entire roster into eight teams.
   a. Each week
      • Team and individual scores are posted for the entire team to see.
   b. End of quarter
      • The winning team receives a special award and privileges.
      • The leader is recognized on the Bobcat Challenge Wall.

Scoring System

• Championship Effort	+2 points
• Winning Effort	+1 point
• Excused from Participation	0 points
• Losing Effort	-1 point

- Community Service   +1 point/2 hours
- Short Study Table Hours   -1 point
- Late for Appointment   -2 points
- Missed Appointment   -4 points
- Athletic Dept. Policy Violations -2 to -10 points
- Dismissed/Quit Team   -10 points
- Academics   +6 to -6 points
- Lifting Results   +5 to 0 points
- Team Competitions   +/- TBD
  ◦ Dodgeball
  ◦ Wii Sports Competition
  ◦ Tug-O-War
  ◦ Dumbbell Relay
  ◦ Home Run Derby
  ◦ Minute to Win It
- Coaches' Discretion   +/- TBD

Magnanimitas
Bill Curry
Georgia State University (Georgia)

We work with our young men every day of the year on a program we call "Magnanimitas." Magnanimitas is Latin for "Greatness of Spirit." We believe every human being is endowed with a God-given potential, a unique gift. We encourage our students to locate that gift, develop it, and give it, first to our team, and then to causes greater than their selfish ones.

Our priorities are the five F's:

1. Faith
2. Family
3. Finish Education
4. Football
5. Fun

Within the context of that set of priorities, we teach accountability. Each student is held responsible to grow a little in each area. We have frequent team and individual meetings on the subject as time permits. During the off-season we meet at least once weekly to teach a concentrated lesson on the leadership component of Magnanimitas. I usually do the teaching, although we occasionally bring in guest lecturers. Also each student-athlete is required to do a specific number of hours of community service each school year. Each of them is monitored and noted and receives positive reinforcement for her or his time on duty. The lessons are tailored to current events, both in our sports culture and in the local community.

Internship Program
Bob Biggs
University of California, Davis (California)

If we as coaches start to give in to the argument that tough environments make it tougher on kids to adjust to the responsibilities of becoming responsible adults, then we just make it easier for them to continue to make excuses. There are too many examples in our program of guys from tough backgrounds making it to professional schools, great job opportunities, and successful relationships to allow student-athletes to use this crutch.

We have established a strong internship program with the internship office on our campus. They teach players how to interview, develop a resume, network, etc. Players are required to complete at least one internship (two is highly recommended) during the winter quarters of their third and fourth years with us.

This effort on our part shows the student-athletes that we genuinely do have their best interests in mind, and that they are not here just to play but also to enhance their career and academic experience with practical experience.

Professional Development for the Players
Larry Kindbom
Washington University (Missouri)

At the beginning of each year, we introduce a theme. It is a short, to-the-point statement that best identifies what we, as an organization, must master to be successful in that given year. Using outside reading and personal anecdotes, I will present the theme to them as something they can incorporate both into their individual lives as well as their roles as team members.

During the summer, I will write a series of five letters and send them to my players through the mail. I tell them to read the letter, put it away for 24 hours, then read it again. This past year the theme was "Finish." For the template of my letters, I used the "Ten Qualities that Employers Consider in Hiring." In each letter, I introduced two of the qualities and tied them in with our theme.

Reasons why I like to use the letters:

- Parents will oftentimes see the letters and begin discussion with the players at home.
- Because it is a series, our players look forward to the next correspondence.
- The players know that you care enough to send the letter, and a short personal thought on each letter makes the players feel even more special.

Summer Service
Jeff Ferguson
Totino-Grace High School (Minnesota)

Totino-Grace is a "Lasallian" Catholic school, and we place an emphasis on service.

In the summer, for a number of years now, our football team volunteers usually four to five times at Feed My Starving Children, packing food that is distributed to those in grave need around the world. It is one part of an educational emphasis on sharing our blessings with others.

Lasallian schools around the world are grounded in the philosophy of St. John Baptist de la Salle, the founder of the Christian Brothers and the patron saint of teachers.

One of St. de la Salle's tenets that our team has embraced as a motto is the phrase "Always with Faith and Zeal." We find it a great way not only to approach the game of football, but to approach one's life. The "Always" part of the phrase is a significant one to challenge oneself with. In talking to the team, we try to impact our players with the importance of that word . . . always. Not *sometimes* with faith and zeal . . . not *when things are going well* with faith and zeal. The real challenge is in trying to live your life ALWAYS with faith and zeal.

Accountability to Others and Responsibility for Others' Actions
Larry Hill
Smithson Valley High School (Texas)

One of the hardest lessons for any young man to learn is to become accountable to others. That is, young men must learn that their actions (good and bad) affect others. Likewise, as coaches we have noticed that young men have a difficult time accepting any responsibility for their peers' actions. For a team to succeed (and a family to succeed), it cannot be acceptable to think, "Well, I did what I'm supposed to do. My teammate's mistake is his own problem."

To combat these attitudes on our team, we instituted the concept of the "The Turk." The Turk is an assigned coach on our staff who has no prescribed duties during our off-season workout time other than to be the coach to which players are sent for a reminder session. The five minutes a group of players may spend with The Turk will not be pleasant. It is not an experience they will want to repeat. The punishment is quick, and then they are back to work. But it constantly reinforces what a team needs to do to become responsible to one another.

For example, we may have a group in the weight room going through a prescribed workout. Each weight rack will have a group of three players, all with an individual printed workout that details exactly how much weight and how many reps each set is to have. Each coach is assigned two to three racks to monitor. At random, the coach will pick an individual player to monitor. The coach will count the reps a player just did, or he may note the weight that was on the bar. The coach will then check that against what the workout sheet prescribes. If the player is not doing what is called for, the entire group will stop what they're doing, leave the weight room, and go to a session with The Turk. The player not following the workout is going for obvious reasons. He is not following the plan. The other two players are going to The Turk because they let it happen on their watch. When the five-minute session is over, the players will rejoin the weight room group.

We have found that The Turk session, though brief, is a constant reminder of teamwork. More than the physical punishment, the reinforcing of the concepts of what is really important makes an impression on our players.

It gives players a reason to be accountable to others (I can't afford to make this mistake. These guys will pay the price with me.) It gives players a reason to practice leadership (don't let a teammate make a mistake that affects us all).

To put a positive spin on it: we didn't avoid punishment together, we succeeded together. We didn't miss workout time to fix a problem for which we all have responsibility, instead we all got our work done. When things get tough during the season, we will not surrender. We will not point fingers and blame someone else. We will not shirk our role in letting it happen. We all helped each other and got to this point. We'll all fight through it together.

From a life lesson standpoint, it is hoped that these same ideas carry over. I will always do my best for my family. I will always realize that what I do will affect my family one way or another. I cannot let others in my family make mistakes. Their mistakes will affect our entire family. I have to have ownership in what all my family does.

The Contract
Chris Ramsey
Newman High School (Georgia)

We use the contract for all forms of discipline . . . quitting, getting in trouble in school, becoming ineligible, etc. The idea is to teach some form of responsibility for the situation the athlete is in, and that the status he enjoyed before has to be earned back.

The length of the contract would be determined by the amount of time before the next season would start. It might take several steps, each allowing the athlete to proceed to the next . . . normally a three- or four-step process.

Example: an athlete has been suspended from school, causing him to miss the remainder of the season. During this time, his grades have fallen, and he is headed to being ineligible for the next season.

1. *Step One.* He must bring in a weekly academic and behavior report from his teachers, as well as attend all weight training/off-season workouts. These must be completed with a good attitude and with the approval of his teachers and coaches to move to step two.

2. *Step Two.* He will be allowed to participate in spring practice, but it will be made clear that he has not earned his way back onto the team until all steps of the contract are completed.

3. *Step Three.* With the approval of his coaches based on effort and attitude, he must complete 90% of the entire summer program to be considered eligible to be reinstated to the team at the start of practice in August.

If all the steps have been completed to the satisfaction of the head coach and his staff, he may be reinstated with the provision that any violation of team rules or policies shall be grounds for immediate dismissal.

Jerry Kill
University of Minnesota (Minnesota)

Standing behind your actions—what you do as well as what you fail to do—is what accountability is. We will never be a team that makes excuses. We will have accountability on and off the field. We either get it done or we do not. As individuals on this team, we will have honesty and integrity in all that we do and say. If we are not honest with ourselves, how can we possibly get better as players, coaches, and people? It is through admitting what we did wrong that we have taken the first step to figuring out how to do it right. As individuals on this team, you must be accountable. As a team, there will be no other way. We offer no excuses. None are accepted.

We must be accountable and responsible for our actions at all times, and in all phases of our lives. We are here to help you deal with whatever circumstances may exist for you. Because we want you to be responsible for your actions, we do not want to be negligent in our presence in your lives, but we must always be responsible and act correctly.

Minnesota Team Rules:

1. *Act right.* Do not embarrass yourself, your team, or your university, and never lie.

2. *Be on time.* Being on time means being five minutes early and waiting to begin; this includes classes, meetings, training room, study table, and practice.

3. *Go to class.* There is no excuse to miss class. Also, turn in all assignments and prepare for all tests. We expect you to sit in the front two rows of class and get to know your professor.

4. *Play hard on game day.* We want to be known as a team that will line up and compete on every snap. We will be the most physical team in the conference. Take pride in playing hard. Great things happen to teams that work hard.

Conclusion

When the light goes on and an individual realizes he has an obligation and a responsibility to be accountable, the changes in that individual are apparent to everyone who knows him. When leadership roles are taken on, it matters not if it is on the football field, or as a husband, community leader, football coach, or captain of industry, the awesome responsibility of being accountable to those you lead is sobering, yet at the same time fulfilling. Life is not always peaches and cream; bad things happen to good people and good organizations. True leaders take responsibility even when the bad thing that happened was not their fault; the leader is responsible.

Abraham Lincoln, whom I admire greatly, had the awesome responsibility of conducting war with fellow Americans. Lincoln said, "I am not bound to win, but I am bound to be true; I am not bound to succeed, but I am bound to live up to what light I have." The light of which he speaks represents the knowledge that we have at any one time to make decisions and reflect on our accountability.

Walter Anderson, a German writer who died in 1962, penned these true and powerful words: "I am responsible. Although I may not be able to prevent the worst from happening, I am responsible for my attitude toward the inevitable misfortunes that darken life. Bad things do happen; how I respond to them defines my character and the quality of my life. I can choose to sit in a perpetual sadness, immobilized by the gravity of my loss, or I can choose to rise from the pain and treasure the most precious gift I have—life itself."

As coaches, we can exhibit through our own lives the value of a life and the precious gift that it is, to let those we lead see in us the person of accountability when things are bad and when things are good.

— 12 —

The Home

In a free society, there are three institutions that nurture children as they mature into adults. The three institutions are the home, the church, and the educational system. The home in America is no longer what it once was in our society. Statistics point to the fact that fatherless homes, dysfunctional two-parent homes, and homes with a negative male role model have adversely affected the children in those homes. Many trace the decline in church attendance to the lack of strong male leadership in some homes. If the home and the church are diminished, then the state educational systems end up with the responsibility of dealing with the social issues created by the change in our society. The importance of the role of the teacher/coach cannot be downplayed, as in many cases the teacher/coach is the last hope to influence for positive change in the lives of our young people.

My own observations and experiences have led me to believe that children from diminished home environments are more likely to grow up unable to figure out who they are and what they want to become in life. Most will grow up with a lack of economic stability, lacking in self-worth as well. And most importantly, many have never been taught a value system or a work ethic. Many do not seem to understand how to build healthy relationships with their peers. Some I have observed developed a tendency to give up on challenges easily. Most young people will imitate what they see in their fathers, and are blessed when they see and emulate positive character traits such as self-control, accountability, courage, and integrity. In the absence of positive male role models, youth will turn to their own peer groups, celebrities, musicians, and sports figures for role modeling. Children from homes with loving, caring parents statistically have a higher chance of succeeding and are most likely to garner the respect of their peers, teachers, and coaches. Therefore, children not living in a positive home environment will likely bring one or more of the negative social issues to the classroom or athletic field.

For negative social behavior to turn positive, and for a life to be changed, the child of the fatherless or dysfunctional home must hear of or see the example of a better way. Leo F. Buscaglia, a noted author, stressed the point that little, positive things can have a profound effect. Buscaglia said, "Too often we underestimate the power of a touch, a smile, a kind word, a listening ear, an honest compliment, or the smallest act of caring, all of which have the potential to turn a life around."

Many experts and statisticians point to the fatherless home as the heart of the societal crisis in America. However, I want to make one point extremely clear. There are thousands of outstanding young men in America who were raised by single moms. Through the mom's love, leadership, hard work, and demonstration of strong character traits, those young men found a value system and a work ethic allowing them to become extremely successful in life. Those moms should be recognized and praised for what they have done. Thankfully, in most cases, there has also been a positive male role model providing a positive influence in the lives of these young men. The positive male influence may have been a dynamic peer, family member, pastor, teacher, or coach. Where there is no positive male role model in the home, even with a magnificent mother's leadership, for young men there needs to be a positive male role model from elsewhere.

Football coaches must accept the fact that very often they must become a mentor, father figure, and positive male role model in the life of each athlete being coached. The great Kansas State coach Bill Snyder, in his book *They Said It Couldn't Be Done*, made an emphatic and true statement when he said, "I think I'm charged by their families to be a father, a mentor, and a teacher to young people. There are lessons of life that will also make you a better player on the field."

When Bill Snyder became the head football coach at Kansas State University, he led one of the greatest turnarounds in the annals of college football. Bill started his program from day one with what he called "Wildcat Goals for Success." Like a father to his children, Coach Snyder gave them a set of goals that have remained current and consistent through the years.

Wildcat Goals for Success
Coach Bill Snyder
Kansas State University (Kansas)

1. *Commitment.* "We want a feeling of commitment from everybody involved in the program, from our players, to our coaches, to our administration and fans. We want everyone committed to a common cause."

2. *Unity.* Come together as never before; there had to be a unity of 120 guys drawing close together based on the commonality of purpose and caring about one another and our team.

3. *Be tough.* The game of football exudes a toughness on the field, but there is also a mental toughness and a toughness to make the hard decisions.

4. *Great effort.* We stress that our players have complete control over each of their goals. Great effort is something every player on our team must have self-control over.

5. *Never give up.* This is the persistent part that every athlete must learn. "It's never over until it's over." Don't give in and never quit in a game or in the classroom.

6. *Refuse to allow failing to become a habit.* You may fail today, but our determination is to succeed the following day with the attitude that success will happen.

7. *Expect to win.* There are times when there is an indication that this game is going to be a difficult one. We might not win this game, but we expect to win it.

8. *Leadership.* We continually encourage our youngsters to be good examples to each other.
9. *Improve every day.* We tell every athlete we want him to have a goal to be a better person, a better student, and a better player every single day.
10. *Self-discipline.* Do it right and don't accept less; this means if you're doing something, do it the way it is supposed to be done and do it that way every time.
11. *Eliminate mistakes* (don't beat yourself). Consciously have control and eliminate mistakes that will keep you from winning.
12. *No self-limitation* (expect more of yourself). Everyone has expectations of other people; we must expect a great deal out of ourselves.
13. *Consistency.* Do all of the things we are charged to do as coaches and players, such as never missing a practice and being on time at meetings—be consistent.
14. *Responsibility.* There has to be accountability with each of our players, coaches, and staff members. Hold yourself accountable to those things over which you have control.
15. *Unselfish.* Team sports require unselfishness; in this day of self-gratification, that is not easy, but it is essential.
16. *Enthusiasm.* "Don't leave home without it." Our coaches are to create an attitude of enthusiasm in their players and in practice.

Coach Snyder's goals touch on a value system, positive character traits, and the basic fundamentals of personal success on and off the football field. Coach Snyder committed himself to being a father figure who would teach positive goals that any father would teach his own children.

Sharing —My Gift

Chapter 4 of this book is about the gift given to me by one of my high school coaches. The gift literally changed my life. The gift was a simple, yet profound concept: "Learn to control your own mind and you can control your future." I trusted my coach and bought into the concept, then realized the concept needed to be expanded into a plan for success. I began to call the concept "The Key to Success," and the mastery of the concept was not easy. However, once mastered, it began to make my life easier. Initially, not knowing what my mind needed to control, it took a little while for what I refer to as the four pillars of success to emerge into a plan. The four pillars were a positive attitude, total effort, self-discipline, and the capacity to really care.

After the key to success became instrumental in my personal development, it became a part of my coaching philosophy, and through the years I taught the concept of "mind control" to my athletes, children, staff, and family members.

"Mind control" can and should be taught in different ways. The concept of mind control and the mastery of the four pillars changed my life. It is a sure fact that if the "key to success" can change the life of an individual who is blessed with the background of values, then it certainly can change the lives of young people who were not blessed with the background I had but who were the products of dysfunctional and fatherless homes. If individuals buy into and master the "key to success," they will be successful no matter their background.

A positive attitude is extremely important, because when things do not go according to plan, the positive attitude allows you to regroup, rethink, and try again. Attaining total effort every day is humanly not sustainable 100 percent of the time, but trying is essential. Early on, the mastery of self-discipline for me disallowed alcohol, drugs, and tobacco. It made me slow to anger and gave me control of my own tongue. Finally, the greatest form of motivation is self-motivation. Self-motivation is ignited by our capacity to really care: care about ourselves, care about others, and care about succeeding.

Discovering the Needs

For the last couple of years, the AFCA staff has hosted several meetings of high school coaches, athletic directors, and executive directors of high school associations from across America. The meetings were purposefully small, so that we could have meaningful discussions of the needs and specific issues faced by all three groups representing high school football. The meetings were held at our national headquarters in Waco, Texas. We mostly just listened to the three groups as they talked about the issues and problems they faced. In one of the sessions with high school coaches from smaller districts in central Texas, this question was asked of me, "Coach Teaff, if for some reason you were only allowed in a single year to teach your players one thing that you believe would change their lives, what would that one thing be?" Without hesitation, I said, "The key to success." Several of the coaches had heard me speak about the key to success in various meetings and in a recent meeting in Dallas, Texas. I spoke on the issue of character development of high school athletes. We discussed the key to success and then went on to another subject. Later I received a phone call from one of the high school coaches in the room asking for a way to implement the key to success in his high school. I drew up a plan of implementation and sent it to the coach. Other coaches have seen it and are excited about it, so I have decided to share it with all coaches. The concept of the key to success will most likely be something that young people from fatherless and dysfunctional homes will not have been taught. My experience has been that when young people are taught the key to success and buy into it, their lives change because they are in control of the powerful forces within them that will determine success in their lives on and off the athletic field.

The Key to Success—Implementation Plan
Grant Teaff

The *key to success* is built around an individual's ability to control their own mind. In controlling one's own mind, specifically concentrate on four mind control functions that, when accomplished, will lead to certain success in any area of involvement.

Think of an individual's aspirations to achieve success in life as a house of success.

Like any structure, a house of success must be built on a firm foundation. In ancient times, huge pillars of stone were used to support the four corners of any building, stabilizing and supporting the structure.

The four pillars that must be mastered through mind-control are:

Pillar 1. Attitude (positive, expecting success, a can-do attitude)

Pillar 2. Total Effort (every day, every way on every play, on and off the field)

Pillar 3. Self-Discipline (control emotions, eliminate poor decisions and stupid mistakes)

Pillar 4. The Capacity to Care (when we emotionally care we emotionally prepare and that motivates us to greater heights).

Note: every coach and staff member should master the *key to success* and live by it, as it is essential for the coaches to live what they teach. "All sermons preached should be validated through the way the preacher lives the sermon." In other words, if you believe in it and you are going to teach it, then you have to use it in your everyday life.

Teaching Mind Control

The head coach should present the plan to the staff.

1. Head coach should discuss each pillar, asking for ideas and comments about the presentations.
2. Have the staff personally prepare for the upcoming two weeks by gathering resource material and planning their presentations.
3. Prepare appropriate signs: bold sigs in appropriate places highlighting the theme of the week, for example, *Attitude.*
4. Coordinators and assistant coaches plan to use a quote, statement, story, or visual aid to draw attention to the pillar being emphasized
5. The head coach's responsibility is to present to the team the *key to success* and each day, before or after practice, do a short presentation magnifying the pillar.
6. On the day preceding the week's game, during a meeting, the head coach should ask the athletes to talk about the pillar from their point of view and what they might have learned about themselves and their ability to control their own mind.

7. At the first team meeting after game day, the head coach should talk about the contribution the concept of mind control had on the victory. If it was a loss, the head coach should be very positive and clearly point out, "With adherence by more of the players to the pillar, a victory could have been attained."

8. Throughout the eight-week application of the *key to success*, the previously studied pillars should become a part of the coaching staff's vernacular. Coaches should use words like, "expect to win," "have positive expectations," "think like a winner," "believe you will win," "commit yourself to making a positive contribution to your team," etc.

The keys to success planned by the coaching staff should be inclusive—the cheerleaders, administration, band, and faculty should all be asked to be a part of the *key to success* initiative.

Imagine an entire school that for eight weeks made an effort to control their attitude, their effort, their self-discipline, and their capacity to really care.

The Parents and Guardians

At the beginning of the year, a meeting should be held asking the parents and guardians to attend. The head coach should explain the concept of the *key to success* and how it will be implemented for the team. He should ask the families to join in, so there will be the same mentality at the athlete's home as there is in the dressing room and the hallways.

Parents need to be shown how the implementation of mind control will positively affect their children's success on the athletic field, but more importantly, their success in the classroom and in the community.

The purpose would be to create a home environment similar to the environment you are creating in the school. Your inclusive effort could very well change your community as well as the lives of some of the parents.

The implementation should start the week before the first ball game.

1. Parent/guardian meeting should be held to enlist the families' involvement in the *key to success*
2. The entire week prior to the first game should be focused on the concept of mind control (*key to success*)
3. The week following the first game will be designated as Week 1
4. Week 1 and Week 2 – Attitude
5. Weeks 3 and 4 – Effort
6. Weeks 5 and 6 – Self-Control
7. Weeks 7 and 8 – The Capacity to Care

With the weeks remaining to the end of the season, playoffs, or bowl games, renew an emphasis on all or parts of the *key to success*.

Tiger Dadz
Chad Rogers
Snyder High School (Texas)

The staff selected trusted, quality men from the community who were vetted and ultimately asked by the head coach to serve as Tiger Dadz. The first group, after being selected as mentors, was trained on the Do's and Don'ts according to local, state, scholastic, and NCAA rules. They were asked to be encouragers, friends, and mentors.

They were asked to stress character, leadership, and accountability. The Tiger Dadz attended practices and games to show their constant support and commitment to the athletes they were mentoring. This program has given each player a positive role model outside the home who cares for them and is someone they can trust and count on when they need to talk to or get advice. Tiger Dadz are trained to be able to incorporate counsel and advice on peer pressure and the importance of respect and attitude.

Each year, the players are very excited about their mentors. They are anxious to know who that person will be. Through Tiger Dadz, the athletes know someone cares about them besides their family and coaches. Tiger Dadz are asked to live what they teach, just as the coaches are asked the same.

Process:

1. Select and vet quality men from the community.
2. All new Tiger Dadz (mentors) must be recommended by current mentors.
3. Once selected, several training sessions are held.
4. Do's and Don'ts according to local, state, scholastic, and NCAA rules are taught.
5. Tiger Dadz are asked to be encouragers, friends, and mentors.
6. Mentors are asked to stress and teach character, leadership, and accountability.
7. Tiger Dadz attend practices and games to show their support and commitment.
8. Each player now has a positive male role model whom he can trust and count on.
9. Counseling and advising on peer pressure are very important.
10. Tiger Dadz teach respect and a positive attitude and praise improved work ethic.

Locals and Legends
Andy McNeely
Plattsburg High School (Missouri)

The Locals and Legends program is designed to provide positive male role models who have graduated from Plattsburg High School, and we team the Legends up with our current high school athletes. All of the Legends played football at Plattsburg. The program in turn feeds itself, as we have been doing this for four years and we have former players wanting to come back and mentor some of our athletes.

Each Thursday night at our team meal, we have one of our senior players and his mentor speak to our team. In this speech they have to cover three criteria:

1. What does playing football at Plattsburg High School mean to the current player? Then the legend speaks on what it meant to him during his playing days. (done by both Local and Legend)

2. What did having a mentor mean to his self-esteem, study habits, self-motivation, and overall decision-making? (done by the Local)

3. Speak on the responsibility he feels with having a young man who relies on guidance from him. (done by the Legend)

These Thursday night team meals have been emotional and quite the team-bonding exercise.

This program has dramatically increased our player graduation rate, our player eligibility, and our attendance at both home and away activities. Our players who have finished the program feel a sense of playing for something bigger than themselves. They feel a responsibility of not letting down their "Legends" who have given much of their time to help guide them.

At the end of the season, we have a banquet for our Legends. This banquet has become quite the tradition. We honor all the Legends for the sacrifices they have made for the betterment of the players in our football program.

The Dog Pound
Keith Willis
Marlin High School (Texas)

Willing, qualified men from the community are paired up with players who have been cut from the team for various reasons. This program provides the players with an opportunity to earn their way back on the team.

With the guidance of the mentors, the players must meet certain requirements set by the coaching staff to be eligible for reinstatement. The requirements are given to the players, mentors, and parents to ensure everyone is clear on the expectations. The mentors are also actively engaged with the team by participating in the chain crew during home games and traveling with the team to help load and unload equipment for away games.

Requirements for Reinstatement

1. Make 22 of 24 two-a-day summer practice sessions
2. Complete 20 hours of community service
3. Pass a drug test

The Dog Pound provides a positive male role model who helps instill accountability, discipline, and respect for authority. The program is a second chance for players to put in the necessary work to be a part of the team and realize they are not entitled to a spot.

In the first year of the program, there were six players who were reinstated to the team by completing the requirements. Going through this program and being on the football team can help save lives, so reaching just one would be a success.

Become a Mentor
Russ Huesman
University of Tennessee—Chattanooga (Tennessee)

We started something recently that I hope makes a difference in some of our at-risk athletes. Instead of getting them mentors or pushing help on them, we are turning *them* into mentors. We are forcing them to grow up by being mentors to at-risk youth at a local boxing club. We are sending seven of our football players who have been discipline issues for us to this gym once a week to become mentors to these athletes who are dealing with problems of their own.

I explained to these athletes that they will not only be helping some at-risk youth, they will be helping themselves. A lot of times when we do community service only the "good ones" volunteer to help, and our athletes with social issues are never involved. I wanted these athletes to know that this is not a punishment, but a chance for them to make a difference in someone else's life. I hope that they respond and see how good their lives are compared to the people they will be mentoring.

Home Visits
Johnny Tusa
Waco High School (Texas)

No kid has ever gone home and put himself in a bad light. So our purpose of home visits was to communicate to the parent what our expectations were and to see what their environment looked like.

We needed to know who was in control of that situation and the thought process of the parent(s). Was there a father? Was he a positive role model? We were trying to get a picture of what the overall circumstances of the family were. These visits heightened our awareness of what our role was going to be with that child.

List of Topics Discussed during the Home Visit

- Last year's assessment (if applicable)
- Classroom/academic expectations
- Football expectations
- Personal expectations
- Spiritual expectations
- Road trip details

Meetings were conducted at all varsity players' homes during the summer. The coaching staff worked with the parents and players to help correct any imbalances in responsibilities and time management to give the child the best opportunity to be a productive student and player.

The home visits were a way to help manage a child for success by understanding their circumstances and providing support where needed. Knowing what kind of support, responsibilities, and home environment the child had helped the coaching staff better understand, interact with, and coach the player.

Alumni Mentors
George Smith
St. Thomas Aquinas High School (Florida)

Coach Smith keeps in contact with certain guys who have played on his football team. These are usually guys whom he feels could help out current or future players at St. Thomas Aquinas. Some of these guys are local. Coach Smith may reach out to a guy if he knows that he is in town and say, "There is a guy here I think you may be able to provide some direction for." Coach may let these two guys talk one-on-one in his office, or the two may meet for lunch to be in a different environment. Many times this creates an ongoing relationship between the current player and the mentor.

Coach Smith also invites mentors to practices and games to keep them engaged. His reasoning is that he wants the current players to see someone who has been through the football program and has had some success in whatever form. There are guys who had a mentor and have gone on to be very successful. These guys come back and keep the cycle going.

This Alumni Mentor program provides the kids with a living example of someone who has been exactly where they are and has lived what the coaches emphasize every day. These guys come back and say the same things the coaches say, but the kids pay more attention because it's coming from someone who has lived it and has come from the same background as them.

Dad's Night
Lee Bridges
John Paul Stevens High School (Texas)

Because we have such a large school district, we do not get to have a parent introduction night at our varsity games. We pick a game of significance and secretly contact the significant adult male in each varsity player's life (father, big brother, grandfather, uncle, etc.), and we invite these men into our dressing room while the team is on the field for pre-game warm-up (the kids do not know that they are going to be there in the dressing room).

When the kids come in, the adult men are there waiting on them, and talk and visit with them about the game or whatever. If a young man does not have someone, we ask his position coach to stand with him. Most of the adult males have been in a dressing room in this situation (some never have) since they were in high school. I say a few words about the importance that each man has brought into his young man's life and thank them for that. I also talk briefly about the things that only men get to share; one of them is this moment and the game of football.

They stand/kneel arm in arm for our team prayer (led by a player in the dressing room), and I give our last-minute instructions and "fire-up" words and break to the field. You need to be out of the doorway or you could get mashed as they leave. We have had some amazing things in these situations—one player's father was able to come home from Iraq, and several have had dads come from other places around the world and the U.S. where they were stationed or deployed.

Conclusion

It is immaterial whether you think of yourself as a father figure, a mentor, or just a positive example. What is important is that as a coach you develop a plan to teach and to influence "beyond the game." You may develop your own methods or use any one of your fellow coaches' suggestions. Whether you use another coach's ideas or develop your own, it is recommended that you include all or part of the following in your teaching and coaching.

Teaching necessities

Developing core values leads to positive character traits. Those you teach should see in you and your staff the values and character traits that you are stressing.

Fairness and consistency in dealing with discipline issues leads to proper behavior and positive leadership, as well as respect.

Remember, your teaching and influence should go far "beyond the game."

Character

"If it's worth doing, it's worth doing right." "If you start it, finish it." Those two extraordinarily instructive quotes are not from a renowned leader, captain of industry, or famous preacher. They are from a great man with only a high school education. That man was my father, Bill Teaff. I loved his words as they became ingrained in my own persona, but I learned the true meaning of his words by watching the man as he lived life on a daily basis. He taught me with words and action. Whether his words were his or from another source, I don't know, but I do know that ultimately his actions verified his beliefs.

Bill Teaff's Lessons on Character

- *"Treat others as you would like to be treated."* In my chosen profession I have applied that lesson; I coached as I wanted to be coached. My dad would use words to plant seeds, and as I grew and matured, he continued to water those planted seeds.
- *"Your word is your bond."* I remember when I first heard the quote at an early age, I questioned my dad, "What is a bond?" He said, "A bond is a binding agreement,

written or oral, so fundamentally it means if you give somebody your word (tell someone you will do something), then you are obligated to do what you said you would do."

- *"Be trustworthy and honest."* I learned a trustworthy person is dependable, reliable, ethical, upright, and honorable. I was told a trustworthy person is responsible and deserving of trust.

- *"Be truthful, never tell a lie."* Dad followed up with an explanation, "If you never lie, you don't have to remember what you said."

- *"Curse words have no place in instructions or in general conversation."* If you feel you have to use curse words to communicate, I would say your vocabulary is woefully lacking.

- *"You are who you are when no one can see you."* Our conduct when we are alone or when we think no one knows who we are shows who we really are.

- *"Never fail because you got outworked."* He also said it in another way, "Do whatever it takes to get the job done." An early development of a work ethic is a foundation for success. My mentality became, "You may have more talent, you may have more resources, but you will never outwork me."

- *"You are responsible for your actions."* To me that statement meant what it said: "Whatever I do in my life and with my life is totally my responsibility."

- *"Love our country, its freedoms and opportunities."* I saw World War II through the eyes of a child when my father and other relatives were serving in the military, seeing the sacrifices and the patriotism of those at home and hearing that men and women were sacrificing their lives for our freedom. I developed a deep respect and love for the United States of America, its flag, and the freedom it provided me to pursue my goals and dreams.

- *"Be generous with your resources."* My father would literally give someone the shirt off his back and constantly served others with his time, talent, and resources. Regarding generosity, he said to me on many occasions, "You just can't outgive God."

Character Defined

The modern definition of character is this: the attributes or features that distinguish an individual. Character is mental and ethical traits. Character is moral excellence and firmness and is the mental and moral qualities distinctive to an individual. I have long sought to surround myself with individuals with positive character traits. Discerning the character of each individual athletic recruit was paramount to my total philosophy. The same held true for staff members, employees, and friends. Who we associate with is essential, because human beings have a propensity to blend into their surroundings.

Growing up in a home in which positive character traits were intentionally taught, I was further impacted by similar words and lessons under the influence of my teachers and coaches. Many of the things I had been taught by my family were verified by my teachers and coaches in the classroom and on the athletic fields. My coaches were family men and men of integrity who cared for me as a person even more than for me as an athlete. The game and the classroom were both challenges for me, but I found a truth: if I applied the work ethic taught by my family, teachers, and coaches, I would succeed, and I did.

Sports Builds Character?

Like thousands who have played the game, I am convinced that the very nature and nuances of the game, when taught properly, build character.

Douglas MacArthur, one of America's great military leaders, said, "Sports is a vital character-builder. It molds the youth of our country for their roles as custodians of the Republic. It teaches them to be strong enough to know that they are weak and brave enough to face themselves when they are afraid. It teaches them to be proud and unbending in honest defeat, but humble and gentle in victory . . . it gives them a predominance of courage over timidity, of appetite for adventure over loss of ease" (Douglas MacArthur as quoted by James Chu).

Another Opinion

I would not be totally honest if I did not say that there are learned men and women who debunk character-building through sports. An eight-year study by Ogilvie and Tutko in 1971 disallowed the concept that competition builds character:

> For eight years, we have studied the effects of competition on personality. On the evidence gathered in this study, we can make some broad-range value judgments. We found no empirical support for the tradition that sport builds character. Indeed, there is evidence that athletic competition limits growth in some areas. It seems that the personality of the ideal athlete is not the result of any molding process, but comes out of the ruthless selection process that occurs at all levels of sport. Athletic competition has no more beneficial effects than intense endeavor in any other field.[24]

Respectful Disagreement

I certainly respect the researchers' conclusion; however, from my own personal experience and involvement with athletics closely for over six decades, I would respectfully disagree.

Many past and present leaders such as General Douglas MacArthur believe strongly in the values that could be and are being taught through sports to the youth of America. After three years of research and work on this book designed to provide solutions to today's social issues, I am thoroughly convinced that teaching a young person to become an individual of character provides a solution for all social issues with which we are now confronted. Helping a young person develop character and integrity is the greatest gift a coach or teacher can give.

The Institute of Ethics

Early in the year 1999, I received a phone call from someone I did not know. His name was Michael Josephson, a lawyer by trade, and as I found out, a passionate evangelical guardian of character development for the youth of America. Mr. Josephson at that early date had already come to the conclusion that our great nation was sinking into the sunset with the potential of America being obscured by the loss of positive character traits in our youth. Mr.

Josephson explained to me his belief that sports, when taught and done properly, could be the great teacher for America from sea to shining sea.

The Summit

Mr. Josephson's organization was called the Institute of Ethics, and he was calling for a summit of men and women across America who were involved with sports. The summit was designed to find ways to increase ethics, sportsmanship, and character-building. The meeting was to be held in Scottsdale, Arizona, on May 25, 1999. I told Mr. Josephson that I would be there to represent thousands of football coaches, the members of the American Football Coaches Association.

I was not sure what to expect, but when I arrived at the summit, I was blown away by the quality of the fifty participants representing most of the stakeholders in sports. There were athletic directors, coaches, and heads of various sporting organizations and associations. Among the notables were John Wooden, legendary basketball coach; sportscaster Bob Costas; and renowned actor Tom Selleck. Fifty invited members of the summit worked for two days and hammered out "The Arizona Accord," whose purpose was to challenge athletic programs to put character-building and sportsmanship ahead of everything else, including winning. The Accord was sent out to conference commissioners, the NCAA, and athletic directors, as well as (through the AFCA) every football coach in our membership. At one meeting John Wooden said that he told his players, "be more concerned with your character than your reputation, because your character is what you really are, while your reputation is merely what others think you are." During the same session, Michael Josephson described character in this way: "Character is doing the right thing when it costs more than you want to pay." I, of course, had never met Tom Selleck, but he was so down to earth and affable that I felt like I had known him for a long time. He was already a huge star by Hollywood standards and since 1999 has had many starring roles in movies and television. Observing him and enjoying his many roles in movies and on television, it is very apparent that the emphasis he placed on positive character development during the summit has been lived out through the roles he has chosen.

Governor Jane D. Hull of Arizona opened the meeting with a pledge of support for the outcome of the group's discussions. In ninety minutes, legendary coach John Wooden, NBC announcer Bob Costas, and Bill Dwyer, sports editor of the *Los Angeles Times*, led an inspiring discussion. The premise of our meeting and the outcome can be summed up with this statement: "Sports can and should enhance the character and uplift the ethics of the nation."

The Accord

The accord declares:

- Participation in sports is a privilege, not a right, and athletes and coaches have a duty to conduct themselves as role models, on and off the field.
- Recruitment discussions for educational institutions must be based on the specific determination that the athlete is seriously considering committing to getting an education and has or will develop the academic skills and character to succeed.
- The academic, emotional, and moral well-being of athletes always must be placed above desires and pressures to win.
- Coaches and athletes must refrain from all forms of disrespectful conduct, including verbal abuse, taunting, trash-taking, and unseemly celebrations. The leadership of high school, youth, and other sports programs must ensure that all coaches, paid or volunteer, are basically competent in character development techniques, first aid, and principles of effective coaching.
- Sports leaders should promote sportsmanship and foster the development of good character by teaching, enforcing, advocating, and modeling the six "pillars of character," which are trustworthiness, respect, responsibility, fairness, caring, and good citizenship.
- All participants pledge to mount extensive communication and training programs throughout their organizations and to seek widespread adoptions of the Accords' principles.

The AFCA's Commitment to the Accord

A press release carried statements from all the participants in the summit. My response read, "The impact of this accord will depend on its implementation. The American Football Coaches Association is deeply committed to the character-building message of this accord. A detailed plan to make character-building a centerpiece of the future of the AFCA will include our publications and conventions and will continue to support the sportsmanship issues by working with the NCAA." Since that time, the AFCA has promoted many initiatives in regard to character development through coaching the sport of football.

Prior to the summit in Arizona, the AFCA joined with the NCAA in emphasizing the importance of sportsmanship in our game. The AFCA has supported tougher penalties by the NCAA and the conferences for any altercations or brawls on the football field. The AFCA called for nationwide consistency in officiating sportsmanship penalties. Over the last nineteen years, we have had more speakers at our convention speaking on leadership and character development than almost any other subjects. The AFCA is still promoting the premise that "sports can and should enhance the character and uplift the ethics of the nation." Although there are cynics regarding the value of sports in character development, the overwhelming majority of those involved in sports believe that not only can we use sports to develop positive character traits, we must.

As coaches, teaching young people to become individuals of character provides an automatic solution to all the social issues we now confront. Helping young people develop character and integrity is another gift coaches can give. Remember these paraphrased words of Edgar A. Guest: those you are teaching learn more about character by watching you than by hearing what you say.

Afterglow

To my knowledge, the majority of the participants in the Arizona summit have continued in their own areas to make a difference in character in America. One example would be Michael Josephson, who created the Josephson Institute of Ethics as a nonprofit organization to honor his parents through the Institute's mission to improve society's ethics by changing personal and organizational decision-making and behavior. Shortly after our meeting in Arizona, the Institute did a preliminary survey called *The 2000 Report Card on America's Youth.* The survey included 8600 high school students, who revealed that the following had occurred in the previous year (1999):

- 71% admitted they had cheated on an exam at least once, and almost half said they had done so two or more times
- 92% lied to their parents; 78% lied to a teacher; 25% said they would lie to get a job
- 40% of males and 30% of females said they had stolen something from a store
- 16% said they had been drunk in school
- 68% said they hit someone because they were angry
- 60% of male students said they could get a gun if they wanted to.

Those statistics, accumulated one year after the summit, verified the need for the summit then, and because of the dramatic increase in fatherless homes since 2000, the need for character development is even greater now.[25]

Developing Positive Character Traits

Character Lessons
Frederick Bouchard
Staley High School (Missouri)

I decided we would begin to institute the principles of *Coaching to Change Lives* by Dennis Parker and D. W. Rutledge. Four years ago, I bought every one of their DVDs and our coaching staff spent a part of each off-season listening to those DVDs and putting those ideas into action. I don't think there are many things we have done as a program that will impact long-term improvement as much as being committed to doing regularly scheduled character development with our team. Truly, I don't believe that more coaching of a technique or fundamental would have made our team as successful as the time we spent doing our character lessons.

Here's how we implemented this program:

- *Pre-season camps and practices.* We would do our lessons in our locker room at the stadium in our teaching area. If we are supposed to be on the field at 8:00 a.m., we would have the required meeting and reporting time for the lesson at 7:30 a.m. If they are going to talk football, we would bring them in at 7:00 a.m. for that conversation or do it after practice.

     Monday: Lesson introduction
     Tuesday: Lesson follow-up
     Wednesday: Lesson follow-up
     Thursday: Closure
     Friday: Comments related to the lesson, implementation, and/or making reference for our future

- *In Season.* School gets out at 2:20 p.m., and the players need to be in their meeting areas at 2:25 p.m. They will meet until 2:45, and practice starts after the meeting.

     Monday: JV, sophomores, and freshmen are often gone (no lesson). Varsity does scouting report and practice.
     Tuesday: Lesson introduction
     Wednesday: Lesson follow-up
     Thursday: Lesson closure
     Friday: Make references to Friday night's game related to the lesson

There are dozens of good "character" programs around, but we hooked into this one and it has worked well for us and our needs. I would strongly recommend this to any football program and any football coach for immediate implementation.

Character Lessons
Randy Allen
Highland Park High School (Texas)

At the close of any practice, there is a moment in which character is systematically taught. This is done through what is called a "listening square." After practice, the players run to the head coach and are then asked to get into a listening square to make eye contact with the coach and use their listening skills. The head coach, or one of his assistants, is assigned a character trait to bring up and talk about for five minutes. Because I strongly believe in this process, I give the coaches a calendar that includes the dates and the topics they are to discuss with the team. I have been inspired as I have listened to coaches talk to their players about a particular character trait. The character traits that we teach in our athletic program are the twenty-six traits listed in the legendary coach John Wooden's pyramid of success:

Work Ethic	Condition	Faith
Friendship	Skill	Competitive
Loyalty	Team Spirit	Greatness
Cooperation	Poise	Patience
Enthusiasm	Confidence	Integrity
Self-Control	Ambition	Reliability
Alertness	Adaptability	Honesty
Initiative	Resourcefulness	Sincerity
Intentness	Fight	

I offer my players a voluntary book study program before school. It is another means by which I can influence my players in developing their integrity and character. We have studied Wooden's devotional book in past years. We met on Wednesday mornings at 7:30 a.m. Each week, one of the athletes was designated to bring donuts. I'm not quite sure if they came for the book study or the sprinkled donuts, but they came. At the beginning of the meetings, a student leader asked if anyone had a prayer request. Each athlete always prayed for the person seated to his right. Each one was also asked to read a paragraph and discuss what was read. Lunch period is an alternative for holding a book study program. At Converse Judson High School, the athletes meet at lunch for "brown bag" meetings. They eat in the field house while discussing the assigned chapter. Having a book study before school or during lunch is a great opportunity for teaching character and also for developing more personal relationships with your players.

Character Coach
Don Carthel
West Texas A&M University (Texas)

We are fortunate to have an FCA Character Coach and Chaplain serve our entire athletic department. He will be beginning his fifth year in this role. One way we use him is to host a Character Class during the fall for our entire incoming freshman class.

His class sessions cover the social topics listed: making wise decisions, time management, personal vision-casting and goal setting, personal discipline, how to treat females properly, and many other lessons that young freshman men face. In addition, he will be teaching a character and leadership development curriculum this year.

Our Character Coach also holds a volunteer mentoring luncheon each Friday in the spring in our cafeteria. This is a very informal time of sharing about life's problems, and relationship building as well as a brief prayer time.

In addition to serving freshman players, our Character Coach meets as needed with our upperclassmen for one-on-one mentoring sessions. I believe all of these "touches" we provide help our athletes with the many social issues they face as college athletes.

Life Skills/Panther Game Plan
Todd Graham
Arizona State University (Arizona)

We have an excellent program linked with our compliance department entitled Life Skills/Panther Game Plan. This program provides guidance and direction to our players from the time they arrive on campus to the day they graduate and leave the program.

The plan is an innovative collection of programs, workshops, and resources to assist student-athletes with valuable tools necessary for success both in college and life after. Some of the program initiatives include the following: academic excellence, athletic achievement, career development/graduate, etc. It is headed up by a member of the university who works closely with our coaching staff and mirrors what the head coach is emphasizing as a teaching point from week to week.

Beyond winning football games, our desire is to help our players become better men through their experience as football players.

Underground Railroad Journey
David Buchanan
Mason County High School (Kentucky)

Unique to our area, we did an Underground Railroad "Journey" with the leadership of our team. The Underground Railroad was a system to assist enslaved people to freedom from the South to the North. Our town, Maysville, Kentucky, sits right on the Ohio River—the dividing line between slave and free. The themes included leadership, service to others, and courage.

The Underground Railroad Journey was led by a national expert on the Underground Railroad who grew up in Maysville. He took our leadership group and me to a home on the Kentucky side of the river and the Rankin House on the Ohio side. At both sites, and on the trip from Maysville to the Rankin House, he told stories and tried to motivate and encourage our guys. His themes were courage, leadership, and service to others.

Judging by their attentiveness and their comments after the journey, it got the attention of the players. Several thought it was one of the best things they had ever done. As a coach, I liked it because it made the leadership/character traits we encourage come alive. They heard about real examples. They saw how those traits changed the world for the better.

Post-Practice Dialogue
Bill Snyder
Kansas State University (Kansas)

We have a series of "Team Goals for Success," which are intrinsic values. We discuss these daily with our players and provide examples, and after practice each day our players break up into pairs (with a different partner each day) and have dialogue about these values and how they impact their lives now and in the future.

Over a period of time, each player is paired with nearly everyone in the program. They are given a topic to discuss, having 1½ minutes each to share their feelings. Some of the countless topics provided are the following:

- Who is the most important person in your life?
- Who is the most inspirational person in your life? Why?
- What was the most difficult time in your life?
- What was the happiest moment of your life?
- Who is your best friend? Talk about him.
- How do you see your life in 20 years? 30 years? . . . etc.

These and many other topics are designed to allow players truly to get to know each other and draw closer together.

Support Staff
Dabo Swinney
Clemson University (South Carolina)

We are very fortunate to have an administration that has allowed us the opportunity to build a strong support staff that surrounds our players.

Director of Player Relations. This position mentors our student-athletes and has an organized, systematic plan of teaching our young men life skills that challenge them to be men of character. The Director of Player Relations also organizes and directs at least two team community outreach events each year.

Freshman Player Development. This position was added to our support staff this past year. It will take the freshmen and mentor them through their entire first year of transition. There are several issues, from homesickness to playing time, that all freshmen must deal with.

Chaplain Ministry. Under the umbrella of FCA, we offer our players counseling, weekly Bible studies, and pre-game devotions.

Reflection
David Taynor
Urbana University (Ohio)

Learning Log

If you are to be successful in life, you must constantly be pursuing growth in all aspects of your life, otherwise known as learning. The log is a plan to encourage self-discipline and accountability as it relates to life-long development.

The objective of the log is to create a sense of accountability by logging our strategic efforts learned through our experiences (emphasis placed on professional development) and increasing our awareness of the effects of our actions.

Developmental Cards

Weekly personal assessments are completed by coaches and players, including strengths and weaknesses. The assessments will be in the areas of character and academics.

Player Journal

Each player journals on the block that is emphasized during that week, highlighting their interpretations and how that block applies personally and programmatically.

Individual Player Meetings

Assistant coaches have academic/character development meetings with each of their position players once a week. Point of emphasis is rotated by area of individual needs for the player.

Player, Personal Development Program
Vic Wallace
Rockford College (Illinois)

I think I originally entered the coaching profession because I loved everything involved in the athletic arena and I did not want to give up athletics with my last college game. A month after graduation, I signed a contract as a high school head coach and began reflecting back to my years of competition and how my coaches had developed me as a person. I have been teaching and learning while I teach ever since.

Being a member of an athletic team is an integral component of a person's education for the future. Through the medium of athletics I teach the importance of respect, responsibility, accountability, and trust. I teach work ethic. I teach self-image and self-respect. I am a big believer in the importance of having a high standard of excellence in everything a person does. I teach "it is fun to set high standards of excellence and high goals." I teach the elements of teamwork: "it is fun to need and fun to be needed." I teach resilience: "it is fun to bounce back after a defeat." I teach persistence: "it is fun to be determined to achieve a goal." It is easy to set a goal. I teach the process of achieving a goal. I teach leadership and how to follow a leader: "it is fun to lead, it is fun to follow."

I sincerely believe the successes of my teams on the field are more directly related to the teaching of these elements of character than they are to the teaching of offense and defense. These character elements are the things I took from athletics and the things my players take into their careers and personal lives. I sincerely believe the values my students learn justify the money spent by the football program as being part of the students' educational experience.

Along with athletic talent, a person's ability to achieve is determined by his specific character and values. I train my staff to develop our players in the fourteen areas listed below. Many coaches leave development of these areas to chance. I believe it is very important to focus on them and teach them. Whatever a player's present level of proficiency in these areas, they can improve through instruction, application, and focus.

During the off-season and as an integral part of pre-season practice, I and my staff will conduct classes teaching and discussing these fourteen areas of concern. In-season, we relate to these daily in normal practice and games. Throughout the year we have one-on-one tutoring sessions for players needing special work on these.

Respect	Standard of Excellence
Responsibility	Team Work
Accountability	Resilience
Trust	Persistence
Work Ethic	Goal Achievement
Self-Image	Leadership
Self-Esteem	Being a Good Follower

Servant Leadership and Becoming a Man of Courage
Wendell Smith, Assistant Head Coach
Ottawa University (Kansas)

I believe one of the best ways to address disrespect and character is our emphasis on *Servant Leadership* and *Becoming a Man of Courage*. If we can develop the Servant-Leader traits on our team, teaching our young men to be *selfless* and to put the needs of others before their own, we will develop a generation of respectful and considerate leaders. Our Servant-Leader emphasis encourages the positive leadership traits of Integrity, Consistency, and Truthfulness. We discuss the importance of Positive Attitude and becoming a Positive Influence. Our attitude as coaches, as well as the attitudes of our players, establishes the prevailing atmosphere for our team. When we demonstrate respect, and *consistently value the needs of others before our own*, we will develop and experience an atmosphere of respect. Our emphasis on Becoming a Man of Courage focuses on *character and integrity*. Courageous leadership requires individual initiative to do the *RIGHT* thing despite what others may think, say, or do. Leadership is positively influencing others to go in a direction other than the one in which they are already headed, initiating change. We encourage doing what is right and standing up for one's beliefs. The Rev. Billy Graham once said, "Courage is contagious. When a brave man takes a stand, the spines of others are often stiffened." Dr. Martin Luther King Jr. once said, "The ultimate measure of a man is not where he stands in moments of comfort and convenience, but where he stands at times of challenge and controversy." Encouraging our young men to make positive choices on and off the field, to stand up for what they believe in, and to become positive influences on our campus and in our community will be life lessons they can utilize long after their playing days are over.

We want our players to become good husbands and fathers, reliable employees, and responsible citizens. We expect their best on the field, in the classroom, on and off campus. We, as coaches, must work to be positive examples and leaders of our players—we must be respectful, and we must be men of integrity and character if we expect the same from our young men.

David Howes
Rio Rancho High School (New Mexico)

First, we attacked social peer pressures by establishing leadership from the inside out. We have a 212 degree leadership council that has the obligation and responsibility of being the "voice" of each individual player. Our coaches and community leaders participate and teach throughout the spring and summer months and focus on education about how to lead one's peers. The council members are voted in by their peers/coaches, and they are extremely proud to represent their fellow student-athletes. We also bought a curriculum from *Character Matters*, and I use this teaching tool throughout the fall season in tandem with our Monday morning scouting report, and in the spring in our C-Team athletic class. We also tag this onto a minimum of four community service projects that benefit various organizations, and this allows our players to utilize their leadership skills running different projects.

Second, I researched mission statements and creeds all over the country to attack character issues and accountability. We developed a creed that combines leadership, team expectations, team philosophy, and school pride. In our first year the creed was preached over and over again, but in year two I made it mandatory to memorize the creed, included it as part of spring season lifting points, and posted two huge creed banners in our locker room and weight room as a constant reminder. I also reference or quote the creed with almost every speech, disciplinary action, and parent meeting, and consistently throughout the entire year.

RAMS CREED

The Rio Rancho Rams football program is built on championship characteristics of *Leadership, Accountability, Trust, Commitment,* and *Respect*. We harvest an individual that understands "loyalty to the team." We have high expectations as a team socially, academically, and athletically. We are passionate about everything we do and commit to excellence. We refuse to underachieve and cheat the team. We honor the Rams that came before us and those that will come after us with loyalty, perseverance, and aggressive effort.

We are the predators not the prey! We are relentless in our attack, we show no weaknesses, we will never quit, we are champions!

We embrace the legacy of Rio Rancho Rams Football and the 5 Championships. We are proud to be the 16th Football team, we are proud to represent Rio Rancho High School, and accept the responsibility that comes along with that.

GO RAMS! PRIDE FOREVER!

Conclusion

"Fame is a vapor. Popularity is an accident. Riches take wings; those who cheer today will curse tomorrow, only one thing endures—character."

—Horace Greely

Having spent the better part of two years researching, writing, and editing this book, I have come to several conclusions. First, we as a nation are facing a multitude of problems. The problem for coaches and teachers is they are on the front line dealing with negative social issues created by a changed American society. Personal experience and further research prove coaches have a profound influence on those they coach. Coaches use the game as a classroom, and they teach the fundamentals of football and the great lessons of life by teaching more than the game.

In my attempt to create applicable resources designed to help coaches deal with social issues, my expectations were verified. Coaches on all levels are extremely caring and amazingly generous with their time, their wisdom, and their proven methods of influencing "beyond the game."

Finally, when coaches/teachers influence their student-athletes in developing core values, the end results invariably will be the emergence of positive character traits. When one possesses a foundation of values, accountability and respect will follow. An understanding will develop regarding so-called free lunches, and players will begin to realize that their only entitlement is opportunity. Finally, they will be more likely to establish a loving home and become husbands, fathers, and role models.

The following quote, often attributed to Frank Outlaw, explains the process in simple vernacular: "Watch your thoughts, for they become words. Watch your words, for they become actions. Watch your actions, for they become habits. Watch your habits, for they become character. Watch your character, for it becomes your destiny."

My final thoughts are, "Values are the fertile earth from which strength of character grows. Once character blooms in an individual, it will endure."

A Coach's Influence
Beyond the Game

Notes

1   Jeff Benedict and Armen Keteyian, "College Football and Crime," *Sports Illustrated*, March 2, 2011, http://sportsillustrated.cnn.com/2011/writers/the_bonus/02/27/cfb.crime/index.html.

2   "Life without Father," PBS Online NewsHour discussion, moderated by Charlayne Hunter-Gault, June 17, 1996, http://www.pbs.org/newshour/bb/youth/fathers_6-17.html.

3   "Appreciating How Fathers Give Children a Head Start," Head Start: An Office of the Administration for Children and Families, Early Childhood Learning & Knowledge Center (ECLKC), U.S. Department of Health and Human Services, http://eclkc.ohs.acf.hhs.gov/hslc/tta-system/family/For%20Parents/Inside%20Head%20Start/Parent%20Involvement/parent_pub_00001_072005.html.

4   Cicero Wilson, "Economic Shifts That Will Impact Crime Control and Community Revitalization," pp. 9-14 in "What Can the Federal Government Do to Decrease Crime and Revitalize Communities?" panel papers from January 5–7, 1998, a joint publication of the National Institute of Justice and the Executive Office for Weed and Seed, U.S. Department of Justice, https://www.ncjrs.gov/pdffiles/172210.pdf.

5   See "Custodial Mothers and Fathers and Their Child Support: 2009," U.S. Census Bureau, issued December 2011, http://www.census.gov/prod/2011pubs/p60-240.pdf.

6   "Fatherless Families," PBS Essays and Dialogues, David Gergen and David Popenoe, May 3, 1996, http://www.pbs.org/newshour/gergen/popenoe.html.

7   "Fatherless Families."

8   "Life without Father."

9   "The Consequences of Fatherlessness," National Center for Fathering (fathers.com), http://www.fathers.com/content/index.php?option=com _content&task=view&id=391.

10 These statistics and their sources are available online at "The Conse-quences of Fatherlessness."

11 Hope Yen, "Roles of American Dads Diverging This Father's Day," Asso-ciated Press, June 15, 2011.

12 Gretchen Livingston, Senior Researcher, and Kim Parker, Associate Direc-tor, Pew Social & Demographic Trends, "A Tale of Two Fathers: More Are Active, but More Are Absent," Pew Research Center Publications, June 15, 2011, http://www.pewsocialtrends.org/2011/06/15/a-tale-of-two-fathers.

13 Sabrina Tavernise, "Married Couples Are No Longer a Majority, Census Finds," New York Times, May 26, 2011, http://www.nytimes.com/2011/ 05/26/us/26marry.html.

14 "The Rights of Unmarried Fathers," Child Welfare Information Gateway, Children's Bureau, U.S. Department of Health and Human Services, June 2010, http://www.childwelfare.gov/systemwide/laws_policies/statutes/ putative.pdf.

15 Tom Osborne, speaking at the Master Coach Series at the AFCA convention.

16 All quotations from this section are from the AFCA convention Master Coach Series.

17 C. Kirk Hadaway and Penny Long Marler, "How Many Americans Attend Worship Each Week? An Alternative Approach to Measurement," Journal for the Scientific Study of Religion 44, no. 3 (2005): 307–22.

18 James MacGregor Burns, Transforming Leadership: A New Pursuit of Happiness (New York: Atlantic Monthly Press, 2003). Cited at http://en .wikipedia.org/wiki/Transformational_leadership.

19 Bernard M. Bass, "Leadership and Performance," New York: Free Press, 1985. Cited at http://en.wikipedia.org/wiki/Transformational_leadership.

20 Joe Ehrmann, quote from a column in The Coach of the America newslet-ter, December 2011. The newsletters can be found at http://www.coachfor america.com/.

21 Leadership quotation of Admiral Arleigh A. Burke is from http://leader shipquote.org/.

22 For the quote from Martin Luther King Jr., see www.MartinLuther KingJr.com/quotes.

23 Adolescent Substance Abuse Knowledge Base, http://www.adolescent -substance-abuse.com/; U.S. Department of Health and Human Services, http://www.hhs.gov/; American Lung Association, http://www.lung .org/; the Kaiser Family Foundation, http://www.kff.org/.

24 Bruce C. Ogilvie and Thomas A. Tutko, "Sport: If You Want to Build Character, Try Something Else," Psychology Today 5, no. 5 (1971): 61–63.

25 Recent report cards can be found on the Josephson Institute website at http://charactercounts.org/programs/reportcard/index.html.